CORRUPTION, ACCOUNTABILITY
AND DISCRETION

PUBLIC POLICY AND GOVERNANCE

Edited by Professor Evan Berman, Victoria University of Wellington, New Zealand.

This series brings together the best in international research on policy and governance issues. Authored and edited by experts in the field, these books present new and insightful research on a range of policy and governance issues across the globe. Topics covered include but are not limited to: policy analysis frameworks; healthcare policy; environmental/resource policy; local government policy; development policy; regional studies/policy; urban policy/planning; social policy.

Titles include:

CORRUPTION, ACCOUNTABILITY AND DISCRETION

EDITED BY

NANCY S. LIND
*Department of Politics and Government,
llinois State University, USA*

and

CARA E. RABE-HEMP
*Department of Criminal Justice Sciences, Illinois State
University, USA*

emerald
PUBLISHING

United Kingdom – North America – Japan
India – Malaysia – China

Emerald Publishing Limited
Howard House, Wagon Lane, Bingley BD16 1WA, UK

First edition 2017

British Library Cataloguing in Publication Data
A catalogue record for this book is available from the British Library

ISBN: 978-1-78743-556-8 (Print)
ISBN: 978-1-78743-555-1 (Online)
ISBN: 978-1-78743-569-8 (Epub)
ISBN: 978-1-83867-928-6 (Paperback)

INVESTOR IN PEOPLE

CONTENTS

LIST OF CONTRIBUTORS

Parwez Besmel	Northern Arizona University, Flagstaff, AZ, USA
Jennifer B. Bethmann	Illinois State University, Normal, IL, USA
Benjamin Bricker	Southern Illinois University, Carbondale, Carbondale, IL, USA
Jaclyn Bunch	University of Alabama, Mobile, AL, USA
Earlene A. S. Camarillo	Western Oregon University, Monmouth, OR, USA
April K. Clark	Department of Political Science, Northern Illinois University, DeKalb, IL, USA
Morgan Foster	Illinois State University, Normal, IL, USA
John Huxford	Illinois State University, Normal, IL, USA
Thomas E. McClure	Illinois State University, Normal, IL, USA
John P. McHale	School of Communication, Illinois State University, Normal, IL, USA
Kerri Milita	Department of Politics and Government, Illinois State University, Normal, IL, USA
Maria A. Moore	Illinois State University, Normal, IL, USA
Philip Mulvey	Illinois State University, Normal, IL, USA
Eric E. Otenyo	Northern Arizona University, Flagstaff, AZ, USA
Michael J. Pomante II	Tulane University, New Orleans, LA, USA
Renee Prunty	Department of Arts and Sciences, Methodist College of UnityPoint Health, Peoria, IL, USA
Cara E. Rabe-Hemp	Illinois State University, Normal, IL, USA
Scot Schraufnagel	Department of Political Science, Northern Illinois University, DeKalb, IL, USA
Mandy Swartzendruber	Kaga:Create, Champaign, IL, USA
Elizabeth Erin Wheat	University of Wisconsin-Green Bay, Brown County, WI, USA

NOTES ON CONTRIBUTORS

Parwez Besmel earned his PhD in Political Science from Northern Arizona University, Flagstaff, in 2016. His PhD dissertation is entitled Prospects of Transitional Justice for Afghanistan. His interests are in the politics of reconstruction and militarization in Afghanistan.

Jennifer B. Bethmann is the Web Accessibility Coordinator for Illinois State University where she recently attained her MS in Communication. Her research interests include media studies, mediated communication, and assistive technologies.

Benjamin Bricker is an Assistant Professor of Political Science at Southern Illinois University in Carbondale. He holds a cross appointment in the SIU School of Law. He received his PhD from Washington University in St. Louis and his J.D. from the University of Illinois College of Law. His first book is *Visions of Judicial Review: A Comparative Examination of Courts and Policy in Democracies*.

Jaclyn Bunch is an Assistant Professor in the Department of Political Science and Criminal Justice at the University of South Alabama. She has a particular interest in state and local relations, federalism, media, and the substantive topics of health care, administration, and budgeting.

Earlene A. S. Camarillo is an Assistant Professor of Political Science at Western Oregon University, Monmouth. She earned her PhD from Northern Arizona University. Her interests are in public administration and health policy. Her work appears in *Public Personnel Management* and the book *Today's Economic Issues: Democrats and Republicans* (2016).

April K. Clark is an Associate Professor in the Department of Political Science at Northern Illinois University. She specializes in the development of political attitudes and behavior with a particular focus on age, period, and cohort differences. She has published on a number of topics, including social capital, political tolerance, interpersonal trust, and environmental politics.

Morgan Foster is a graduate assistant at Illinois state University where she is pursuing a degree in criminal justice sciences. She sits on the advisory board for the academic organization, Breaking Barriers, where she assists female undergraduate students in the criminal justice major push past the patriarch and pave their own way in the criminal justice field as leading women.

John Huxford teaches classes on news literacy and cultural influences on society, on and coordinates the Journalism Program in the School of Communication at Illinois State University. He was formerly a reporter, editor, and feature writer and spent nearly 20 years in journalism. His research centers on the textual and visual construction of news.

Nancy S. Lind is a Professor of Politics and Government at Illinois State University, USA, where she has taught for over 30 years. She has won University Distinguished Teaching and Service Awards and had edited/co-edited/co-authored over a dozen books as well as written several peer reviewed journal articles. Her specialties are Public Administration and Policy and American Politics.

Thomas E. McClure is the Director of Legal Studies and an Associate Professor of Politics and Government at Illinois State University. He served as a judicial law clerk for the Illinois Appellate Court for two years and engaged in the private practice for 26 years. He has earned the top Martindale Hubbell rating of AV and has been recognized as an Illinois Super Lawyer six times.

John P. McHale is a Professor in the School of Communication at Illinois State University. His past books include *Saintly Sex: John Paul II, Gender, Sex & the Catholic Church* (2014), *Convergent Media Writing* (2016), and *Communicating for Change* (2004). McHale has received over 10 awards for his film work, including the Walter Cronkite Civic Engagement Leadership award at the United Nations.

Kerri Milita is an Assistant Professor at Illinois State University. She received her PhD in Political Science from Florida State University in May 2014. Her research interests include elections, election laws, and direct democracy. Recently, her works have appeared in *Political Behavior*, *State Politics & Policy Quarterly*, *Electoral Studies*, and *PS: Political Science & Politics*.

Maria A. Moore coordinates the Mass Media Program in the School of Communication at Illinois State University where she teaches media law, ethics and management courses. She has 30 years of television station experience and is the recipient of seven regional Emmys. Her research focuses on whistleblower or leaked sources for investigative reporting, First Amendment issues, multimodal media production, collaborative learning, and civic engagement.

Philip Mulvey is an Assistant Professor in the Department of Criminal Justice Sciences at Illinois State University. Prior to entering academia, he was the Project Manager for the Northwestern Juvenile Project as part of the Health Disparities and Public Policy program at Northwestern University.

Eric E. Otenyo is a Professor of Public Administration at Northern Arizona University. His books include: *Trade Unions and the Age of ICTs in Kenya* (2017), *E-Government: The Use of Information and Communication Technologies in Administration* (2011); *Managerial Discretion in Government Decision Making: Beyond the Street Level* (2007), and *Comparative Public Administration: The Essential Readings* (2006).

Michael J. Pomante II is a Visiting Assistant Professor at Tulane University. He received his Doctor of Philosophy degree from Northern Illinois University in 2016. He has been published in *American Politics Research* and is the co-author of *Historical Dictionary of the Barack Obama Administration*.

Renee Prunty is an instructor in political science and communication at Methodist College of UnityPoint Health. Her research interests include constitutional law, early American government, education policy and pedagogy. She has two master's degrees from Illinois State University, in communication and political science.

Cara E. Rabe-Hemp is a Professor in the Department of Criminal Justice Sciences at Illinois State University, USA. In 2010, Cara was awarded the University Research Initiative Award, in 2014 she was inducted into the College of Applied Sciences and Technology Academy of Achievement, and in 2016 she was awarded the College of Applied Sciences and Technology Outstanding Researcher Award.

Scot Schraufnagel is a Professor and Chair in the Political Science Department at Northern Illinois University. He is a former US Peace Corp volunteer serving in Sierra Leone, West Africa. His research interests include legislative politics, political parties, and comparative election laws.

Mandy Swartzendruber serves on the board of directors for Kaga:Create, a nonprofit that works to encourage Native American youth to express themselves through art. She has an MS in public service from Illinois State University, and previously served as an AmeriCorps fellow with the East Central Illinois Area Agency on Aging.

Elizabeth Erin Wheat is an Assistant Professor in Public and Environmental Affairs (Political Science) at the University of Wisconsin-Green Bay. Her research focuses on environmental law at the Court of Appeals. environmental justice, water policy, trafficking of endangered species, and the use of simulations in the classroom.

INTRODUCTION

Cara E. Rabe-Hemp and Nancy S. Lind

The corruption of public officials in the United States (U.S.) and its corrosive impact on public policy, political stability, and democratic institutions earns it a spot among the most current public crises. In the past decade, the public has been barraged with stories of political corruption, including Illinois governor Rod Blagojevich's attempt to sell Barack Obama's vacant Senate seat and lobbyist Jack Abramoff's conviction for conspiracy and fraud for his pay-for-play racket in the nation's capital. Not surprising then is the public's perception that political corruption is getting worse. In a recent U.S. poll, 60% of people said that corruption has increased over the last two years. This perception has devastating consequences for governance, as faith in the government and its accompanying interactions is quickly turning to political apathy. This collection of chapters provides the key elements needed to understand the nature and prevalence of corruption in public governance, as well as the devastating public policy consequences. This text explores the implications of public governance corruption on political stability, public trust, and policymaking, as well as recommendations for how to establish controls on discretion and stricter regulations to increase accountability and corruption control in public governance.

NATURE AND PREVALENCE

In 2015, Chapman University released a report entitled *Survey of American Fears*. Of the 89 potential fears that the survey queried, the majority of Americans reported being either "afraid" or "very afraid" of federal government corruption (Rappell, 2015). Why is the public so afraid? One explanation for increased public fear is that the public is simply more aware of corruption. Today, stories of corruption are a prominent feature of public life. The media plays an important role in defining for the American people which political issues are important, as well as holding public officials accountable for their corrupt behavior. This is an imperfect system, resulting at times in a "punishing avalanche of negative publicity," and in other cases a total ignorance of corruption and incompetence (Entman, 2012, p. 1).

Bolstering this explanation are official statistics that suggest little change in corruption in the past decade. For example, the annual "Corruption Perceptions Index" produced by Transparency International, which provides yearly information on how U.S. citizens view their government and how it compares to other nations globally, shows the rates of U.S. corruption largely unchanged from previous years. In comparison to other countries, the U.S. and other democracies are less corrupt than emerging economies, such as Asia, Africa, and Latin America as well as formerly communist economies such as Russia. Prosecutions for corrupt behavior show similar trends. In their 2016 article, Cordis and Milyo reported that contrary to conventional wisdom, corruption convictions of public officials are not increasing. Instead, convictions are consistent over time and mostly involve low-ranking federal and local officials. These official statistics illustrate that while the U.S. is not one of the most corrupt countries, corruption exists in America. With statistics of corruption largely unchanged in the past decade, how do we explain an increased perception of corruption by the America people? Richard White provides a possible answer in his 2013 article, "What counts as corruption," arguing that the definition of corruption is what has changed, revolving around the concepts of self-interest and undue influence.

In defining corruption, the Founding Fathers spent considerable time and energy discussing the discretionary power of public officials and the best methods to hold them accountable for their actions. In the framer's view, corruption is the opposite of public virtue. A republican form of government requires that public officials act as *citizens*, concerned for the public good, and not merely as private, self-interested individuals. Through this lens, corruption is defined as self-interest placed above public interest. For example, in New York in the 1800s, Tammany Hall secured votes in exchange for jobs and aid and then used their political powers to gain graft from their position. In another example, Albert Fall, the Secretary of the Interior (1921-1923) accepted a bribe to secretly lease federal oil reserves, infamously called the Teapot Dome Scandal. To combat corruption, the Founding Fathers set up structural provisions designed to encourage public virtue and reduce the temptation to lord private interests over the public good, including a ban on gift-giving from foreign sovereigns without congressional approval and limits on the additional positions that members of Congress could simultaneously hold. Their assumption that public officials would hold a concern for the public good, over private interest, was important to combatting corruption.

By comparison, corruption currently equates to outright bribery or quid-pro-quo exchanges. Gone is the more nuanced approach of how undue influence permeates governance. This is because today influencing the government is defined as a First Amendment right, rather than as a risk for corruption. It is how we, as a public, influence our government and let our public officials know what we value as they represent us (Teachout, 2014). However, there is a fine line between our ability as a public to influence governmental leaders and corruption. After all, at the heart of corruption is the discretionary power of public officials to make decisions. Amundsen (1999) reminds us that the basis of corruption is that the official misuses public power for *private* benefit.

PUBLIC POLICY CONSEQUENCES

Has the corrupting influence of money in the American political process rendered officials incapable of governing the American people? When we look at campaigns, the measure of a successful campaign revolves around money, rather than votes. For this reason, the money associated with campaign funding, where it comes from, how it influences political decisions, and so on, are increasingly concerning for many Americans. The groundbreaking 2010 Supreme Court ruling in *Citizens United v. Federal Election Commission*, that freedom of speech prohibited the government from restricting independent political expenditures by nonprofit corporations, for-profit corporations, labor unions and other associations, only exacerbated this issue. In his State of the Union address in 2010, President Barack Obama criticized the *Citizens United* ruling,

> With all due deference to separation of powers, last week the Supreme Court reversed a century of law that I believe will open the floodgates for special interests – including foreign corporations – to spend without limit in our elections. I don't think American elections should be bankrolled by America's most powerful interests, or worse, by foreign entities. They should be decided by the American people.

To give the reader a sense of how this works, let's look at fundraising for the 2014 Congressional elections. In 2014, 5.4 million Americans donated to congressional campaigns, political parties, or political action committees. However, this number is misleading as the top 100 individuals and organizations gave almost as much as the bottom 4.75 million contributors did.

In other words, "100 individuals and organizations gave 60% of the money contributed" (Lessig, 2015, p. 15). The power of the dollar in elections have led many to argue that the way campaigns are funded in the U.S. means that citizens do not have equal representation. Instead, the corrupting ability of the few to influence elected officials makes candidates open to their influence. This leaves Americans increasingly convinced that the game of government is rigged in favor of the elite and the powerful. Charles Lewis, founder of the Center for Public Integrity, succinctly described the situation: "Our political process has increasingly become an accepted system of legal corruption" (Edsall, 2014, n.p).

Of course, campaigns are not the only potential for corruption. The Federal Bureau of Investigation (2017) cautions Americans that corruption "can affect everything from how well our borders are secured and our neighborhoods protected to how verdicts are handed down in courts to how public infrastructure such as roads and schools are built" (n.p.). This is because part of the responsibility of public officials is to allocate rights over public resources in the name of the state or the government. When the government awards contracts based on inappropriate and fraudulent criteria, they not only mishandle taxpayer dollars, they also deprive honest companies an opportunity for lucrative business. There are recent examples including, contractor spending during wartime, sexual harassment in local governance, and the undue influence of lobbyists and the corporations that employ them illustrating how all sectors of public governance, municipal, state and federal may be vulnerable to corruption.

IMPLICATIONS FOR GOVERNANCE

Because of persistent reports of corruption in American politics, public confidence in governance is waning. In a 2015 Gallup poll, only 11% of Americans reported a great deal or quite a lot of confidence in Congress, compared to 33% for the President, and 32% for the U.S. Supreme Court (Gallup, 2015). The democratic idea of a federal republic, that a group of elected officials represents the interests of a larger group of people, is at risk. Public distrust in the form of low voter turnout and a lack of public participation suggests that political apathy has largely taken hold of American politics. While distrust of government is nothing new, it can lead to negative consequences, including being more bureaucratic, less effective, and less capable of responding to the public's needs. The continued lack of confidence in governmental officials weakens the authority of the state. To understand this, we must acknowledge how governance differs from government. Frank Weil provided an excellent description in his 2015 Blog in the *Huffington Post* when he stated, "Government is only ONE arm of modern society and it derives its legitimacy and powers from its taxes, spending, laws, and regulations (n.p.)." Governance, on the other hand, which is the focus of this book, includes the relationships between the constitutional branches of government, including the agencies as well as relationships with the media. Governance is a broader term than government. Corruption leads to an inability to carry out the basic role of governance, jeopardizing the framework for our social order (Bok, 2001). In the words of Transparency International (2017), "corruption is one of the greatest challenges of the contemporary world. It undermines good government, fundamentally distorts public policy, leads to the misallocation of resources, harms the private sector and private sector development and particularly hurts the poor (p. 1)." Corruption of public governance not only undermines the effectiveness of the political system, it also results in corrupt public policymaking on the most pressing issues facing Americans today, such as the management of war, health care, crime, and banking. These policies influence the provision of public services to the American people. Finally, corruption hits our pocketbooks by siphoning off tax dollars. The Federal Bureau of Investigation estimates that public corruption costs the U.S. government and the public billions of dollars each year (FBI, 2017). Worldwide estimates show that the cost of corruption equals more than five percent of the global Gross Domestic Product (2.6 trillion dollars), with over 1 trillion dollars paid in bribes each year (World Economic Forum, 2017). This translates to increasing business costs, waste and inefficiency in public resources, and destabilization of the rule of law.

These risks warrant a careful look at the nature and etiology of corruption with an eye toward drafting controls on discretion and rules for accountability. Accountability is defined by its ability to reduce the opportunities for corruption, maladministration, or legal impropriety that come to people in positions of power (Castiglione, 2017). Historically, strict regulation and oversight mechanisms have been designed to encourage ethical decision-making and punish violators. However, in *Corruption in America*, Zephyr Teachout argues that these efforts have been largely unsuccessful, as regulating corruption has bedeviled lawyers, politicians, and political philosophers. Instead, the future of accountability may lie in solutions that allow for greater transparency and accountability in governance. For example, the expanded access that citizens and the media have to influence governance could be a vehicle to mobilize accountability in governance by restraining the discretion of public officials to utilize their office for personal gain. Future solutions

to combatting corruption may involve strengthening protections for whistleblowers, a careful look at the power of judicial review in accountability, and
greater transparency in the election process.

ORGANIZATION OF THE BOOK

The book is divided into four parts, Part I: Etiology; Part II: Permeation
of Corruption in Governance; Part III: Policy Issues; and Part IV: Oversight
and Accountability. The first two chapters comprising Part I are concerned
with the etiology of corruption in public governance. In Chapter 1, *Measuring
Corruption: Transparency International's "Corruption Perceptions Index"*,
April K. Clark captures the complexity of why it is hard to measure corruption. She provides a comprehensive overview of the various definitional
challenges and tools used for measuring and analyzing corruption including
the widely used "Corruption Perceptions Index" produced by Transparency
International. Clark examines the perceived severity of political corruption
in the U.S. and how it influences the regulation of political corruption. She
concludes that corruption hinders the government's ability to act and is a
powerful determinant of political support across widely varying political,
cultural, and economic contexts.

Chapter 2, *The Price of Corruption in Congress*, written by Michael J.
Pomante II and Scot Schraufnagel, reviews five major scandals that have
rocked Congress since the 1970s, Korea-gate, ABSCAM, Keating 5, House
Banking Scandal, and Abramoff/DeLay Lobbying Scandal. Bolstered by this
review and their analysis of the American National Election Study data, they
assert that scandal definitely influences congressional disapproval and public trust in government. Specifically, Pomante and Schraufnagel uncover an
important increase in congressional disapproval and an eroding of trust in
the national government associated with congressional scandals, leading to a
less effective Congress when disapproval grows and trust shrinks.

Part II of the text presents the influence of corruption, discretion, and
accountability on public governance at the different levels of government.
Chapter 3, *Legislative Scandals in the United States*, presents the state of
corruption in the American legislative system, a decade after the infamous
scandal surrounding powerful lobbyist Jack Abramoff who claimed to have
"bought" influence in nearly half of all United States congressional offices.
Kerri Milita and Jaclyn Bunch review the notorious scandal that culminated in the arrest of Bob Ney (R-OH), chairperson of the powerful House
Administration Committee, which oversees federal elections, the resignation

of then-House Majority Leader Tom DeLay (R-TX), and the incarceration of Abramoff himself. Milita and Bunch argue that today in Congress, it is business as usual, with lobbyists influencing Congress through the same old avenues: the revolving door, whereby former members of Congress or congressional staff leave public service to work for lobbying firms and lobby former colleagues for campaign contributions and gift giving. In sum, a decade after the Abramoff scandal, Congress is still vulnerable to corruption.

Chapter 4, *Campaign Contributions and Vote Buying* by Renee Prunty and Mandy Swartzendruber examines whether campaign contributions equate with vote buying in U.S. Presidential campaigns. This chapter reviews the intricacies of campaign finance with special attention directed to how the decision in *Citizens United* contributed to a drastic increase in campaign spending resulting in the perception of citizens that influence is bought. The authors conclude that while there is no direct evidence that those contributing more money to campaigns have a greater influence on policy, the public may find it hard to believe.

Chapter 5, *Do Contributions to Judicial Campaigns Create the Appearance of Corruption*, written by Thomas E. McClure, presents the relationship between integrity ratings of Illinois trial judges and campaign contributions through the Illinois State Bar Association's judicial poll integrity scores of 253 elected judges. McClure's results suggest that judge's integrity scores decline as the amount of attorney contributions increases, the number of reported attorney contributors enlarges, and the number of large attorney contributors grows. The author concludes with a radical solution to corruption in judicial campaigns: abolishing judicial elections.

Finally, in the last chapter of Part 2, Chapter 6, *Media Coverage of Corruption and Scandal in the 2016 Presidential Election: Fantasy Themes of Crooked Hillary and Corrupt Businessman Trump*, John P. McHale illustrates how media coverage of corruption can uniquely affect voter attitudes and public policy formulation and implementation. By tracing the competing narratives offered in media coverage of the 2016 Presidential election, the dramatic characters, Crooked Hillary and Corrupt Businessman Trump, are constructed, resulting in a very nasty electoral process. McHale argues that in 2016, our nation may have hit a new low in Presidential campaigns.

Part III of the text, Policy Issues, starts with Chapter 7, *Crime, Injustice and Politics* written by Cara E. Rabe-Hemp, Philip Mulvey, and Morgan Foster. The authors examine the role of crime, politics, and media imagery in electoral politics, arguing that crime is one of the most enduring political issues of this century and that, in turn, politicians have played a fundamental role in constructing criminal justice policies. Rabe-Hemp, Mulvey, and Foster

present the history of the "get tough" rhetoric, increasingly popular with politicians that led to the War on Drugs, zero-tolerance policing, and mandatory
sentencing. These criminal justice policies have produced the highest incarceration rate in the world, vastly overcrowded prisons, and increased police
militarization, but no resulting decrease in crime. Today these strategies are
associated with the reduced legitimacy of public officials and disproportionate consequences for poor and minority communities. The authors argue that
while no politician is going to argue that we need more crime, given that politicians can shape the scope, explanations, and consequences of crime, they
need to use their discretion to be honest about the reality of crime.

Sex scandals have rocked American politics since Alexander Hamilton paid
for silence regarding his affair with another man's wife in 1791. In Chapter
8, Eric E. Otenyo and Earlene A. Smith analyze the accountability of a very
specific form of sex scandal – sexual harassment in police agencies. *Mayors'
and Citizen Attitudes toward Sexual Harassment in Police Departments* analyzes public and mayoral reactions to reported cases of sexual harassment
and misconduct in police departments. Through the lens of agenda setting,
this chapter explores case studies of sexual harassment within police agencies,
concluding that currently these issues are largely obscured from the public, as
they have not been problematized as a crisis that would trigger political action.
The authors define several implications for policymaking including, stricter
reprimands for sexual harassment, the increased empowerment of female
officers, and the increased awareness of the public to mobilize accountability.

In Chapter 9, *Wars in Iraq and Afghanistan: Contractor Corruption and
Election Campaigns*, Eric E. Otenyo and Parwez Besmel examine the extent
to which reports of contractor corruption in the leadership of the Iraq and
Afghan wars influenced the political agendas of Presidential candidates. The
authors argue that while accounts of corruption following the invasions of
Iraq and Afghanistan have been widely reported, they have not become a core
campaign and governance issue in election cycles. This finding suggests that
the framing of corruption needs to be targeted to generate concerned voters and a reduction in corruption. The authors argue that the public should
be outraged because the opportunity costs of corruption are colossal and
undermine democratic institutions, which in the end will lower the quality of
administrative practices and policy implementation.

Part IV, Oversight and Accountability, explores recommendations for how
to establish controls on discretion and strict regulation to increase accountability and corruption in public governance. Chapter 10, Citizens United *and
Political Accountability*, by Benjamin Bricker, examines the role that the 2010
case, *Citizens United v. FEC* has played in curbing corruption in campaign

spending in U.S. elections. Bricker argues that the Court's decision serves to redirect the focus of accountability away from those who seek to sway election outcomes through massive election spending and toward efforts by the government to regulate that type of spending. The practical result has been to allow for the creation of new organizations that can take in unlimited amounts of money while also effectively hiding the source of funds from disclosure. Instead, the author encourages solutions that embody greater disclosure and accountability in government.

Chapter 11, *Judicial Review*, by Elizabeth Erin Wheat provides a historical look at judicial review and its power to maintain separation of powers in the U.S. political system. Specifically, through laws passed by Congress or regulations enacted by federal agencies, these branches of government draft policies with the expectation that the judicial branch will enforce them. The courts, however, were designed to uphold the Constitution and rule on the constitutionality of the laws and regulations. In other words, while judicial opinions can have the effect of creating policy, this is a different purpose than the Founding Fathers intended. Judicial review gives the courts the authority to review Congress, the President, federal agencies, and itself, promoting legal and effective public policy. This makes it an increasingly important tool for accountability.

Chapter 12, *National Security Whistleblowers and the Journalists Who Tell Their Stories: A Dangerous Policy Dance of Truth-finding, Truth-telling, and Consequence*, written by Maria A. Moore, John Huxford, and Jennifer B. Bethmann acknowledges the whistleblower as a crucial resource in journalism's attempts to make accountable those who wield power and misuse it through corruption. The media have increasingly become modern mechanisms for enforcing accountability. By examining case studies of those who have braved the government's anger, this chapter examines not only the circumstances of these breaches but also their political and legal repercussions. The authors establish the importance of stronger policy protections for National Security whistleblowers, resulting in positive conclusions for both the public and those who disclosed the information as a means of controlling political corruption.

In sum, this text provides a modern look at the corruption of public officials in the United States, including its devastating impact on governance in the form of public policy and political stability. What the reader will find is that many themes cut across the multiple levels of government represented in this book – namely the pervasiveness of corruption in American governance and their impact on the public institutions and citizens that public officials are sworn to serve. Viewing the similarities of corruption across all levels of government informs solutions to make accountable those public officials who

misuse their discretionary power. Modern mechanisms for enforcing accountability highlight the power and responsibility of the people to identify and
combat corruption in governance.

REFERENCES

Bok, D. (2001). *The Trouble with Government.* Cambridge, MA: Harvard University Press.
Castiglione, D. (2017). Accountability. *Britannica.* Retrieved from https://www.britannica.com/topic/accountability
Edsall, T. (2014, August 5). The value of political corruption. *New York Times.* Retrieved from https://www.nytimes.com/2014/08/06/opinion/thomas-edsall-the-value-of-political-corruption.html?_r=0
Entman, R. M. (2012). *Scandal and Silence: Media Responses to Presidential Misconduct.* Cambridge, UK: Polity.
Federal Bureau of Investigation. (2017). *Public Corruption.* Retrieved from https://www.fbi.gov/investigate/public-corruption
Gallup. (2015). *Confidence in Institutions.* Retrieved from http://www.gallup.com/poll/1597/Confidence-Institutions.aspx
Obama, B. (2010). *State of the Union Address.* Retrieved from https://obamawhitehouse.archives.gov/the-press-office/2016/01/12/remarks-president-barack-obama-%E2%80%93-prepared-delivery-state-union-address
Rappell, C. (2015, October 25). What's the scariest thing in America? Government corruption. *Washington Post.* Retrieved from https://www.washingtonpost.com/news/rampage/wp/2015/10/28/whats-the-scariest-thing-in-america-government-corruption/?utm_term=.ebcc2ceb3846
Transparency International. (2017). *Corruption Perceptions Index.* Retrieved from www.transparency.org/cpi
Teachout, Z. (2014). *Corruption in America: From Benjamin Franklin's Snuff Box to Citizens United.* Cambridge, MA: Harvard University Press.
Weil, F. (2015). Government vs. Governance. *The Blog Huffington Post.* Retrieved from http://www.huffingtonpost.com/frank-a-weil/government-vs-overnance_b_6858646.html
White, R. (2013). What counts as Corruption? *Social Research, 80*(4), 1033–1056.
World Economic Forum. (2017). *Global Agenda Councils Anti-Corruption.* Retrieved from http://reports.weforum.org/global-agenda-council-2012/councils/anti-corruption/

PART I

ETIOLOGY

CHAPTER 1

MEASURING CORRUPTION: TRANSPARENCY INTERNATIONAL'S "CORRUPTION PERCEPTIONS INDEX"

April K. Clark

ABSTRACT

Citizens are demanding better performance from governments and they are increasingly aware of the costs of poor management and corruption. In view of scarce resources and the major transformations already underway in the global economy, identification and awareness of good governance and preventing corrupt practices have become key to ensuring structural reforms and critical investments necessary for encouraging, sustaining, and enhancing economic growth and competitiveness. Political corruption severely undermines government legitimacy and weakens the development of political, economic, social, and environmental structures.

Keywords: Corruption Index; governance; measuring corruption; trust in government

Corruption, Accountability and Discretion
Public Policy and Governance, 3–22
Copyright © 2017 by Emerald Publishing Limited
All rights of reproduction in any form reserved
doi:10.1108/S2053-769720170000029001

INTRODUCTION

An essential component to any democracy is government legitimacy. If citizens feel that the government's power is not legitimate, the government's ability to act is hindered and, in the most drastic cases, a crisis of public accountability and revolution occurs. It is well-established that citizens in countries with higher levels of political corruption express more negative evaluations of the political system's performance and exhibit lower levels of trust in public servants (Anderson & Tverdova, 2003; Li, Xu, & Zou, 2000; Tanzi & Davoodi, 2001; Treisman, 2000). These findings provide strong and systematic evidence that the informal political practice of corruption compromises important democratic principles and, as such, is a powerful determinant of political support across widely varying political, cultural, and economic contexts. Likewise, when there is a lack of accountability from public officials, corrupt acts become more attractive and easier to pursue (Linz & Stepan, 1996; Rose-Ackerman, 1999).

Few topics in political science stimulate as much interest as political corruption. This research seeks to contribute to this literature by broadening our understanding and approaches to identifying corrupt behavior. Political corruption severely undermines governmental legitimacy and weakens the development of political, economic, social, and environmental structures. However, because it is usually a covert activity, corruption is notoriously hard to measure. A core question then: is it possible to measure political corruption, and if so, how? This chapter begins by discussing why such a seemingly straightforward question is actually quite complex. Then, it provides a comprehensive overview of the various definitional challenges and tools used for measuring and analyzing corruption including the more established and widely used indicator the "Corruption Perceptions Index" provided by Transparency International. Next, it reports how the United States (U.S.) ranks according to the different measurement methods and identifies, as a result of the specific corruption indicators employed (e.g. institutional performance, budget accountability, political financing, etc.), where the biggest political corruption risks in the U.S. government exist. It concludes with a brief discussion of how common the U.S. public perceives the problem of political corruption to be – both over time and at various levels of government – and what these results mean for the future of American democracy. More specifically, this section will permit us to examine if and how perceptions of corruption influence citizens' interactions with government as well as provide a better understanding of citizens' policy preferences for regulating political corruption.

DEFINING CORRUPTION

Corruption is a constant political threat to the world's democracies. Yet, like all contested and complex phenomenon, corruption is hard to measure. The definitional problem stretches beyond violations of legal rules to popular conceptions of right and wrong. Thus, definitional debates are often grounded in "objective" versus "subjective" origins of corruption (Johnston, 1986; Scott, 1972). Several definitions of political corruption have been proposed and are broadly based on criteria that emphasize the legal, public interest, or public opinion characteristics of political corruption (Heidenheimer, [1970] 1989; Scott, 1972).

The legalistic criteria for defining political corruption suggests that political behavior is corrupt when it deviates from legal and public duty norms for private gain. Although it is not without its critics (Berg, Hahn, & Schmidhauser, 1976; Peters & Welch, 1978a), the legalistic criteria is one of the most prominent definitions found in the corruption literature. A second approach defines corruption as any act or acts that threaten or betray the public or common interest. While the public interest definition significantly broadens the range of behavior considered corrupt, it simultaneously enables political elites to claim almost any act is in the public interest (Peters & Welch, 1978a). Third, the public opinion notion of political corruption is based on popular conceptions of political acts, which are deemed corrupt, or not. This approach focuses our attention on political behavior that is perceived as corrupt as constructed from the invocation of values and traditions deeply rooted in the existing political culture (Johnston, 1986).

However, as public opinion surveys reveal, citizens are often uncertain or quite ambivalent in their assessments of wrongdoing. Different people conjure up different ideas of what constitutes alleged corrupt behavior. The variation from individual to individual makes measurement difficult and more unreliable. While widespread agreement exists that political corruption is a significant problem, it is clear that no universally accepted definition is likely to emerge. Likewise, it is also worth noting that no matter the definition used, the occurrence of political corruption can vary in degree and kind (Peters &Welch, 1978a). In short, a variety of definitional approaches exists but the major approaches can be divided into the more limited objective approach that interprets corruption as restricted to violations of formal rules and laws. Conversely, the subjective approach provides a broader definition, which includes any action that is simply perceived as corrupt.

Even though there are conceptual problems associated with the measurement of corruption, the available evidence suggests that one of the most commonly employed definitions of political corruption draws upon Nye's (1967) proposed formal definition which generally begins with the misuse of public office (elective or appointive) for private benefit (personal, close family, private clique) (Potter & Tavits, 2012; Rose-Ackermann, 1999; Schwindt-Bayer & Tavits, 2016). While this narrowest definition of political corruption excludes many interesting political phenomena, it offers major empirical and measurement advantages over broader definitions (Meier & Holbrook, 1992). This approach to political corruption – the public office for private gain definition – provides a more precise concept that is more straightforward to detect.

Regardless of the definition of political corruption used, the concept captures an array of practices and offenses (Peters & Welch, 1978a). The term political corruption covers a broad range of acts and behavior, but classification of the various forms includes bribery, extortion, cronyism, nepotism, patronage, graft, and embezzlement. Bribery is payment (in money or in kind) given to or taken by a state official to circumvent public policies and processes for competitive advantage and profit. Public office can also be abused for personal benefit even if no bribery occurs, through patronage and nepotism, the theft of state assets, or the diversion of state revenues. These challenges, in part, explain the shortage of studies that systematically analyze political corruption.

In short, no definition exists that is considered universally acceptable as capturing all forms, types, and degrees of political corruption. Consequently, no unanimously accepted classification is likely to emerge. However, the contemporary definition centering on the "private gains made by public officials" has been adopted by many scholars (Lambsdorff, 2007; Nye, 1967; Rose-Ackermann, 1999; Schwindt-Bayer & Tavits, 2016), because it is both concise and broad enough to include most forms of corruption (for a contrasting view, see Kaufmann, 2005). The advantage of this approach is that it places the public sector and public officials at the center of the phenomenon. Differentiating the various forms of corruption is vitally important to the construction of a valid measurement approach. The next section addresses the issue of measurement.

MEASURING CORRUPTION

The use of power by government officials for illegitimate private gain is typically done in secret and thus, the concept of political corruption is notoriously difficult to measure. There exists a number of competing measurement tools that reflect the enduring array of definitional challenges in understanding corrupt behavior. Some offer interesting insights and compelling evidence of the wide range of the types of activities or transactions that might fall within the concept. This section provides a comprehensive overview of the various approaches and tools used for measuring and analyzing corruption including the more established and widely used indicator, the "Corruption Perceptions Index" provided by Transparency International.

As a clear indication of the scale and depth of the complexity of political corruption, a wide range of possible measures based on a variety of different definitions of the concept have emerged. The debate over which measurement strategy is appropriate is evident in the disparate results obtained by studies employing different indicators. The existing approaches to measuring political corruption are often parsed into the objective (experience-based) or subjective (perception-based) measurement approaches. As a phenomenon, political corruption cannot be measured directly and in that sense, all available measures are based to some degree on subjective renderings such as estimates of corrupt activity originating from the number of federal convictions for "official corruption" or individual renderings by observers and/or participants. As such, the precise level of corrupt activities will never be known.

Pure objective measures refer to attempts to provide precise estimates of the level of corruption by using objective data (Bandiera, Prat, & Valletti, 2009; Di Tella & Schargrodsky, 2003; Duncan, 2006; Ferraz & Finan, 2008; Golden & Picci, 2005; Olken, 2006, 2007; Reinikka & Svensson, 2004). Such an approach has relied on actual quantifications such as corruption investigations, prosecutions, and convictions. This approach has been helpful for understanding the nature and circumstances surrounding corruption as captured by international trading transactions (Bhagwati, 1974); official statistics and media reports (Liu, 1983; Pharr, 2000; Rose-Ackerman, 1978); official expenditures reports (Golden & Picci, 2005; Olken, 2006); as well as other valuable practices to measure actual corruption.

Since *pure* objective measurements are relatively rare, another type of "objective" data are experience-based indicators based on more demonstrable political corruption occurrences. Experience-based measures are designed to tap into citizens' or business entities actual experience with corruption such as when a public official solicits or extorts a bribe (Kurtz & Schrank, 2007; Mocan, 2008; Seligson, 2002, 2006; Treisman, 2007). These experience-based indicators are not objective in the sense of being comparatively verifiable, but they are an attempt to move from opinions towards real experiences. Thus, these survey-based measures attempt to elicit truthful reporting of actual personal experiences with bribery or obtaining public services or contracts through interactions with government officials (Dreher, Kotsogiannis, & McCorriston, 2007). For example, questions about corruption put to firms are often prefaced by "in your experience, what share of annual sales do firms like your own pay in unofficial payments to public officials?" (European Bank for Reconstruction & Development, 2017). The advantage of this measurement approach over existing "objective" indicators includes the availability of data for a large cross-section of countries, and corruption levels do not need to be inferred indirectly from indicators such as wasteful spending or other suspicious activities.

Given that political corruption is inherently difficult to directly measure – owing to its illegal and clandestine nature, almost all studies use *subjective* indicators of corruption. Rather than providing an actual observation of political corruption, perception-based indicators gauge opinions of corruption by a variety of different sources (political elites, business experts, the public, etc.) (Mishler & Rose, 2001; Smith, 2010; Tverdova, 2011). Subjective measures include surveys consisting of business elites' opinions about conducting business within a given country or citizens' perceptions of corruption. Such perception-based surveys include questions designed to gauge opinions regarding the prominence of corruption in government. For example, perception-based questions assess "How serious is the issue of corruption?" or "Do you think corruption in government is getting worse, is getting better, or is about the same as it has been?" Researchers can glean valuable insights from these questions including the public's feelings on how corrupt politicians and government are; specific incidents of corruption; as well as demonstrate valuable trend changes in corruption perceptions over a long period. In fact, in an April 2016 poll preceding the U.S. presidential election, "corrupt government officials" was identified as among the greatest fears – beating out terrorist attacks and money troubles – by the American public (Chapman University, 2016). According to researchers, despite some shift from 2015 to 2016 in the range of items mentioned, the top fear of political corruption was also number one in the previous year.

Yet, some have expressed concern that indicators of corruption perceptions do not necessarily reflect the actual prevalence of corruption in a country (Heywood & Rose, 2014; Kurtz & Shrank, 2007; Razafindrakoto & Roubaud, 2010). A number of empirical studies present results that raise serious concerns about whether perception-based indicators are useful as either a general assessment of political corruption or for testing hypotheses about the causes or consequences of corruption (Kaufmann et al., 2007; Kurtz & Schrank, 2007; Olken, 2009; Treisman, 2007). Among the chief objections is that perception-based measures may reflect opinions rather than the actual presence of corruption. Previous studies show that public perceptions of corruption are only weakly correlated with individual "experience-based" survey results. Further, empirical research demonstrates that the inconsistency is not constrained to views expressed by the public. In fact, rather large disparities in corruption perceptions and experiences have been uncovered among elite samples as well. For example, expert evaluations and opinions of business elites about the perceived quality of political institutions have been shown to be an ineffective indicator of the real quality of institutions within a country (Glaeser, LaPorta, López-de-Silanes, & Shleifer, 2004; Mocan, 2008). Endogeneity (i.e. a loop of causality between the independent and dependent variables) is also a point of concern, as it remains unknown whether low institutional quality encourages corruption or the other way around (Dreher, Kotsogiannis, & McCorriston, 2007). Moreover, there is evidence that perception-based indicators are more susceptible to systematic biases either because individuals' beliefs are biased, or because of a reporting bias reflecting a differential propensity to report corruption that is conditioned by an individual's beliefs about corruption (Bradburn, 1983; Kurtz & Schrank, 2007).

In recent years, scholarship has begun to examine the *gap* between people's perceptions versus actual experiences with political corruption (Treisman, 2000; 2007). A comparison of perception- and experience-based measures reveals that important disparities exist between the measurement approaches and, in large part, these studies illustrate the value that objective measures offer for assessing political corruption levels. Perceptions of corruption are likely partial to certain types of political corruption (e.g. bribery) but less capable of distinguishing between different forms of corrupt acts (e.g. grand versus petty corruption), or realizing its impact (Kenny, 2006; Knack, 2006). Likewise, it has been argued that objective-experience based measures are unlikely to be biased towards the views of elites such as the business community or reflect the political attitudes of rating experts (Kaufmann et al., 2007; Kaufmann & Kraay, 2008). However, while these early attempts suggest there might be differences between perceptions and experience, and illustrate the progress that can be achieved using objective measures, they have focused on a particular geographical region, activity, or industry. Thus, despite notable contributions to the measurement debate, the results are limited and not well-suited for assessing the different measurement frameworks or the studies employing them.

In sum, measuring political corruption is nearly as difficult as defining it. Many and varied measurement approaches exist in the literature. Keeping in mind the criticisms leveled against both subjective and objective corruption indicators, we now consider one of the most widely used international indicators that is based on both perceptions and actual corruption experiences: Transparency International's Corruption Perceptions Index.

TRANSPARENCY INTERNATIONAL: CORRUPTION PERCEPTIONS INDEX (CPI)

While many of the political corruption studies have relied on perception-based or experience-based indicators, a different approach is built on aggregate corruption and governance indicators. These so-called "second generation" (Johnston, 2000) or "composite" (Arndt & Oman, 2006) measures have been constructed by combining a number of individual underlying variables, compiled from a wide variety of existing data sources. Although several aggregate indicators exist, one of the most frequently used is Transparency International's Corruption Perceptions Index (CPI). First launched in 1995, the CPI has been widely credited with putting the issue of corruption on the international policy agenda. The CPI is produced annually and ranks democratic countries in terms of the degree to which corruption is *perceived* to exist among public officials and politicians. The CPI is a composite index composed by drawing on 13 different polls and surveys – a "poll of polls" – from 11 independent institutions gathering corruption-related data from expert and business surveys carried out by a variety of independent and reputable institutions (Transparency International [TI], 2016; see Table 1 for a summary of the different sources of the 2016 CPI).

The CPI captures information pertaining to the administrative and political aspects of corruption with survey questions relating to bribery and kickbacks in the public sector, embezzlements of public funds, and evaluations of the strength and effectiveness of anti-corruption efforts in the public

Table 1. Sources of the CPI 2016.

1. African Development Bank Governance Ratings 2015
2. Bertelsmann Foundation Sustainable Governance Indicators 2016
3. Bertelsmann Foundation Transformation Index 2016
4. Economist Intelligence Unit Country Risk Ratings 2016
5. Freedom House Nations in Transit 2016
6. Global Insight Country Risk Ratings 2015
7. IMD World Competitiveness Yearbook 2016
8. Political and Economic Risk Consultancy Asian Intelligence 2016
9. Political Risk Services International Country Risk Guide 2016
10. World Bank — Country Policy and Institutional Assessment 2015
11. World Economic Forum Executive Opinion Survey (EOS) 2016
12. World Justice Project Rule of Law Index 2016
13. Varieties of Democracy (VDEM) Project 2016

Source: Transparency International, 2016 (file:///C:/Users/a1563778/Downloads/CPI_2016_SourceDescriptionDocument_EN.pdf)

sector (TI, 2015). Countries are ranked using a scale of 0-100 where 0 equals the highest level of perceived corruption and 100 equals the lowest level of perceived corruption. The lower-ranked countries in the index are plagued by untrustworthy and badly functioning public institutions like the police, legislature, and judiciary. Even where anti-corruption laws exist, they are often ignored in practice. People frequently face situations of bribery and extortion, rely on basic services that have been undermined by the misappropriation of funds, and confront public official indifference when seeking redress from authorities that are "on the take" (TI, 2016). In contrast, higher-ranked countries tend to have higher degrees of press freedom, access to information about public expenditures, stronger standards of integrity for public officials, and independent judicial systems (TI, 2016). However, high-scoring countries are not immune to political corruption. Citizens in higher-ranked countries are subjected to closed-door deals, conflicts of interest, illicit finance, and patchy law enforcement that can distort public policy and exacerbate corruption at home and abroad.

The most recent results of the CPI (in 2016), indicate that over two-thirds of the 176 countries and territories in that year's index fell below the midpoint of the 0 (highly corrupt) to 100 (very clean) scale (TI, 2016). With a score of 90, Denmark and New Zealand tied for the top spot, indicating very little political corruption. Conversely, Somalia coming in with ten points scored dead last among the 176 countries evaluated – indicating political corruption is a serious problem facing the country. Moreover, the low global average score of 43 indicates endemic public sector corruption exists worldwide. Top-scoring countries are by far outnumbered by countries where citizens face the real impact of corruption on a daily basis. Regionally, sub-Saharan Africa, Eastern Europe, and Central Asia are the areas identified as having serious political corruption problems. The Middle East and North Africa score slightly better but this region is also plagued with high corruption levels. In comparison, the EU and Western Europe with five of its member states (Denmark, Finland, Sweden, Switzerland, and Norway) ranked among the top six countries on the index, reflecting the region's commitment to anti-corruption efforts.

Although widely credited with playing a critical role in moving universal attention to the issue of political corruption, the index has been criticized both on methodological grounds and usage practices (Andersson & Heywood, 2008; de Maria, 2008; Hawken & Munck, 2009; Heywood & Rose, 2014; Razafindrakoto & Roubaud, 2010; Thomas, 2010; Weber, 2008). A criticism associated with the CPI, and corruption perception indices in general, is the contention that they have more to do with individual estimations concerning the frequency of corruption rather than the actual occurrence of corruption.

This does not necessarily negate the importance or usefulness of the CPI as perceptions are an essential element in forming the public's viewpoint towards the performance of the government and political leaders (Treisman, 2000).

The CPI also looks solely at perceptions of public sector corruption as perceived by experts only. However, private sector actors have also at times played very significant roles. Some compelling empirical findings about the scale and scope of corruption in the private sector come from academic scholarship. A recent study of large shareholders and top officers of more than 20,000 publicly traded firms in 47 countries provides convincing evidence that conflicts of interests permeate developing and developed countries alike (Faccio, 2006). Elsewhere, Ufere, Perelli, Boland, and Carlsson (2012) find that entrepreneurs are active (not passive, as typically portrayed in the literature) bribers, having developed highly sophisticated bribery practices supported by a large network of other actors such as government agents, politicians, and technocrats. These are just some examples of the part played by the private sector in the corruption problem that is entirely overlooked by the CPI.

A different critique questions the validity of the practice of constructing indices from a variety of different data sources. The CPI is an aggregate indicator comprised of a series of different surveys each with its own unique definition and conceptualization of political corruption. This approach is problematic becomes it assumes that respondents share a similar assessment practice resulting in a high degree of accuracy in what is perceived as low/high corruption. However, considering the extant literature, it would not be very surprising to discover considerable unreliability in the high/low rankings (Knack, 2006; Søreide, 2006). A related problem associated with aggregated corruption indicators is the loss of conceptual clarity (Rohwer, 2009). Aggregate indicators, such as the CPI, combine the views of a large number of individuals residing in developing and developed countries that are obtained from survey responses compiled from a diverse variety of private, non-governmental, and international entities. As such, it is unclear what the findings reached employing a composite corruption indicator actually reveal as the form or type of corruption and their meaning vary from country to country (Thompson & Shah, 2005).

Notwithstanding definitional and measurement concerns, more than at any time in the past, we now have better evidence of actual corruption and know a lot more about the corruption that people actually experience in their daily lives. At the same time, we have a greater awareness of the causes and consequences of political corruption. At the level of ordinary citizens, there are a number of data sources that provide insight into citizens' experiences and perceptions of political corruption that have important implications for system support and effectiveness. Furthermore, other assessment tools such as the

Business Environment and Enterprise Survey (BEEPS) turns the spotlight onto the business community – making the connection that corruption is not limited to the public sector, but involves businesses as well (Faccio, 2006; Ufere et al., 2012). In addition, a recent trend in the field of corruption measurement has been toward "actionable" measures that pinpoint specific features of corruption that directly link to where policy reforms can be made. They have also been helpful in the development of explanations for what might be causing corruption, as well as helping to decide both what particular action should be implemented and assessing whether it has worked (United National Development Program, 2008). In short, the very best of these measurement practices are useful for identifying site trends and to illustrate the scale and scope of particular types of corruption. Nevertheless, like Transparency International's CPI, they alone cannot provide a definitive accounting of political corruption. In the end, the recommended best practices solution is employing a mixed-methods approach that relies on "multiple sources of quantitative data, qualitative narrative analysis, and real-life case studies to "paint a picture" of corruption in a country, sub-national, or sector context" (UNDP, 2008, p. 8).

POLITICAL CORRUPTION IN THE U.S.

Although less so than in other countries, political corruption has plagued the U.S. throughout its relatively short history. In fact, allegations of political corruption date back as far as the 1700s. The U.S. government has tried to curtail corruption at numerous times by passing legislation (e.g. Pendleton Act) or implementing regulations (e.g. the Obama Administration's ethics reform), but these efforts may do little to change the public's attitudes regarding political corruption. Political corruption in the U.S. is a complex phenomenon which can be assessed at the global, national, and state level.

The U.S. ranked 18 (among the 176 countries evaluated) with a score of 74 points out of 100 on the 2016 Corruption Perceptions Index reported by Transparency International (TI, 2016). According to the CPI rankings, corruption is a relatively rare occurrence in the U.S. – the country averaged 74.7 points from 1995 until 2015, reaching an all-time high of 78 points in 2000 and a record low of 71 points in 2010.

Within the U.S., which states are more corrupt? Well, depending on how you define corruption, it could be Louisiana, or New York, or Kentucky, or Georgia (Enten, 2015), and then there is the District of Columbia. Few cities have experienced the rash of corruption charges that the District has faced. In the space of two years, three city council members, Michael Brown,

Kwame Brown, and Harry Thomas Jr., resigned and plead guilty to corruption or embezzlement charges not to mention the investigation into Mayor Vincent Gray's 2010 campaign. Per capita, with only 602,000 residents and a per capita conviction rate of 16.02 per 10,000 residents, no state comes anywhere close to the number of officials convicted (Simpson et al., 2012).

A number of studies examining the impact of corruption in the American states identify conviction rates of public officials for violations of federal corruption laws as a valid and reliable measure (Glaeser & Saks, 2006; Liu & Mikeseli, 2014; Meier & Holbrook, 1992). The theoretical and empirical evidence confirms that the number of public official convictions is an objective and consistent measure to capture state-level corruption. In addition to confirming a great deal of face validity, the results of these studies show considerable accord with outcomes using a similar objective measure of corruption (see for example, Johnston, 1983; Nice, 1983) as well as exhibiting a positive correlation with subjective (or perception-oriented) indices of corruption compiled from elite and/or mass survey data (Glaeser & Saks, 2006; Meier & Holbrook, 1992; Peters & Welch, 1978b). Indeed, averaging conviction data based on the number of public officials (federal, state, and local) compiled by the U.S. Department of Justice for the period 1976–2008, Liu & Mikeseli show that the top ten corrupt states are (from most convictions to least) Alaska, Mississippi, Louisiana, North Dakota, South Dakota, Tennessee, Alabama, Illinois, Montana, and New York (2014). On the least corrupt side, we find Oregon followed by Washington, Minnesota, New Hampshire, Utah, Iowa, Nebraska, Colorado, Vermont and Wisconsin. These considerations notwithstanding, the available evidence suggests that there is considerable agreement that the extent to which the mass public accurately perceives political corruption affects the functioning of U.S. democracy.

PUBLIC PERCEPTIONS OF CORRUPTION IN THE U.S.

This section considers the extent to which the U.S. public perceives political corruption to be a problem – both over time and at various levels of government – and what these impressions might mean for the future health of American democracy. More specifically, this section permits us to examine the perceived severity of political corruption in the U.S. and if/how perceptions of corruption influence citizens' interactions with government and views about policy preferences for regulating political corruption. Keeping in mind the somewhat erratic availability of political corruption survey items and the definitional and measurement challenges discussed previously, much of the focus will be on interpreting public opinion data to ascertain "how" and "what" the American public thinks about political corruption over time. To facilitate the longitudinal discussion, where possible, comparisons of responses for slightly different worded questions will occur.

Responses based on several nationally representative surveys reveal a broad consensus among the American public that political corruption is an important and pervasive problem facing the country (Streb & Clark, 2009). Although the question wording is slightly different, multiple polling organizations have asked about people's views regarding the importance of corruption. The results all tell a familiar story: most of the public say that corruption in government is an "extremely" or "very" important issue to them. A recent Gallup survey reports that a full 87% of Americans deemed reducing corruption as either extremely or very important – placing this issue second only to the economy and job creation, and ahead of the budget deficit, terrorism, and Social Security, as among the top priorities for the next president (Gallup, 2012). Moreover, while there is considerable partisan polarization over a host of political issues, reducing government corruption enjoys support from voters on both sides of the partisan aisle. While supporters of the Democratic and Republican presidential candidates disagreed on how best to address the major issues facing the country, they both rated reducing government corruption among their top priorities for the next president (46% vs. 45%, respectively) (Gallup, 2012).

Virtually no one believes that corrupt political leaders are "not a problem at all." Further, trend analyses based on several Gallup polls indicate that while the numbers have fluctuated slightly since 2007, the percentage who see government corruption as a pervasive problem has never been less than a majority in the past decade. More disconcerting is the *growing* number of Americans – 67% in 2007 as compared to 75% in 2014 – who believe government corruption is more widespread (Gallup, 2015a). In a similar vein, Americans believe that "corrupt political leaders" are a significant problem in the U.S. The results of three separate Pew Research Center surveys conducted in 2002, 2006, and 2007 showed that roughly 80% of the U.S. adults believed that "corrupt political leaders" are a "very/moderately" big problem (Pew Research Center, 2006, p. 57). Also troubling is the discovery that the public's corruption concerns extend to specific institutions of government. Americans give Congress dismal marks for its performance with more than half saying they believe corruption on Capitol Hill is commonplace. Recent Gallup surveys taken in 2014 and 2015 showed that a majority of Americans believed most members of the U.S. Congress are corrupt and roughly, three-in-ten believed their own member is corrupt (Gallup, 2015b).

The picture is slightly more positive when the public evaluates the degree of political corruption in local or state government. According to the results of an *ABC News/Washington Post* poll, 33% of Americans believed that corruption in state government was "widespread" and 24% said the same when asked about their local government (*ABC News/Washington Post*, 2006). Likewise, additional evidence supports the view that the public perceives federal government corruption as more pervasive than at other levels of government. Specifically, when asked which level of government was *most* corrupt – "the federal government, your state government, or your local government," more than half (59%) of the public pointed to the Washington establishment as the main source of the problem as opposed to the 15% and 13% who identified their local or state governments (NPR/Kaiser/Kennedy School, 2000, p. 1).

These findings provide compelling evidence that the American public is overwhelmingly troubled by political corruption. Regardless of variations in question wording, large majorities consider "government corruption" as a "serious," "important," or "big" problem. Certainly, this is unfortunate news for those concerned about the health of American democracy. The emergent consensus is that the public sees corruption as endemic in government and importantly, the public appears to be growing increasingly cynical about the magnitude of political corruption – contributing to concerns about government performance, effectiveness, and dissatisfaction with democracy. In fact, 65% of Americans are dissatisfied with the nation's system of government and how well it works, the highest percentage in Gallup's trend since it began in 2001 (Gallup, 2014). Indeed, a recent report indicates that the global rise of populist leaders and movements in general, and Donald Trump's presidency in the U.S. in particular, may partially reflect rising concerns about government corruption (TI, 2017). Judging by the recent successes of populist candidates at the ballot box, it is clear that they have been able to exploit public disenchantment with "the corrupt system" and present themselves as the "only way out" (TI, 2017). For example, U.S. presidential candidate Donald Trump's "Drain the swamp" reference for reforming Washington D.C. clearly resonated with U.S. voters. Likewise, there is strong academic evidence that corruption was a salient issue for many anti-establishment voters in post-Communist countries (Bagenholm, 2013; Engler, 2015). To add insult to injury, the historical evidence suggests that populist leaders use the corrupt political establishment (or anti-corruption) message to drum up support, but are only likely to exacerbate – not control – corruption as it continues to permeate into governing institutions.

POLITICAL CONSEQUENCES AND POLICY PREFERENCES

The question that remains is whether there is reason to be concerned with the public's perceptions about political corruption. We began this chapter by arguing that political corruption could affect government performance, legitimacy, effectiveness, and ultimately, the degree of system support among the populace. While some disagreement exists over the consequences of political corruption (Johnston, 1986), a voluminous literature has documented the harmful effects corruption has on a nation's social, political, and economic life (Montinola & Jackman, 2002; Rose-Ackerman, 1999). Many of these studies present persuasive evidence regarding the effects of corruption on economic development and income inequality (Gupta, Davoodi, & Alonso-Terme, 2002; Li et al., 2000; Tanzi & Davoodi, 2001); on influencing investment (domestic and/or foreign) (Anderson & Tverdova, 2003; Mauro, 1998a; Seligson, 2002; Treisman, 2000); in the development of political attitudes such as political and interpersonal trust, efficacy, and the principles of democratic accountability, equality, and openness (Anderson & Tverdova, 2003; Rothstein & Stolle, 2008; Seligson, 2002); and in the quality of public services and the public workforce (Gupta et al., 2002; Mauro, 1998b). Likewise, it is well known that political attitudes and values such as greater trust in government and efficacy can be important determinants of political participation and engagement, as well as other activities with real consequences for shaping political leadership and public policy.

Corruption undermines the legitimacy of institutions and processes and distorts policies and priorities. Corrupt elites can change either national policies or the implementation of national policies to serve their own interests at some cost to the populace, as it is typical for public spending to be diverted to sectors where corruption benefits are the greatest (Mauro, 1998a). While the precise cost of misdirected public policies caused by government corruption is difficult to determine, there is no doubt that a price is paid by the public – especially the most vulnerable in society (such as women, children, elderly, persons with disabilities) who depend more on public services and public goods and have limited or no means to look for alternative private services. Since little attention is paid to whether the needs of the collectivity are served by works or services purchased with side payments, corrupt elites flourish at the expense of the general population (Tanzi, 1998).

CONCLUSIONS

Political corruption is one of the oldest and most perplexing phenomena existing in society. While no formal consensus exists on a definition of corruption, a commonly held conceptualization is the "misuse or abuse of entrusted power for private gain" (Nye, 1967: 419). The possible causes of corruption are many and quite complex. While theories abound, the means to control it are not fully understood. Still, political corruption generally thrives in settings with poorly designed economic policies, where education levels are low and civil society is underdeveloped, and the accountability of public institutions is weak. At the same time, there are many consequences of corruption that have implications for economic, social, and political development. While disagreement continues, it is generally believed that the harmful consequences of corruption are more numerous and convincing than any beneficial exchange that might result from engaging in corrupt practices. Consequently, political corruption increases the costs of doing business while simultaneously decreasing the quality of public services and goods, and can intensify income equality and poverty. High scale corruption also dissipates political legitimacy and hinders democratic development.

A number of strategies and reforms have been proposed for reducing corruption. There is no single best practices solution when it comes to the design and implementation of anti-corruption strategies. Rather, the success of corruption reform is often dependent upon whether the proposed plan takes into consideration the country's context and main corruption challenges. As such, anti-corruption policymaking has taken different shapes and forms and been implemented in a variety of ways, with mixed results. Yet, among the existing anti-corruption strategies, international organizations identify institutional strengthening (e.g. national ownership of anti-corruption strategy design) and establishing or improving the monitoring and evaluation system (e.g. an active civil society and media enterprise), as key features to fighting corruption and improving governance (TI, 2013). Even still, the literature and real world experience shows that – either due to a lack of political will or simply due to a poorly designed strategy – anti-corruption reform implementation remains a challenge (Hussmann, 2007; McCusker, 2006).

REFERENCES

ABC News/Washington Post. (2006). Monthly poll #1. Retrieved from http://www.icpsr.umich.edu/icpsrweb/ICPSR/studies/4654

Anderson, C. J., & Tverdova, Y. V. (2003). Corruption, political allegiances, and attitudes toward government in contemporary democracies. *American Journal of Political Science*, *47*(1), 91–109.

Andersson, S., & Heywood, P. M. (2008). The politics of perception: Use and abuse of Transparency International's approach to measuring corruption. *Political Studies*, *57*(4), 746–767.

Arndt, C., & Oman, C. (2006). Uses and abuses of governance indicators. *OECD, Development Centre Studies, Paris*.

Bagenholm, A. (2013). The electoral fate and policy impact of "anti-corruption parties" in Central and Eastern Europe. *Human Affairs Post disciplinary Humanities & Social Sciences Quarterly*, *23*(2), 174–195.

Bandiera, O., Prat, A., & Valletti, T. (2009). Active and passive waste in government spending: Evidence from a policy experiment. *American Economic Review*, *99*, 1278–1308.

Berg, L. L., Hahn, H., & Schmidhauser, J. R. (1976). *Corruption in the American political system*. Morristown, NJ: General Learning Press.

Bhagwati, J. N. (1974). Illegal transactions in international trade. In J. N. Bhagwati (Ed.), *Anatomy and consequences of exchange control regimes* (pp. 64–81). Amsterdam and New York: North-Holland-American Elsevier.

Bradburn, N. M. (1983). Response effects. In P. H. Rossi, J. D. Wright, & A. B. Anderson (Eds.), *Handbook of survey research* (pp. 289–328). New York: Academic Press.

Chapman University (2016). *Survey on American Fears*. Retrieved from http://www.chapman.edu/wilkinson/research-centers/babbie-center/survey-american-fears.aspx

de Maria, W. (2008). Measurements and markets: Deconstructing the corruption perception index. *International Journal of Public Sector Management*, *21*(7), 777–797.

Di Tella, R., & Schargrodsky, E. (2003). The role of wages and auditing during a crackdown on corruption in the City Buenos Aires. *Journal of Law and Economics*, *46*, 269–300.

Dreher, A., Kotsogiannis, C., & McCorriston, S. (2007). Corruption around the world: Evidence from a structural model. *Journal of Comparative Economics*, *35*(3), 443–466.

Duncan, N. (2006). The non-perception based measurement of corruption: A review of issues and methods from a policy perspective. In J. G. Sampford (Ed.), *Measuring corruption* (pp. 131–162). London, UK: Ashgate Publishing.

Engler, S. (2015). Corruption and electoral support for new political parties in Central and Eastern Europe. *West European Politics*, *39*(2), 278–304.

Enten, H. FiveThirtyEight. (2015). *Ranking the States from Most to Least Corrupt*. Retrieved from https://fivethirtyeight.com/datalab/ranking-the-states-from-most-to-least-corrupt/

European Bank for Reconstruction & Development. (2017). *World Bank Business Environment and Enterprise Performance Survey*. Retrieved from, http://ebrd-beeps.com/

Faccio, M. (2006). Politically connected firms. *American Economic Review*, *96*(1), 369–386.

Ferraz, C., & Finan, F. (2008). Exposing corrupt politicians: The effects of Brazils publicly-released audits on electoral outcomes. *Quarterly Journal of Economics*, *123*(3), 703–745.

Gallup (2012). Americans *Want Next President to Prioritize Jobs, Corruption*. Retrieved from http://www.gallup.com/poll/156347/Americans-Next-President-Prioritize-Jobs-Corruption.aspx

Gallup (2015a). *In U.S., 65% Dissatisfied with How Gov't System Works*. Retrieved from http://www.gallup.com/poll/166985/dissatisfied-gov-system-works.aspx

Gallup (2015b). *Majority of Americans See Congress As Out of Touch, Corrupt*. Retrieved from http://www.gallup.com/poll/185918/majority-americans-congress-touch-corrupt.aspx

Glaeser, E. L., LaPorta, R., López-de-Silanes, F., & Shleifer, A. (2004). Do Institutions Cause Growth? *Journal of Economic Growth*, *9*(3), 271–303.

Glaeser, E. L., & Saks, R. E. (2006). Corruption in America. *Journal of Public Economics, 90,* 1053–1072.

Golden, M., & Picci, L. (2005). Proposals for a new measure of corruption, illustrated with Italian data. *Economics and Politics, 17*(1), 37–75.

Gupta, S., Davoodi, H., & Alonso-Terme, R. (2002). Does corruption affect income inequality and poverty? *Economics of Governance, 3,* 23–45.

Hawken, A., & Munck, G. L. (2009). Do You Know Your Data? Measurement Validity in Corruption Research. Working Paper, School of Public Policy, Pepperdine University.

Heidenheimer, A. J. [1970] (1989). Perspectives on the perception of corruption. In A. J. Heidenheimer, M. Johnston, and V. T. LeVine (Eds.), *Political corruption: A handbook.* New Brunswick, NJ: Transaction.

Heywood, P. M., & Rose, J. (2014). "Close but no cigar": The measurement of corruption. *Journal of Public Policy, 34*(3), 507–529.

Hussmann, K. (Ed.). (2007). Anti-corruption policy making in practice: What can be learned for implementing Article 5 of UNCAC? Report of six country case studies: Georgia, Indonesia, Nicaragua, Pakistan, Tanzania, and Zambia, U4 Report 1. Retrieved from file:///C:/Users/a1563778/Downloads/2914-anti-corruption-policy-making-in-practice. pdf

Johnston, M. (1986). The political consequences of corruption: A reassessment. *Comparative Politics, 18*(4), 459–477.

Johnston, M. (2000). Measuring the new corruption rankings: Implications for analysis and reform. In A. J. Heidenheimer & M. Johnston (Eds.), *Political Corruption 2000.* New Brunswick, NJ: Transaction Press.

Kaufmann, D. (2005). Back to Basics — 10 Myths About Governance and Corruption. *Finance & Development, 42*(3). Retrieved from http://www.imf.org/external/pubs/ft/ fandd/2005/09/basics.htm

Kaufmann, D., Kraay, A., & Mastruzzi, M. (2007). Worldwide governance indicators project: Answering the critics. *World Bank Policy Research Working Paper* No. 4149. Retrieved from https://ssrn.com/abstract=965077

Kaufmann, D., & Kraay, A. (2008). Governance indicators: Where are we, where should we be going? *The World Bank Research Observer, 23*(1), 1–30.

Kenny, C. (2006). Measuring and reducing the impact of corruption in infrastructure. *World Bank Policy Research Working Paper 4099.* Retrieved from http://siteresources.worldbank. org/INTINFNETWORK/Resources/wps4099.pdf

Knack, S. (2006). Measuring corruption in Eastern Europe and Central Asia: A critique of the cross-country indicators. *World Bank Working Paper 3968.*

Kurtz, M., & Schrank, A. (2007). Growth and governance: A defense. *Journal of Politics, 69*(2), 563–569.

Lambsdorff, J. G. (2007). *The institutional economics of corruption and reform.* Cambridge University Press.

Li, H. L., Xu, C., & Zou, H. F. (2000). Corruption, income distribution, and growth. *Economics and Politics, 12*(2), 155–182.

Linz, J., & Stepan, A. (1996). Toward consolidated democracies. *Journal of Democracy, 7,* 14–33.

Liu, A. P. (1983). The politics of corruption in the People's Republic of China. *American Political Science Review, 77*(3), 602–623.

Liu, C., & Mikesell, J. L. (2014). The impact of public officials' corruption on the size and allocation of U.S. state spending. *Public Administration Review, 74*(3), 346–359.

Mauro, P. (1998a). Corruption and the composition of government expenditure. *Journal of Public Economics, 69,* 263–279.

Mauro, P. (1998b). Corruption: Causes, consequences, and agenda for further research. *Finance and Development*, 11–14. Retrieved from http://conferences.wcfia.harvard.edu/sites/projects.iq.harvard.edu/files/gov2126/files/mauro_1998.pdf

McCusker, R. (2006). Review of anti-corruption strategies. Technical and background paper, Australian government. Retrieved from http://www.aic.gov.au/media_library/publications/tbp/tbp023/tbp023.pdf

Meier, K., & Holbrook, T. M. (1992). I seen my opportunities and I took'em: Political corruption in the American states. *Journal of Politics*, *54*, 135–155.

Mishler, W., & Rose, R. (2001). What are the origins of political trust? Testing institutional and cultural theories in post-Communist societies. *Comparative Political Studies*, *34*(1), 30–62.

Mocan, N. (2008). What determines corruption? International evidence from microdata. *Economic Inquiry*, *46*(4), 493–510.

Montinola, G. R., & Jackman, R. W. (2002). Sources of corruption: A cross-country study. *British Journal of Political Science*, *32*(1), 147–170.

NPR-Kaiser-Kennedy School Poll Attitudes Toward Government. Retrieved from http://www.npr.org/programs/specials/poll/govt/gov.toplines.pdf

Nye, J. S. (1967). Corruption and political development: A cost-benefit analysis. *The American Political Science Review*, *61*(2), 417–427.

Olken, B.A. (2006). Corruption and the costs of redistribution: Micro evidence from Indonesia. *Journal of Public Economics*, *90*, 853–870.

Olken, B.A. (2007). Monitoring corruption: Evidence from a field experiment in Indonesia. *Journal of Political Economy*, *115*, 200–249.

Olken, B. A., (2009). Corruption perceptions vs. corruption reality. *Journal of Public Economics*, *93*(7–8), 950–964.

Peters, J. G., & Welch, S. (1978a). Political corruption in America. *American Political Science Review*, *72*, 974–984.

Peters, J. G., & Welch, S. (1978b). Politics, corruption, and political culture: A view from the State legislatures. *American Politics Quarterly*, *6*, 345–356.

Pew Research Center. (2006). America's Immigration Quandary - No Consensus on Immigration Problem or Proposed Fixes. http://www.people-press.org/2006/03/30/americas-immigration-quandary/ (Accessed March 23, 2017)

Pharr, S. J. (2000). Officials' misconduct and public distrust: Japan and the trilateral democracies. In S. J. Pharr & R. D. Putnam (Eds.). *Disaffected democracies: What's troubling the trilateral democracies?* (pp. 173–201). Princeton, NJ: Princeton University Press.

Potter, J. D., & Tavits, M. (2012). Curbing corruption with political institutions. In S. Rose-Ackerman and T. Søreide (Eds.). *International handbook on the economics of corruption, Volume Two* (pp. 52–79). MA: Edward Elgar Publishing.

Razafindrakoto, M., & Roubaud, F. (2010). Are international databases on corruption reliable? A comparison of expert opinion surveys and household surveys in sub-Saharan Africa. *World Development*, *38*(8), 1057–1069.

Reinikka, R., & Svensson, J. (2004). Local capture: Evidence from a central government transfer program in Uganda. *Quarterly Journal of Economics*, *119*, 679–705.

Rohwer, A. (2009). Measuring corruption: A comparison between the Transparency International Corruption Perceptions Index and the World Bank's Worldwide Governance Indicators. *CESifo DICE Report*, *7*(3), 42–52.

Rose-Ackerman, S. (1978). *Corruption: A study in political economy*. NY: Academic Press.

Rose-Ackerman, S. (1999). *Corruption and government*. Cambridge University Press.

Rothstein, B., & Stolle, D. (2008). The state and social capital: An institutional theory of generalized trust. *Comparative Politics*, *40*(4), 441–459.

Schwindt-Bayer, L. A., & Tavits, M. (2016). *Clarity of responsibility, accountability, and corruption.* New York: Cambridge University Press.

Scott, J. C. (1972). *Comparative Political Corruption.* Englewood Cliffs, NJ: Prentice-Hall.

Seligson, M. (2002). The impact of corruption on regime legitimacy: A comparative study of our Latin American countries. *Journal of Politics, 64*(2), 408–433.

Seligson, M. (2006). The measurement and impact of corruption victimization: Survey evidence from Latin America. *World Development, 34*(2), 381–404.

Smith, D. J. (2010). Corruption, NGOs, and development in Nigeria. *Third World Quarterly, 31*(2), 243–258.

Søreide, T. (2006). Is it wrong to rank? A critical assessment of corruption indices. *Working paper,* Chr. Michelsen Institute. Retrieved from https://www.cmi.no/publications/2120-is-it-wrong-to-rank

Streb, M. J., & Clark, A. K. (2009). The public and political corruption. In M. A. Genovese & V. A. Farrar-Myers (Eds.). *Corruption and American politics* (pp. 275–304). NY: Cambria Press.

Tanzi, V. (1998). Corruption and the budget: Problems and solutions. In A. K. Jain (Ed.). *Economics of corruption* (pp. 111–128). Norwell, MA: Kluwer Academic.

Tanzi, V., & Davoodi, H. (2001). Corruption, growth, and public finances. In A. K. Jain (Ed.). *The political economy of corruption* (pp. 89–110). London: Routledge Press.

Thomas, M. A. (2010). What do the worldwide governance indicators measure? *European Journal of Development Research, 22,* 31–54.

Thompson, T., & Shah, A. (2005). Transparency International's Corruption Perceptions Index: Whose Perceptions Are They Anyway? Washington, DC: World Bank. Retrieved from https://pdfs.semanticscholar.org/6106/ce11dbfe3bbf3fbc21c571957fcb8492c132.pdf

Transparency International (2013). Anti-corruption helpdesk: Providing on-demand research to help fight corruption. Retrieved from http://www.transparency.org/files/content/corruptionqas/Good_practices_in_anti-corruption_strategy.pdf

Transparency International (2015). Corruption perceptions index 2015. Retrieved from https://www.iaca.int/images/news/2016/Corruption_Perceptions_Index_2015_report.pdf

Transparency International (2016). Corruption perceptions index 2016. Retrieved from http://www.transparency.org/news/feature/corruption_perceptions_index_2016

Transparency International (2017). Corruption and inequality: How populists mislead people. Retrieved from http://www.transparency.org/news/feature/corruption_and_inequality_how_populists_mislead_people

Treisman, D. (2000). The causes of corruption: A cross-national study. *Journal of Public Economics, 76*(3), 399–457.

Treisman, D. (2007). What have we learned about the causes of corruption from ten years of cross-national empirical research? *Annual Review of Political Science, 10*(1), 211–243.

Tverdova, Y. V. (2011). See no evil: Heterogeneity in public perception of corruption. *Canadian Journal of Political Science, 44*(1), 1–25.

Ufere, N., Perelli, S., Boland, R., & Carlsson, B. (2012). Merchants of corruption: How entrepreneurs manufacture and supply bribes. *World Development, 40*(12), 2440–2453.

United National Development Program – Global Integrity. (2008). A Users' Guide to Measuring Corruption. Retrieved from https://www.un.org/ruleoflaw/files/8%20A%20Users%20Guide%20to%20Measuring%20Corruption_2008.pdf

Weber A. C. (2008). How much do perceptions of corruption really tell us? *Economics: The Open-Access, Open-Assessment E-Journal, 2,* 2008-3. Retrieved from http://www.economics-ejournal.org/economics/journalarticles/2008-3

CHAPTER 2

THE PRICE OF CORRUPTION IN CONGRESS

Michael J. Pomante II and Scot Schraufnagel

ABSTRACT

The research uncovers an increase in the disapproval of Congress and a drop in public trust in government associated with exposed congressional corruption in the post-Watergate era. The tools Congress holds to punish members caught up in scandal are discussed and the chapter considers five major scandals to rock Congress since the 1970s. Importantly, we uncover evidence that government institutions and actors are somewhat resilient and can bounce back after experiencing negative public sentiment for a period of time. Yet, it seems in the aftermath of exposed corruption, the corresponding drop in public support has policy implications. We determine that movement in public disapproval of Congress and overall trust in government help explain public law output and the ability of Congress to pass its contemporary legislative agenda.

Keywords: Congress; disapproval; public policy; scandal; trust in government

Corruption, Accountability and Discretion
Public Policy and Governance, 23–42
Copyright © 2017 by Emerald Publishing Limited
All rights of reproduction in any form reserved
doi:10.1108/S2053-769720170000029002

INTRODUCTION

When people talk about the government in the United States, it is common to hear references to corruption or crooked politicians. Indeed, a recent study by the Pew Research Center found only 34% of Americans basically trust government. Importantly, the perception of corruption whether it reflects reality, or not, has potentially important implications. When politicians are not trusted by large proportions of the citizens they represent, it is not difficult to imagine policymaking will be affected. For instance, we know in the United States, historically, that trust in government is higher during the first two years of a new president's term, in what is commonly referred to as a honeymoon period. Not surprisingly, it is during these honeymoon periods that Congress has passed many landmark public policies (Coleman, 1999, 828). We can also note, anecdotally, that following crises like the Great Depression, the terrorist attacks of 9/11, and the Great Recession of 2008 Congress is more prone to produce new public policies, arguably because public demand for action is greater.

In this chapter we explore the relationship between congressional scandal and congressional disapproval and trust in government and test whether fluctuating levels of disapproval and trust have policymaking implications. In short, our concern is to better understand how corruption influences governance or the ability of Congress to do its job. In a society like the United States, which embraces individual liberty, there is already a public predisposed to skepticism about collective or government action. When this situation is exacerbated by the corrupt behavior of elected officials, or even the perception of corruption, the situation may become grimmer for policymakers tasked with passing laws to keep pace with an evolving political landscape. It is important to have as complete an understanding as possible of how corruption, whether imagined or real, influences collective governance.

Notably, corruption is a difficult topic to study for a couple of reasons. First, researchers in the social sciences tend to want to study observed phenomena. Unfortunately, those who commit corrupt acts do everything they can to hide their activities (Boylan & Long, 2003, p. 421). Second, corruption is difficult to define. Broadly speaking, political corruption refers to any undesirable or unlawful act by a political actor (Heidenheimer, Johnston, & LeVine, 1989, 8–9). More directly, scholars note, political corruption is the act of using one's public office for personal gain (Johnson, LaGountain, & Yamarik, 2011; Rose-Ackerman, 1978). Still others tie political corruption directly to abuses of public trust (Goel and Nelson, 1998; Meier and Holbrook, 1992; Schlesinger and Meier, 2002). The lack of a concrete or agreed upon definition, however, is only part of the story. As it turns out, the simple perception of corruption can have implications for quality governance.

Michael Johnson (1986) argues that the public views any action of personal taking, official theft, misrepresentation, and favoritism as corrupt behavior, whether these events actually occur or not. Fig. 1 below shows aggregate public perceptions of corruption in the United States as assessed by Transparency International. The darker line is perceived corruption and the lighter line depicts how the United States ranks, compared to other countries around the world (Transparency International, http://www.transparency.org/research/cpi/overview). Using either metric, we learn that over the past 20 years, the United States has not seen an improvement in public perceptions

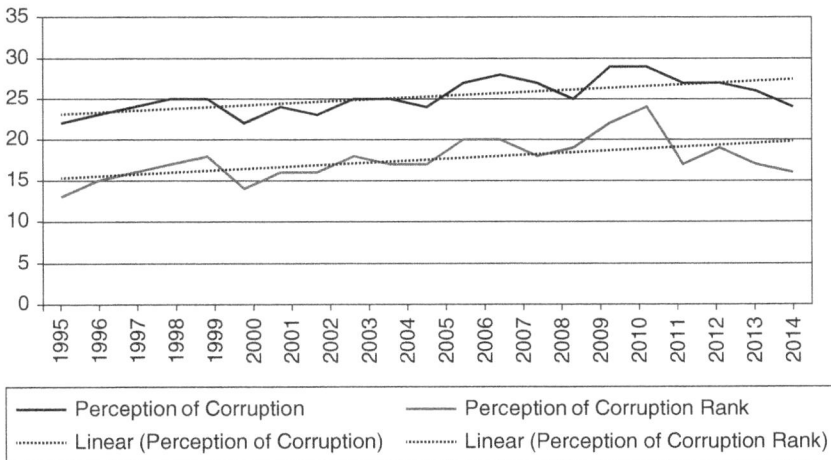

Fig. 1. Perceived Corruption in the United States: 1995–2015.
Data adapted from: Transparency International Corruption Perception Index (last accessed 3/27/2017).
Note: Transparency International first started to rank countries "by their perceived levels of corruption, as determined by expert assessments and opinion surveys" in 1995 (transparency.org, last accessed 3/29/2017). Over the years there have been minor changes to the scale that is used for assessment. From 1995 to 1997, the organization used a 10-point scale with two decimal places. In 1998 they removed one decimal place because they stated it suggested a level of accuracy that the assessment did not have. Then in 2010 they moved to a 100-point scale. In order to present the data in a consistent manner, data points which had two decimal places were rounded to the nearest tenth and values that were on a 10-point scale were multiplied by 10 to bring them in line with the current 100-point scale. Last, for the sake of presentation, scale values have been reversed, so that larger values indicating greater perceived corruption.

of corruption. In fact, the perception of corruption, and the country's rank compared to other countries, has increased slightly. In other words, in the contemporary period, public perceptions of corruption remain a real concern.

What we look to study, specifically, is whether scandal in the legislative branch produces a measureable drop in public approval of Congress and trust in government. In the past, researchers have found that higher levels of government corruption, generally, associate with more negative evaluations of the political system and government employees (Anderson & Tverdova, 2003). Scholars also note that without adequate levels of public trust, government leaders will lack support for their policy decisions (Gamson, 1968), which in turn has the ability to reduce citizen compliance with the rule of law (Barber, 1983; Levi, 1997; Tyler, 1990). Still more, it is argued that if citizens withhold their trust, government legitimacy suffers (Easton, 1965; 1975). What is missing from this body of research, however, is a thorough understanding of the manner in which exposed congressional corruption influences the ability of the legislative branch to execute its lawmaking responsibilities.

We learn that congressional scandals, in the contemporary period, have influenced congressional disapproval positively and government trust negatively. Moreover, we find an empirical relationship between varying levels of congressional disapproval and government trust and policymaking success in the form of public laws produced, as well as topical legislative productivity. It seems the price of corruption transcends whatever punishment is meted out to individual legislators caught up in scandal. The implications are for society as a whole. The chapter begins with a brief elaboration of congressional wrongdoing; we then elaborate five congressional scandals from the contemporary period, which provide the empirical foundation for the hypothesis testing that follows.

CONGRESSIONAL SCANDALS

In the U.S. Constitution, the power to remove an executive or judicial branch official for "high crimes and misdemeanors" is given to Congress through the power of impeachment (U.S. Constitution, Art. 1, Sec. 2, Clause 5). But, Article 1, Section 5, Clause 2 of the Constitution also expressly authorizes Congress to discipline its own members for "disorderly behavior" and criminal or civil misconduct. Jack Maskell (2016, p. i) notes the purpose of allowing Congress to punish its own was a way to prevent any "discredit" from descending upon the legislative branch. Yet, when members of Congress have been caught in corrupt acts, or scandalous behavior, it is rare for the institution to actually take action. Instead, voters are given the option to levy punishment in the next election cycle, by voting the implicated members out of office. If voters do not replace the accused member, the wrongdoing is often deemed insufficiently important to justify official action. Importantly, the reluctance to employ official sanctions, we will learn, does not prevent increasing public disapproval of Congress as an institution.

On occasion, Congress has felt the need to take action against a member because of activities while in office. When Congress decides to punish a member it can take one of three paths: Reprimand, censure, or expulsion. The least severe is a reprimand, which is only available in the House of Representatives. A reprimand requires majority support on a House resolution, while the member is "standing in his place," or through the adoption of a committee report (Maskell, 2016, p. 13). Similar to a reprimand, but more embarrassing for the member, is censure. A censure is issued through a majority vote in either the House or Senate, and if the resolution is passed, it is read aloud by the Speaker of the House or the presiding officer in the Senate. In addition to the public ridicule, the member is typically removed from any leadership positions he/she holds within their congressional party organization or on legislative committees. The most severe punishment a member can receive is expulsion. A member can be expelled from Congress by a two-thirds vote of the members who are present and voting in their respective chamber.

Since the 1970s, ten members of the House have been reprimanded. Nine of the ten for scandalous actions, including but not limited to, the use of their office for personal gain and failure to report campaign contributions. One member, Joe Wilson (R-SC), was reprimanded for disorderly behavior. This occurred after he interrupted President Barack Obama's speech to a joint session of Congress in 2009. The most recent and only woman to receive a reprimand from the House was Laura Richardson (D-CA) in 2012. She was found guilty of breaking House rules, which prohibit the use of official congressional staff to work on election campaigns.

Over this same time period, five members of the House have been censured. In each case the member participated in scandalous behavior, multiple times. The corruption came in the form of payroll fraud, personal use of campaign funds, sexual misconduct, and the failure to pay taxes. The most recent member of the House to be censured was Charles B. Rangel (D-NY) in 2010, for misuse of congressional letterhead, inappropriate use of a rent-controlled facility as a campaign headquarters, and a failure to pay taxes. In the same time period two members of the Senate have been censured.

Herman Talmadge (D-GA) in 1979 and David Durenberger (R-MN) in 1990, were both censured for multiple accounts of financial misconduct.

Since the 1970s, two members have been expelled from the House, Michael J. Myers (D-PA) in 1980 and James A. Traficant (D-OH) in 2002. Both were convicted of bribery, with Traficant also being found guilty of defrauding the government, receipt of illegal gratuities, obstructing justice, filing false tax returns, and racketeering. No Senators have been expelled in modern times, but several have resigned prior to a vote being held to remove them from office. In 1982, Harrison A. Williams (D-NJ) resigned after being accused of bribery in the ABSCAM scandal. In 1995, Bob Packwood (R-OR) resigned following charges of sexual misconduct and abuse of power. Most recently, John Ensign (R-NV) in 2011 was charged with financial improprieties stemming from an extramarital affair and he resigned his seat before any punitive vote could be held.

As it turns out, it is somewhat common for a member, caught in some significant scandalous behavior, to strategically vacate their position to prevent embarrassment and defeat in the next election cycle. For instance, following the release of the House Ethics Committee report which singled out members of the House of Representatives for their excessive overdrawn accounts in the House Banking Scandal, four members (Robert J. Mrazek [D-NY], Robert W. Davis [R-MI], Carl C. Perkins [D-KY], and Ed Feighan [D-OH]) retired after completing their term in the 103rd Congress (1993–95).

When we compare turnover of members of Congress, caused by strategic retirement, loss in a primary election, or loss in the General Election, there is decidedly more turnover in election cycles that takes place after a significant congressional scandal has been exposed. At the end of a two-year congressional term, without a newsworthy or notable scandal, the mean number of members who do not return is 68.2. Yet, when a scandal breaks and members of Congress are implicated in wrongdoings, the mean number of members who do not return increases to 82.9. If a member who has been caught-up in scandal is lucky enough to win re-election, they on average still lose electoral support. Research notes a drop of five (Basinger, 2012; Dimock & Jacobson, 1995) to ten (Welch & Hibbing, 1997) percentage points in the average margin of victory for members implicated in scandal.

FIVE CONTEMPORARY CONGRESSIONAL SCANDALS

We are defining the "contemporary" period as post-Watergate, starting with the 93rd Congress (1973–75). The Watergate scandal was of such immense proportions that public approval and trust in government has never recovered. For instance, the PEW Research Center keeps track of trust in government and has chronicled the results of six national surveys prior to the Watergate scandal (PEW). In these surveys, the American National Election Study asked a random sample of the American public the following question: "[d]o you think you can trust the federal government to do the right thing" (American National Election Study, 2015). The average values for the six surveys, prior to Watergate, indicate that 64% of Americans felt they *can* trust the government to do the right thing "almost always" or "most of the time." In the 1958 survey, 73% of Americans trusted government. Post-Watergate the average level of support is about half the pre-1974 average, and in 2017, only about 19% of respondents claim to trust government. By limiting the analysis to post-Watergate we have made things more difficult for ourselves because trust in government, and disapproval of Congress, have less room to vary. In addition, a study of the contemporary period reduces the possibility of faulty inferences, which can be drawn when conducting empirical tests using data from a time period that is fundamentally different from the modern era. Once each of the five scandals has been defined we will test whether these events had a measurable effect on disapproval of Congress and government trust.

Koreagate

The first major congressional scandal to occur post-Watergate was "Koreagate," which took place from 1976 to 1978. The two-year time span from mid-1976 to mid-1978 represents the period of discovery, indictments, and public awareness. Approximately 30 members of Congress attempted to work with the Korean Central Intelligence Agency (KCIA), allegedly taking bribes in an effort to boost the influence of South Korean policy objectives. News reports suggested 30 members of Congress may have taken part in the scheme. In the end, only ten members were directly implicated. At the heart of the scandal, the KCIA had agreed to parse out commissions, from American rice sales to South Korea, to members of Congress who helped establish policies favored by the South Korean government. Congressman Richard T. Hanna (D-CA) was the main actor in Congress. He and other members of the House purportedly accepted payments ranging from $100,000 to $200,000 each time they were contacted for a favor. When the story of the bribery broke, the scandal became known as Koreagate, a reference to the Watergate scandal, which preceded it. Of the ten implicated members, only Hanna was convicted. He was sentence to 6 to 30 months in prison, and served 12 months. Three other representatives received a censure by the House, and two others who were charged were subsequently acquitted.

ABSCAM

In March of 1978, the Federal Bureau of Investigation (FBI) commenced a sting operation in an effort to catch government officials accepting bribes in return for political favors. The trap was set for more than 30 government officials, including members of Congress. In the end, seven members of Congress (six from the House and one from the Senate) were convicted of bribery and conspiracy in individual trials, which took place throughout 1981. Each of the politicians was caught on videotape accepting bribes from a fictitious Arabian company called Abdul Enterprises. The company was purportedly seeking favors ranging from private immigration bills, that would allow foreigners associated with Abdul Enterprises into the country, to building permits and licenses for casinos in Atlantic City. The congressional scandal remained newsworthy throughout 1982 and we code the scandal as lasting from the beginning of 1980 until the end of 1982.

Keating Five

In 1989, five U.S. Senators were caught improperly interfering in an investigation of Charles H. Keating. The scandal became newsworthy early in 1990 and received considerable news coverage through the end of 1991. Keating was being investigated by the Federal Home Loan Bank Board (FHLBB) because the company he was leading, Lincoln Savings and Loan, had gone bankrupt and the federal government was left to bailout the company's customers. Because deposits at the savings and loan were government insured, the scandal ended up costing American taxpayers three billion dollars. This scandal became known as the Keating Five for the five Senators, Alan Cranston (D-CA), Dennis DeConcini (D-AZ), John Glenn (D-OH), John McCain (R-AZ), and Donald Riegle Jr. (D-MI), who had intervened in the investigation on behalf of Keating. In the end, Keating was convicted in both federal and state courts of fraud, racketeering, and conspiracy. He served four and a half years in prison before his convictions were overturned in 1996.

In 1991, the Senate Ethics Committee determined that Cranston, DeConcini, and Riegle had interfered with the FHLBB's investigation. However, Cranston was the only one to receive a formal scolding, but the Senate stopped short of censuring the California Democrat. Senators McCain and Glenn were criticized for exercising poor judgment by the Senate investigative committee. Although all five senators, arguably, participated in unacceptable behavior, no one stepped down from their position before the end of their term, and both Glenn and McCain subsequently won re-election campaigns.

House Banking Scandal

Early in 1992, the House Banking scandal broke. Later that year, the public became aware that some members of Congress routinely withdrew cash from the House Bank, before their paychecks were deposited, effectively taking money from the bank when they had a zero balance. In addition, the House Bank had a very generous overdraft protection policy, which allowed members to write checks when there were insufficient funds in their accounts to cover the checks. Although the scandal did not result in any actual loss of public monies, the perception of scandal shook Congress. The public seemed to easily grasp the nature of the scandalous behavior as it was routinely characterized by the media as members of Congress bouncing checks. The scandal continued to receive considerable public attention through the first half of 1993 and the scandal played a prominent role in the large amount of turnover, which occurred in the 1994 midterm elections. In the end, 77 House members either resigned or were ousted from office in the 1994 elections. Many of the worst offenders in the House Banking Scandal chose retirement rather than electoral defeat (Banducci & Karp, 1994, 279–80).

Abramoff/DeLay Lobbying Scandal

The Jack Abramoff lobbying scandal was first exposed early in 2005. On March 9, 2006, Abramoff was sentenced to five years and ten months in prison, in addition to restitution of 21 million dollars. What led to his conviction was a series of scandals which included defrauding his Native American clients, bribery of public officials, a plot to control the courts of Guam, bank fraud, and payments to thinktank employees to report favorable reviews or analyses that would benefit the policy positions of his clients. Although

Abramoff's reprehensible behavior was far reaching, only a few members of Congress got caught up in the scandal. Two members who were connected were Bob Ney (R-OH), the chair of the House Administration Committee, and Tom DeLay (R-TX), the House Majority Leader. Both members ended up stepping down from their leadership positions, in part, because of their associations with Abramoff. DeLay, importantly, was a very high profile member of Congress and his name was associated with the Abramoff scandal throughout 2006. As part of the investigation several other members were implicated when it became public they had been on golfing excursions with Abramoff. This information was used in subsequent congressional election cycles by their opponents as a means to discredit them. The last of the connected members, Tom Fenney (R-FL), lost his re-election bid in the 2008 election cycle.

THE CONSEQUENCES OF SCANDAL

Political scientists have linked trust in government to evaluations of incumbent politicians and government institutions (Feldman, 1983; Hetherington, 1998; Williams, 1985). In addition, some have specifically drawn a connection between political corruption and government trust (Chanley, Rudolph, & Rahn, 2000; Garment, 1991; Orren, 1997). Still others have found a direct link between the unethical behavior of elected members of Congress and levels of public trust (Chanley, Rudolph, & Rahn, 2000). None of these studies, however, can be construed as the final word. Arguably, more work needs to be done to better understand the role corruption can play in compromising quality governance and competent policymaking. This research looks to trace congressional scandal to public disapproval of Congress and government trust and then test for effects on lawmaking.

Corruption and Congressional Disapproval

Fig. 2 demonstrates the public's disapproval ratings of Congress post-Watergate. Although disapproval ratings are not available for every quarter, of every year since 1974, we are fortunate that the Gallup polling organization has been asking the American public the same exact question during the entire time period of this study. Specifically, the Gallup organization asks individuals "[d]o you approve or disapprove of the way Congress is handling its job" (Gallup, 2010). The figure below reports the average percentage of respondents during each

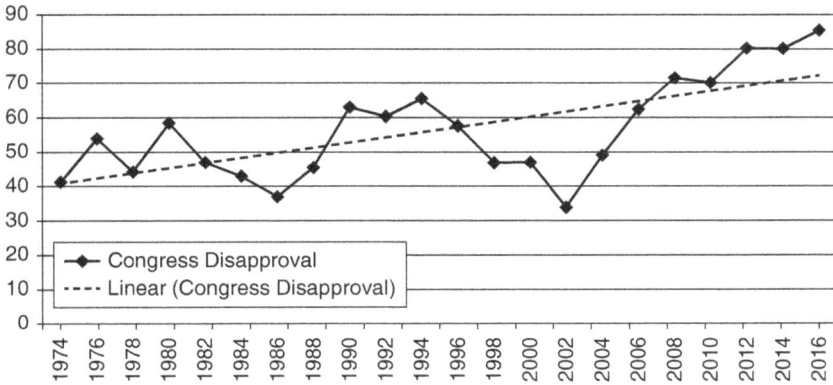

Fig. 2. Congressional Disapproval: 1974–2016.
Data adapted from: Gallup (http://www.gallup.com/poll/1600/congress-public.aspx; last accessed 4/01/2017).

biennial Congress who disapprove. It is important to note there is considerable variation in the timeline. For instance, shortly after the terrorist attacks of September 11, 2001 congressional disapproval drops rather dramatically. Indeed, the 107th Congress (2001–03) receives the lowest rating (33.9) during the time period studied. However, this effect fades, and we can note disapproval ratings in excess of 80% for the most recent Congresses. What we wish to learn is whether the scandals outlined above can help predict some of the overall movement in disapproval over time. It is important to note that scholars have found one of the best predictors of congressional approval is presidential approval (Mondak, Carmines, Huckfeldt, Mitchell, & Schraufnagel, 2007), arguably due to the blanket feelings toward government that presidential approval or disapproval enlists (Bernstein, 2001).

In Fig. 3, we display bar graphs representing disapproval ratings before and after each scandal broke. Most specifically, we use the average of the six most current measures of disapproval before the scandal became newsworthy and the average disapproval rating for the six surveys after media coverage of the scandal commenced. We use an average of six surveys to avoid bias that might result from the anomalous findings of only one or two surveys, in effect, to provide a more robust test that change has actually occurred.

Although the public tends to have a limited attention span when it comes to political scandals, Fig. 3 suggests the public expresses their disapproval immediately following each of the dishonorable episodes, apart from

ABSCAM. The null finding for ABSCAM might occur because the scandal became newsworthy soon after Koreagate, when disapproval was already high. Alternatively, the null findings for ABSCAM may be attributed to the reality that it is more difficult to pin down the actual start and end date of salacious news coverage of this particular scandal. We note disapproval goes up after Koreagate and stays right around 45% through the ABSCAM years (1980–82). Fig. 3 also demonstrates that after the three most recent congressional scandals, congressional disapproval increases significantly. Importantly these scandals seem to affect disapproval of Congress regardless of the number of members who participated in the scandalous behavior, the nature of the scandalous acts, or whether or not there was any official sanctioning of implicated members.

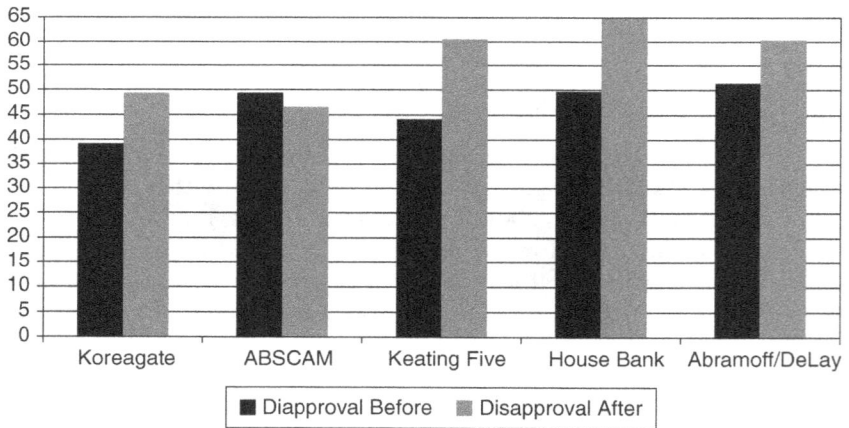

Fig. 3. Public Disapproval of Congress Before and After Major Scandals. Data adapted from: Gallup (http://www.gallup.com/poll/1600/congress-public.aspx; last accessed 4/01/2017).

Corruption and Government Trust

To measure government trust we use the American National Election Study data, available since 1958, and compiled by the PEW Research Center. Recall, the question we use asks survey respondents whether they trust the "federal government to do what is right." We add the number of respondents who answer, "just about always," to those who answered, "most of the time"

(PEW Research Center). All the surveys that took place in a two-year Congress are added up, and divided by the number of surveys conducted for display in Fig. 4. Note, in Fig. 4, higher values indicate a greater level of trust.

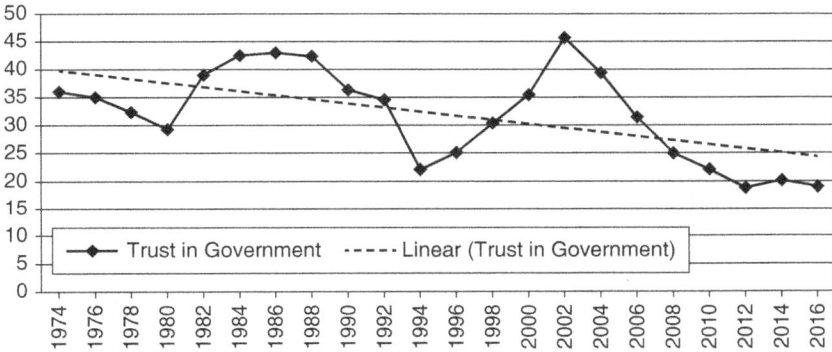

Fig. 4. Percent of U.S. Respondents Who Trust the Government to Do What Is Right: "Most of the Time" and "Almost Always."
Data adapted from: PEW Research Center's accumulation of the American National Election Study Time Series Cumulative Data File (http://www.people-press.org/2015/11/23/public-trust-in-government-1958-2015/; last accessed 4/1/2017).

Interestingly, the single survey which produces the *lowest* level of trust was conducted on October 4, 2011, during a time when the media was consistently covering a possible government shutdown. The failure of Congress and the president to agree on an operating budget was causing gridlock. We can note that over the entire period examined, trust in government has decreased and this occurs after leaving out the much higher levels of trust that existed before the Watergate scandal. Notably, by 2016, the two-year moving average value falls below 20%. What we wish to ascertain, however, is whether the rise and fall of trust, in the past 40 years or so, can be explained by the five congressional scandals outlined above.

Fig. 5 displays average values from the six surveys that preceded the scandal becoming public and the six surveys that most immediately follow the scandal making national headlines. We learn that the ABSCAM scandal does not associate with a drop in trust in the same manner as other scandals. As noted earlier, this may occur because of the close temporal proximity of the scandal to Koreagate or from an insufficient density of media coverage of the scandal. We can note, again, the three more recent scandals do associate with measureable change. With the two most recent scandals, trust levels drop precipitously. Next, we will turn to testing whether vacillation in government trust, and congressional disapproval ratings, has implications for congressional policymaking.

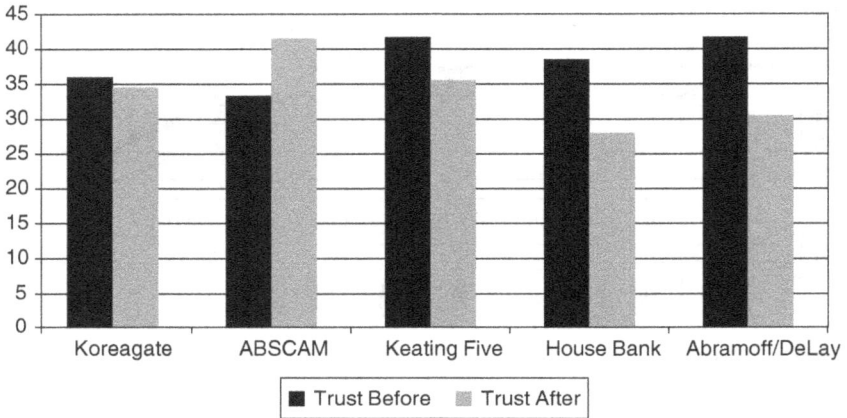

Fig. 5. Public Trust in Government before and after Major Congressional Scandals. Data adapted from: PEW Research Center (http://www.people-press.org/2015/11/23/public-trust-in-government-1958-2015/; last accessed 4/1/2017).

THE EFFECT OF DISAPPROVAL, TRUST, AND SCANDAL ON POLICYMAKING

In this section, we test the effect the two-year average values of congressional disapproval, and government trust, have on meaningful congressional output. Specifically, the following models explore how changing levels of disapproval, trust, and scandal, influence congressional policymaking using two distinct outcome variables intended to tap competent policymaking. The first is a simple count of the number of public laws enacted by each Congress. This measure is often used by media outlets as evidence of a Congress that is either getting things done or is gridlocked. It is an incomplete measure, to be certain, because it does not address the quality of the legislation passed. Moreover, the measure does not account for the length of the bill passed or the potential that a single bill may change multiple public policies. Importantly, the most common type of bill passed in the time period studied, only addresses a single public policy and the bill itself is only a single page in length. Moreover, in a mass society like the United States there is always a legislative agenda and a plethora of pressing societal concerns. In effect, the demand for legislation is always present so the volume of public laws should tell us something about whether Congress is performing responsibly.

Because any measure of a concept like competent policymaking is incomplete it is important to test things in more than one way. The second output variable we use is topical legislative productivity and the measure is drawn from the *Congressional Digest*, which has been reporting on salient issues facing each Congress since the 1920s. Specifically, the *Digest* covers either 9 or 10 topics each year or 18 to 20 issues per Congress. The *Digest* brings these topics up because editors at the journal consider the issue a pressing public matter, facing the contemporaneous Congress. We use the percent of the *Digest* topics that subsequently are addressed by new laws in the concurrent Congress as our indicator of competent policymaking. For a complete elaboration of this measure of congressional productivity, see Dodd and Schraufnagel (2017, 210–211). In both sets of models we are examining the 22 post-Watergate Congresses, the 93rd (1973–75) through the 114th (2015–17).

Our key explanatory variable in these tests is a one Congress lag of either *Congressional Disapproval* or *Trust in Government*. We lag these average values because arguably a change in disapproval or trust would not affect congressional policymaking straightaway or instantaneously, but instead would have a more extended effect. To illustrate our measurement strategy, we use average disapproval or trust in the 102nd Congress (1991–92) to predict policymaking in the 103rd Congress (1993–94) and so forth. The lag of our primary explanatory variables reduces the sample size, for these tests, to 21 Congresses.

We also include a dummy variable in each model equal to "1" for each Congress that witnessed scandal. The intention here is to control for the scandal itself and any synchronous distraction in policymaking caused by the alleged corruption. Specifically, we score the 94th (1975–76) through the 97th (1981–82) Congresses "1" to account for the Koreagate and the ABSCAM scandals. Also, the 101st (1989–90) through the 103rd (1993–94) to account for the Keating Five and House Bank scandals. Last we score the 109th (2005–06) Congress "1" to account for the Abramoff/DeLay scandal. All other Congresses are scored "0" for this consideration.

Next, we include three control variables. The first is *Presidential Honeymoons*, which are routinely found to associate with more policymaking (Coleman 1999; Binder 2003). The Congress after a November presidential election is scored "1" and other Congresses "0." We also control for the six

Quasi-Divided Governments that occur in the time period studied. These are Congresses where the two major political parties split majority control of the two chambers. Previous research (Dodd & Schraufnagel, 2017) finds this partisan arrangement to be especially deleterious when it comes to congressional policymaking. Last, we control for partisan swings in control of Congress, which ought to lead to more policymaking (Binder, 2003). Specifically, we use *Total Seat Change* or the total number of seats in the House of Representatives and Senate that witness a switch from one party to the other. Large movement, or partisan swings, ought to lead to more productivity.

Table 1 presents the results of our test of the influence of congressional disapproval and scandal on the two outcome variables explained above. We can note that congressional disapproval is associated negatively with policymaking. There are fewer public laws and less topical legislative productivity when the lagged value of congressional disapproval is taking on higher values. We can also note that Congresses defined, in part, by a current scandal produces less topical legislation. In this second model, Presidential Honeymoons and Total Seat Change also perform as hypothesized.

Considering the first model, the coefficient for Congressional Disapproval (−4.96) suggests about five less public laws, on average, for each one percent

Table 1. The Effect of Scandal and Congressional Disapproval on Policymaking.

Predictor Variables	Exp. Sign	Public Laws Passed Coefficient (s.e.)	Topical Legislation Passed Coefficient (s.e.)
Congressional Disapproval (Lagged)	Neg.	−4.96 (1.93)*	−.28 (.16)*
Scandal	Neg.	11.90 (46.22)	−7.13 (4.10)*
Presidential Honeymoons	Pos.	−5.88 (27.24)	6.78 (3.09)*
Quasi-Divided Government	Neg.	−67.98 (45.28)†	0.04 (4.47)
Total Seat Change	Pos.	0.36 (1.23)	0.56 (0.13)***
Constant		770.4 (116.9)***	16.7 (8.6)*
F-Statistic		5.28**	6.73**
Adjusted-R^2		0.52	0.59
d-Statistic		1.90	1.93
n		21	21

Notes:***$p < 0.001$; **$p < 0.01$; *$p < 0.05$; †$p < 0.10$ (one-tailed tests)
Prais-Winsten Regression to Account for Data Arrayed over Time and Possible Serial Correlation of Standard Errors (s.e.).

increase in public disapproval during the time period studied, all else being equal. Considering topical legislative productivity, a one percent increase in disapproval is associated with about a quarter percent drop (−0.28) in the percentage of these legislative matters that become law. A contemporaneous scandal is associated with about a seven percentage point (−7.13) drop in topical legislative productivity. In some respects, the fact that the control variables do not perform as well in the first model makes sense. The sheer volume of laws produced arguably can be strategic and manipulated by congressional operatives in ways that are not as predictable.

Table 2 presents the results of our test of the effect of government trust and scandal on policymaking. We used the same set of predictor variables, but now test the lag of government trust. We obtained very similar results. It turns out that congressional disapproval and trust in government are closely related. The lagged values of these two variables are correlated at $r = 0.87$ ($p < 0.001$). If there is any notable difference in the two models, it is that Government Trust seems to affect competent policymaking even more than congressional disapproval. The coefficient from the first model in Table 2 (9.94), which uses the number of public laws as the dependent variable, suggests about ten more laws, on average, associated with a one percent increase in public trust. Also notable, and consistent with existing research, after

Table 2. The Effect of Scandal and Trust in Government on Policymaking.

Predictor Variables	Exp. Sign	Public Laws Passed Coefficient (s.e.)	Topical Legislation Passed Coefficient (s.e.)
Trust in Government (Lagged)	Pos.	9.94 (2.88)**	0.40 (0.21)*
Scandal	Neg.	0.97 (41.03)	−6.62 (3.77)*
Presidential Honeymoons	Pos.	−16.72 (23.45)	5.65 (3.23)*
Quasi-Divided Government	Neg.	−70.22 (39.58)*	0.04 (4.47)
Total Seat Change	Pos.	0.10 (1.07)	0.53 (0.11)***
Constant		192.5(110.9)‡	−10.2 (8.3)
F-Statistic		7.45***	6.62***
Adjusted-R^2		0.62	0.58
d-Statistic		1.78	1.93
n		21	21

Notes:***$p < 0.001$; **$p < 0.01$; *$p < 0.05$; ‡$p < 0.10$ (one-tailed tests)
Prais-Winsten Regression to Account for Data Arrayed over Time.

controlling for other considerations, we find an average decrease in public law output of over 70 public laws under conditions of quasi-divided government. Total Seat Change, again, is an important predictor of Topical Legislation Passed after controlling for other considerations.

CONCLUSION

Our main thesis is not that scandal causes or effects public policy directly. Instead our position is that scandal influences congressional disapproval and trust in government. We are then able to show that movement in congressional disapproval and trust in government effect public policy. When members of Congress are involved in corrupt behavior, both voters and the institution of Congress have the ability to punish those involved. We note considerable inconsistency, however, in the likelihood and severity of individual punishments received by members of Congress since the 1970s. Yet, and importantly, there seem to be societal costs which transcend any individual punishment members of Congress receive. Specifically, we have uncovered an important increase in congressional disapproval and an eroding of trust in the national government associated with congressional scandals. The five scandals discussed and analyzed in this chapter are not the only bad press that Congress has received in the post-Watergate era. They are, however, indicative of high profile incidents that have received considerable public attention for a relatively narrow period of time. The limited news coverage allows for an empirical test of pre- and post-disapproval and trust ratings. Specifically, we have uncovered movement in disapproval and trust associated with four of the five scandals. This suggests, and largely affirms, our suspicion that alleged, or real, congressional scandal has implications for quality governance.

What becomes relevant, next, is whether we can trace vacillation in disapproval and trust to policymaking. In this case, we have conducted a total of four tests using two very dissimilar dependent variables. The first outcome variable was, simply, legislative output or public laws produced. Although this measure does not tap the landmark status of laws being written, it does tell us something about the willingness and ability of the legislative branch to perform its constitutionally prescribed duties. One can easily imagine in an open-mass society like the United States there is always demand for policy change. What we know now is that less of this gets addressed when public disapproval is gaining and public trust is waning. Moreover, when we set before Congress a defined agenda, determined by a nonpartisan publication (the *Congressional Digest*), the same result holds true. Congress completes less of its agenda when disapproval grows and trust shrinks. Importantly, other predictor variables in these models perform reasonably well, lending construct validity to our measurement strategies. In the end, we conclude there is, indeed, real-world implications for quality governance and effective policymaking associated with congressional scandal.

REFERENCES

American National Election Study. (2015). *Codebook*. Retrieved from http://www.electionstudies.org/studypages/anes_timeseries_cdf/anes_timeseries_cdf_codebook_var.pdf

Anderson, C., & Tverdova, Y. V. (2003). Corruption, political allegiances, and attitudes toward government in contemporary democracies. *American Journal of Political Science, 47*(1), 91–109.

Banducci, S. A., & Karp, J. A. (1994). The electoral consequence of scandal and reapportionment in the 1992 House elections. *American Politics Quarterly, 22*, 3–26.

Barber, B. (1983). *The Logic and Limits of Trust*. New Brunswick, NJ: Rutgers University Press.

Basinger, S. J. (2012). Scandals and congressional elections in the post-Watergate era. *Political Research Quarterly, 66*(2), 385–398.

Bernstein, J. L. (2001). Linking presidential and congressional approval during unified and divided governments. In J. R. Hibbing, & E. Theiss_Morse (Eds.), *What Is It about Government that Americans Dislike?* (pp. 98–117). New York: Cambridge University Press.

Binder, S. A. (2003). *Stalemate: Causes and Consequences of Legislative Gridlock, 1947–96*. Washington D.C.: Brookings Institution Press.

Boylan, R. T., & Long, C. X. (2003). Measuring public corruption in the American states: A survey of state house reporters. *State Politics and Policy Quarterly, 3*(4), 420–438.

Chanley, V. A., Rudolph, T. J., & Rahn, W. M. (2000). The origins and consequences of public trust in government: A time series analysis. *Public Opinion Quarterly, 64*, 239–256.

Coleman, J. J. (1999). Unified government, divided government, and party responsiveness. *American Political Science Review, 93*(4), 821–835.

Dimock, M. A., & Jacobson, G. C. (1995). Checks and choices: The House Bank scandal's impact on voters in 1992. *The Journal of Politics, 57*(4), 1143–1159.

Dodd, L. C., & Schraufnagel, S. (2017). Party polarization and productivity in Congress. In L. C. Dodd, & B. I. Oppenheimer, *Congress Reconsidered* (11th ed., pp. 207–236). Washington D.C.: Sage/Congressional Quarterly Press.

Easton, D. (1965). *A Systems Analysis of Political Life*. New York: Wiley.

Easton, D. (1975). A Re-assessment of the concept of political support. *British Journal of Political Science, 5*, 435–457.

Feldman, S. (1983). The measure and meaning of trust in government. *Political Methodology, 9*, 341–354.

Gallup. (2010). http://www.gallup.com/poll/145238/Congress-Job-Approval-Rating-Worst-Gallup-History.aspx

Gamson, W. A. (1968). *Power and Discontent*. Homewood, IL: Dorsey.

Garment, S. (1991). *Scandal: The Crisis of Mistrust in American Politics*. New York: Random House.

Goel, R. K., & Nelson, M. (1998). Corruption and government size: A disaggregated analysis. *Public Choice, 97*, 107–120.

Heidenheimer, A., Johnston, M., & LeVine, V. (1989). *Political Corruption: A Handbook*. New Brunswick, NJ: Transaction.

Hetherington, M. J. (1998). The political relevance of political trust. *American Political Science Review, 92*, 791–808.

Johnson, M. (1986). Right and wrong in american politics: popular conceptions of corruption. *Polity, 18*, 367–397.

Johnson, N. D., LaFountain, C. L., & Yamarik, S. (2011). Corruption is bad for growth (even in the United States). *Public Choice, 147*(3/4), 377–393.

Levi, M. (1997). *Consent, Dissent and Partiotism*. New York: Cambridge University Press.

Maskell, J. (2016). *Expulsion, Censure, Reprimand, and Fine: Legislative Discipline in the House of Representatitives*. Washington DC: Congressional Research Service.

Meier, K. J., & Holbrook, T. (1992). I seen my opportunities and I took 'em: Political corruption in the American States. *Journal of Politics, 54*, 135–155.

Mondak, J. J., Carmines, E. G., Huckfeldt, R., Mitchell, D.-G., & Schraufnagel, S. (2007). Does familiarity breed contempt? The impact of information on mass attitudes toward congress. *American Journal of Political Science, 51*(1), 34–48.

Orren, G. (1997). Fall from grace: The public's loss of faith in government. In J. S. Nye, P. D. Zelikow, & D. C. King (Eds.), *Why People Don't Trust Government*. Cambridge, MA: Harvard University Press.

Pew Research Center. http://www.people-press.org/2015/11/23/public-trust-in-government-1958-2015/

Rose-Ackerman, S. (1978). *Corruption: A Study in Political Economy*. New York: Academic Press.

Schlesinger, T., & Meier, K. J. (2002). The targeting of political corruption in the United States. In A. Heidenheimer, & M. Johnson, *Political Corruption*. New Brunswick, NJ: Transaction Publishers.

Tyler, T. R. (1990). *Why People Obay the Law*. New Haven, CT: Yale University Press.

Welch, S., & Hibbing, J. R. (1997). The effects of charges of corruption on voting behavior in congressional elections, 1982–1990. *Journal of Politics, 59*, 226–239.

Williams, J. T. (1985). Systemic influence of political trust: The importance of perceived institutional performance. *Political Methodology, 11*, 125–142.

PART II

PERMEATION OF CORRUPTION IN GOVERNANCE

CHAPTER 3

LEGISLATIVE SCANDALS IN THE UNITED STATES

Kerri Milita and Jaclyn Bunch

ABSTRACT

Just over ten years ago, the American legislative system was rocked by a series of scandals surrounding powerful lobbyist Jack Abramoff who claimed to have "bought" influence in nearly half of the United States congressional offices. The Abramoff scandal brought public attention to three critical areas of corruption in congressional politics: loopholes in gift-giving laws, campaign finance, and the revolving door. For instance, why are lobbyists allowed to buy a meal for congressional representatives if they are both standing up but not if they are sitting down? Why is sharing a simple meal with an elected official banned but allowed so long as campaign contribution checks are exchanged (i.e., the mystery of the $5,000 hamburger)? And just how much does it cost to buy your congressman? We explore these areas of corruption that were brought to light in 2006 by "the biggest political scandal of the century," and examine how things have, or in some instances, haven't changed in the years since the Abramoff scandal broke. Does Congress run cleaner today? Or is it still politics as usual?

Keywords: Congress; corruption; Abramoff; campaign finance; revolving door; loopholes

Corruption, Accountability and Discretion
Public Policy and Governance, 45–60
Copyright © 2017 by Emerald Publishing Limited
All rights of reproduction in any form reserved
doi:10.1108/S2053-769720170000029003

INTRODUCTION

"The great tragedy in American politics is what is legal, not what is illegal."
— Jack Abramoff

In 2005, the American legislative system was rocked by a series of scandals surrounding powerful lobbyist Jack Abramoff. At the root of this controversy was Abramoff's claim that he had "bought" influence in nearly half of the United States congressional offices. Abramoff immediately became the face of the "biggest political scandal of the century" (Schmidt & Grimaldi, 2005). What began as a simple indictment over misappropriating clients' funds quickly unraveled to reveal a complicated and interconnected web of congressional corruption. In one short year, the scandal culminated in the arrest of Bob Ney (R-OH), chairman of the powerful House Administration Committee which oversees federal elections, the resignation of then House Majority Leader Tom DeLay (R-TX), and the incarceration of Abramoff himself.

Following investigations by the House, Senate, and Department of Justice, it was discovered that *at least* four-dozen members of Congress had indisputable ties to Abramoff and had engaged in unethical, though not necessarily illegal, activities such as allowing the influential lobbyist to pay for "fact-finding missions" to golf courses in Scotland (Cowen, 2013). The sizable roster of congressmen and congressional staff entangled with Abramoff sits in stark contrast to the actual number of resignations and convictions that resulted from the scandal. Abramoff himself would later lament that most of his unscrupulous dealings were legal; that they were simply the result of exploiting blatant loopholes in ethics rules, loopholes intentionally left open by members of Congress to benefit themselves (Abramoff, 2011).

Following his three and half year stint in prison Abramoff hit the media circuit. This move appeared to be motivated by his crusade to highlight three key avenues of legislative corruption, avenues he used to secure influence in Congress; avenues that, he assures us, remain open even today. The three main pathways of lobbyist influence over legislators are (1) the revolving door, whereby former members of Congress or congressional staff leave public service to work for lobbying firms and lobby former colleagues, (2) campaign finance, and (3) gift-giving while in office.

The revolving door, Abramoff noted, is perhaps the easiest, most immediate means of obtaining legislative access. Under this mechanism, members of Congress or congressional staff will agree to job offers in lobbying firms while they are still acting in their capacity as public servants; in the months or years during which they are still elected officials or staffers, their future employer effectively "owns" the office (Abramoff, 2011; Vidal, Draca, & Fons-Rosen, 2012). Similarly, while federal laws prohibit campaign contributions exceeding $5,000, the political action committee (PAC) system allows lobbyists to donate unlimited sums of money to non-profit groups (PACs) that produce television advertisements on candidates' behalves (Magleby & Nelson, 1990). Additionally, while lobbyist-to-legislator gift-giving is technically prohibited under House and Senate ethics rules, gifts such as food, drink, or lobbyist-sponsored travel are allowed provided that the goods are received during fundraisers, charity events, or "fact-finding missions," whereby members of Congress must physically travel to obtain some "policy-relevant information" (Committee on Ethics, 2016a).

In this chapter, we will explore these three key avenues of lobbyist influence over Congress using the infamous Abramoff scandal as a guidepost. We explore these areas of corruption that were brought to light over ten years ago by "the man who bought Washington," and examine how things have, or in some instances, have not changed in the years since the Abramoff scandal broke. Does Congress run cleaner today? Or is it still politics as usual? We conclude our discussion by introducing several policy reforms aimed at directly addressing Abramoff's three gaping loopholes whereby special interests secure daily influence over the lawmaking process.

THE REVOLVING DOOR

Speaking from experience, Jack Abramoff has shed light on the pathways of financial corruption in the United States Congress. By far, the most influential path to power in the lobbyists' playbook is use of the revolving door. The revolving door refers to the tendency for members of Congress or their staff to leave office and immediately work for a powerful lobbying firm on K Street, peddling influence with their former legislative colleagues. Oftentimes, a lobbyists' influence over a congressional office comes not from immediate financial boons, such as gifts and campaign contributions, but rather from future employment prospects.

The goal of lobbyists in this process is to ingratiate incumbents and staffers in Congress to the interests of their firm, accomplished with promises of future employment and financial gain. In exchange, staffers and members of Congress work on behalf of the lobbyist, their future employer. Members of Congress have authorized the insertion of language into bills that enables privileges and benefits for their future employers. Abramoff admitted that he, on several occasions, lobbied members of Congress to add language into reform bills to authorize backdoor licenses to Native American tribes' casino gambling. In a 2011 interview, he noted that "[What we did] was craft language that was so obscure, so confusing, so uninformative, but so precise…to change the US code. Public law 100-89 is amended by striking section 207(101.668,672). The only person that knows what that [strike] does is the [committee] chair [Bob Ney], and he stuck it in there" (Abramoff, 2011).

After Jack Abramoff's sentencing, numerous incumbents were pressed on their relationship with Abramoff and were forced to admit that they felt compelled to work with Abramoff because he had the connections and networks to get them where they wanted to go, both during and after their political career. In an interview with *60 Minutes*, Abramoff asserted that he could influence policy by offering representatives and staffers lucrative positions within either his own firm or with related companies with whom he had establish a network. These offers were tied to promises of enormous increases to their salaries once they left the Hill. Abramoff famously said "the minute I offered him [or her] a job…that was it. We owned them" (Abramoff, 2011).

Unsurprisingly, prestigious congressional committees are among the most likely to be targeted by lobbying interests (Cox & Magar, 1999). Since the early 2000s, the Committees on Ways and Means, Appropriations, and Energy and Commerce have been the top three targeted committees in the U.S. House. The number of revolvers is just as impressive in the Senate, with the three most "revolved" committees in the Senate boasting over 400 former staffers now working as registered lobbyists (Center for Responsive Politics, n.d.). These heavily targeted committees in both the House and the Senate are the keystones of legislative functioning, controlling congressional spending, taxing, national and state energy production, and business operations, respectively.

Despite Abramoff's incarceration and subsequent call for change in the media circuit, the revolving door keeps spinning. After the November 2010 election, more lobbyists secured staff position jobs for the 112th Congress than during the two previous years (Webber, 2011). The U.S. Senate has seen comparable numbers of staffers and legislators leaving office to eventually work as lobbyists. Again, we tend to see these staffers/legislators turned lobbyists among the more influential committees within the chamber. The Senate Committees on Finance, Judiciary, Appropriations, Health, Education, Labor and Pensions, as well as Commerce, Science and Transportation all have seen attrition to the revolving door in triple digit numbers.

Finally, there is much to be said about the industries and lobbying firms that tend to offer employment to previous congressmen. While employment in a lobbying firm alone is not illegal, nor is it confirmation that there were favors exchanged while in service, it is certainly indicative of the potential for influence. And, if we are to trust the testimony of Jack Abramoff, these figures are likely signs of significant and successful lobbying efforts.

While the name Jack Abramoff rose to the collective conscious of Americans following the salient scandal and subsequent media tour, his case is far from atypical. One additional revolving door case study is the career of Billy Tauzin, a former Republican member of Louisiana's House delegation. Tauzin was originally elected to office in 1980 and served for 25 years, finally leaving in 2005. During his time in Congress, he served on prominent committees, including sitting as chair of the Energy and Commerce Committee. However, he is most notably known for his role and influential contributions to a multitude of healthcare and healthcare reform laws, including shepherding President George W. Bush's Medicare Part D proposal through the legislative process. Medicare Part D was viewed by many analysts as a financial windfall for the prescription drug industry. According to the Kirkpatrick and Wilson (2010):

> [Tauzin] set up his first hunting club — *which included lobbyists as dues-paying members* — in the early 1990s on a property about a hundred miles from the Capitol on the Eastern Shore of Maryland where he likes to shoot ducks. When the Congressional publication "Roll Call" first reported Mr. Tauzin's million-dollar purchase of the Texas ranch in 2003, his spokesman said that the House Ethics Committee had approved of the clubs and that Mr. Tauzin himself paid the same dues as other members. News of the purchase also fueled rumors around Washington that Mr. Tauzin, still presiding over major pieces of legislation, was seeking more lucrative work. In 2004, the Motion Picture Association of America reportedly offered him a salary of about $1.5 million to become its top lobbyist. Then PhRMA (*Pharmaceutical Research and Manufacturers of America*) lured him away from Congress with its $2 million-a-year offer.

Here we see loopholes in action as a congressman establishes a forum that enables lobbyists to openly affiliate with congressional staff. Why was this acceptable? Because he also paid dues to his own club. This fine distinction is often the difference between ethical and unethical behavior.

In 2005, Tauzin became President and CEO of Pharmaceutical Research and Manufacturers of America (PhRMA), which, since 2000, has brought over 50 former legislators and staffers into employment. Tauzin has spent most of his post-congressional career lobbying for pharmaceuticals, but has also represented other industries, including trucking, health services, telephone utilities, and oil-and-gas. Much of Tauzin's lobbying work has been completed in his time at PhRMA, or in his two subsequent positions; serving as Special Legislative Counsel for the lobbying firm Alston & Bird from 2010 to 2014, or independently as a Partner at Tauzin Consultants.

A similar trajectory marks Albert's Wynn's path to the revolving door. Wynn was an eight-term Democrat who served Maryland in the House of Representatives from 1993 to 2008. What is interesting in the Wynn case is that he accepted a position at a major lobbying law firm, Dickstein Shapiro LLP, prior to the completion of his congressional term. Wynn continued to serve in an influential position on the House Energy and Commerce Committee for months while revolving out almost immediately after losing the 2008 primary election, requiring his district to hold a special election to fill the vacancy for the remaining 6 months of his term (Birnbaum, 2008). Upon taking a position at Dickstein Shapiro, Wynn was barred, due to current reform laws, from actively lobbying his former colleagues, but instead engaged in "counsel" at the firm.

While serving as a partner at Dickstein Shapiro, which has a revolving door personnel count of 36 known "revolvers," he advised clients on "how Congress works and what strategies or tactics that would be helpful, where information can be obtained, what the timing ought to be of certain activities, [and] who members of Congress are that might be receptive" (Schouten, n.d.). However, the failing reach of reform is not just evident in the advising activities revolvers participate in but also the rate at which they still revolve – a trend that has not apparently slowed at all. Wynn has since moved on to a new lobbying firm, Greenberg Traurig LLP, a firm that is also known for hiring former legislators and staffers. According to FEC reports, in 2016 alone, Greenberg Traurig has given nearly $1.5 million in campaign related contributions to members of Congress, only serving to further confound the concerns for corruption.

CAMPAIGN FINANCE

Perhaps the most infamous incident of the Abramoff scandal was the indictment of House Majority Leader Tom DeLay. DeLay was the target of two separate investigations involving the U.S. House Committee on Ethics and the Department of Justice. Both investigations charged that DeLay had received political donations in exchange for granting favors to Abramoff's clients—such as the use of skyboxes at sporting events to hold fundraisers for DeLay where Abramoff himself footed the bill (Wendland, 2005). Abramoff also admitted to exceeding the federal donation limit of $5,000 by channeling money to DeLay through a PAC (Resnick, 2013).

The DeLay indictment, Abramoff argued is indicative of a much broader problem regarding American campaign finance. The PAC system effectively allows deep pocketed interests to donate potentially millions of dollars to candidates, albeit indirectly. PACs are non-profit groups dedicated to raising and spending money for the election or defeat of candidates. They can contribute up to $5,000 to a federal candidate. However, their real power, according to Abramoff, is their ability to take unlimited contributions from private entities and produce televised advertisements on behalf of candidates with the sole condition that the ads be "issue oriented" (Hasen, 2000).

In practice, the current PAC system allows lobbyists and interest groups to "double dip" in campaign donations to candidates. Abramoff himself donated money to key members of Congress and kept within the $5,000 limit. However, he was also able to channel money through several PACs that would then donate an additional $5,000 each to favored candidates. Thus, Abramoff's $5,000 donation to Tom DeLay exceeded the $5,000 cap by many tens of thousands of dollars — all technically *within* the confines of current campaign finance law.

If we examine the financial contributions that PACs have made to Democratic and Republican congressional candidates within the last 20 years, a single important pattern emerges: money follows power. Broadly, the party with the most PAC donations to its candidates was the party that controlled Congress during that election cycle. Between 2000 and 2006, Republicans retained majority control over both chambers of Congress and simultaneously, received the majority of financial contributions from PACs, according to FEC records. Similarly, in 2008, when Democrats reclaimed power in the House and Senate, Democratic candidates saw a surge in fundraising from these non-profits. Republican candidates would once again see an advantage following the Democrats' loss of the House between 2010 and 2012. PACs, just as Abramoff warned, appear to donate strategically to whichever party is in power and can assist with the group's policy concerns. More importantly, the total dollar amount of PAC contributions to candidates is substantial. From January to September 2016, over $385 million was contributed to congressional candidates through both direct financial donations and in-kind contributions (e.g. providing a large private home for a fundraiser and supplying the event with food).

The amount of money that PACs donate to candidates, however, pales in comparison to the total amount of internal fundraising that these non-profit groups can accomplish. Official campaign finance records have noted the amount of money raised and reported to the FEC each year for the last two decades. These records also show the total amount raised by PACs relative to the total amount directly donated to candidates. There are three main takea-way points from examining the last two decades of the FEC's campaign finance records. First, PAC fundraising is on the rise. In 2000, a presidential election year, PACs raised a mere $550 million. Between January and September of 2016, however, PACs raised well over $1.5 billion. Second, PACs raise far more money than they donate to candidates. Today, only about one fourth of PAC revenue is redirected to candidates. A supermajority of PAC revenue is directed toward television advertising on behalf of candidates (West, 2014). Third and finally, financial contributions to candidates are remarkably stable over time. PACs are donating about the same dollar amount to candidates each election cycle—no more, no less. Rather, it is the financial investment in televised advertisements that are increasing each election cycle.

As televised ads comprise the single most expensive aspect of campaigns, candidates are undoubtedly relieved to see PACs take on this mantle so that they can redirect their war chest coffers elsewhere (Burton, Miller, & Shea, 2015). PAC advertisements not only allow candidates to refocus their spending efforts on mobilization and outreach, they enable candidates to avoid direct mudslinging as PAC advertisements have become the primary source of negative advertisements during campaign season (Beckel, 2013). By helping to indirectly finance candidates' reelection bids, PACs, and their lobbyist backers, can forge strong collaborative relationships with policy-makers.

In the years following the Abramoff scandal, however, the United States Supreme Court issued one of the most famous rulings this century: *Citizens United vs. FEC*. The Citizens United ruling created a new breed of PAC referred to informally as the SuperPAC. SuperPACs, like PACs, must report their donors to the FEC and, unlike PACs, are forbidden from coordinat-ing with candidates, as their independence grants them unlimited fundrais-ing powers and places virtually no restrictions on how they can spend their money (Kang, 2013). In other words, SuperPACs are not required to limit their advertising to policy issues; they are free to air "express advocacy" ads (e.g. ads that instruct viewers to "vote for" x). Thus, as Abramoff remarked in a post-incarceration interview, it is highly unlikely that the corrupting influences within our campaign finance system have seen any improvement since his scandal broke in the late 2000s (Klein, 2011). If anything, the sway of lobbyists over legislators has increased since the Abramoff years, as ree-lection is more expensive than ever and candidates are all too happy to rely on PACs and SuperPACs to do their dirty work (i.e. negative advertising) for them.

THE GIFT THAT KEEPS ON GIVING

In the wake of the Abramoff scandal, the U.S. House and Senate tightened their admittedly lax gift-giving laws. Today, a member of Congress cannot take a gift (i.e. anything with monetary value) from a registered lobbyist. This includes lobbyist-sponsored travel on what were previously dubbed "fact-finding missions," whereby members of Congress could allow lobbyists to pay for travel and expenses, airfare and hotel, if the travel was necessary to investigate matters of policy. This former travel allowance led to the famed "golf-trips to Scotland" (Abramoff, 2011). Members of Congress were given free travel on private jets to exotic locations to dine at the best restaurants, all at lobbyists' expense. Abramoff remarked that at one point he spent over $1 million each year on tickets to sporting events and concerts to distribute to members of Congress, their staff, and the members' most valued constituents.

Perhaps one of the most famous non-Abramoff related scandals pertaining to gift-giving is former Alaska Senator Ted Stevens. Stevens, a longtime senator, maintained a cozy relationship with major Alaskan oil firms (and, notably, failed to report the gifts procured through this relationship). The oil company Veco allegedly renovated Stevens' Alaskan cabin into a two-story "chalet," complete with a state of the art hot tub, several viewing decks, and a large garage, all free of charge. Journalists estimated that the renovations totaled around $250,000 (Nasaw, 2009). In return, the Alaskan Senator was accused of using his seniority and powerful committee assignments to cut bureaucratic red tape and reduce government regulations on the oil company. Charges of corruption against Stevens were eventually dropped in 2009 after accusations of a mistrial. Stevens faced no formal consequences.

Currently, congressmen are now forbidden from accepting any gift valued at $25 or over, save for tokens received from immediate family members. Congressmen are also not allowed to attend any event with a monetary cover charge without paying the total amount of attending, including cover, food, and drink, themselves. The goal of these reforms was, purportedly, to restrict the undue influence of lobbyists over lawmakers and the legislative process.

However, it should come as no surprise that several loopholes were left, perhaps intentionally, open. For instance, members of Congress may still attend lobbyist-sponsored events so long as there is either no cover charge to enter or the event is, in theory, open to the public (Committee on Ethics, 2016). Thus, a lobbyist can still provide complimentary food and drink if anyone could technically attend and receive those same benefits as well. The catch is that "open to the public" events such as these are not publicized or publicly announced, and thus the public has no way of knowing that they are also able to attend (Abramoff, 2011). The open and free event ends up being attended by only the lobbyist and the legislator.

Exceptions to the gift rule have also been made for campaign events such as rallies or fundraisers (Committee on Ethics, 2016a). Lobbyists can host lavish fundraisers for members of Congress, often fronting the costs of the venue, food, drink, and travel to and from the event. These infamous fundraisers are notorious for behind the scenes influence peddling and policy promises that are made by congressmen in attendance (Abramoff, 2011). And perhaps this should come as no surprise; lobbyist fundraisers are famed for introducing the concept of "bundling," whereby lobbyists gather dozens, sometimes hundreds, of individual $5,000 checks from various donors and present them to the candidate at the event ($5,000 being the maximum amount that any single individual may contribute to a candidate within one election cycle). It is not uncommon for one of these fundraisers to bring in over $200,000 in donations to a congressman's war chest (Eggen & Farnam, 2011).

While it is technically illegal for a member of Congress to accept a meal at a restaurant from a registered lobbyist, there are several loopholes that can easily be exploited to allow such a meeting to take place. For instance, congressmen cannot have a meal with a lobbyist while sitting down. However, a meal can be had if both parties are standing up, as this implies a casual, inexpensive atmosphere (Abramoff, 2011). Moreover, the lobbyist and congressman can sit down, dine together, and have the lobbyist pick up the tab so long as the lobbyist presents the congressman with at least one check made out to the congressman's election fund by a third party—as this qualifies the meeting as a fundraiser, for which a formal exemption to the gift rule applies (Committee on Ethics, 2016a). Abramoff noted that this loophole is cheekily referred to among Washington insiders as the "$5,000 hamburger."

In short, there is little evidence that the reforms enacted in the wake of the Abramoff scandal have done anything to clean up the politics of gift giving in Congress. Lawmakers intentionally limited the scope of reforms (Abramoff, 2011). Purposeful exemptions were carved out to allow members of Congress to retain their privileged relationships with registered lobbyists, arguably their strongest and most loyal fundraisers.

POLICY REFORMS

In this section, we describe several potential policy reforms for each of the three areas of corruption and scandal that were brought to light in the wake of the Abramoff scandal. We opt to keep each proposed reform within the confines of what is already possible within our extant political system (e.g. we do not prescribe policy changes that would require, for instance, a national initiative or referendum to be adopted). These changes would require those currently in power, and potentially benefiting from deregulation, to opt into regulating themselves and their activities more stringently. While it is unlikely that leaders on either side would adopt these policy prescriptions unprompted, when sufficient public pressure is placed on members of Congress, there is a strong incentive to adopt the policies being demanded by the public (Kingdon, 1977). That is, when an issue is salient and public demands are clear, the public tends to get what it wants on matters of policy.

Halting the Revolving Door

Currently, there is a two-year "cooling off" period whereby members of Congress are forbidden from registering as lobbyists and lobbying their former colleagues. This provision, formerly called the Honest Leadership and Open Government Act, was adopted in late 2007 and signed into law by President George W. Bush following the Abramoff scandal. The bill also established a one-year "cooling off" period for legislative staff. During the so-called "cooling-off" period, neither legislative staff nor former members may formally lobby Congress.

While this reform may seem laudable it changed very little regarding how the revolving door in Washington functions. There are three key flaws with this policy reform. First, both former staff and members of Congress can still immediately go into lobbying — they just simply cannot lobby their former colleagues in the legislative branch. Thus, we see many former staff and members lobbying, for instance, executive branch agencies directly following their exit from public service, biding their time until their "cooling-off" period expires.

Second, even though former staff and members of Congress cannot immediately lobby their former colleagues, they can be employed by lobbying firms and act as non-lobbying policy consultants. Notably, this role does not require these former public servants to register to lobby. Under the Lobbying Disclosure Act of 1995, three criteria must be met for an individual to qualify as a lobbyist: the individual must (i) make more than $3,000 over 3 months from lobbying, (ii) have spent more than 20% of his or her time lobbying for a single client over 3 months, and (iii) have more than one lobbying contact.

Failure to meet all three criteria means that an individual is not required to register as a lobbyist and is, thus, not subject to the "cooling-off" period.

In recent years, there has been a sizable drop in the number of registered lobbyists, a drop that coincides with the enactment of lobbying restrictions in the late 2000s (Goodwin & Baccellieri, 2016). For instance, the number of registered D.C. lobbyists peaked in 2007 at around 15,000. Today, as of early 2017, that number stands just over 9,700. Many of these individuals that no longer register to lobby still engage in the same activities, a practice now being referred to as "shadow lobbying" (Auble, 2013). Perhaps most prominently, Newt Gingrich, former Republican Speaker of the House, was accused during the 2012 Republican presidential primary of engaging in shady lobbying practices, having made millions of dollars acting as a "policy consultant" to companies such as Freddie Mac. In his capacity as a consultant, Gingrich met with members of Congress to discuss his clients' policy concerns and never registered as a lobbyist.

Finally, the provision in the Honest Leadership and Open Government Act does not prohibit legislative staff or members of Congress from accepting future job offers while they are still serving in office. Abramoff noted during multiple interviews that offering a public servant a future job is the most surefire way to obtain policy influence in the office, as the future employer effectively now "owns" the staff or member (2011). Moreover, because these job offers are taken up months or years after the initial offer, they are virtually impossible to track.

To truly halt the revolving door, there should be an extended moratorium on elected officials and their staff entering the lobbying or consulting profession. Individuals that opt for a career in public service should ideally, by default, be locked out of the profession of lobbying. Moreover, former members of Congress and their staff should be banned from ever accepting payment or paychecks, in any form, from lobbying firms, regardless of whether the member or staff ever registers as a lobbyist. We should also implement a two-year "cooling off" period that applies to *any* organization that currently employs a lobbyist in Washington to prevent instances such as Gingrich's alleged "shadow lobbying" on behalf of Freddie Mac.

The goal behind these stringent reforms is to fundamentally change the incentive structure who runs for Congress and who opts to work as legislative staff. Nearly half of all members of Congress that leave office go on to work in a formal capacity as a lobbyist. Today, part of the expectation of working in Congress is that you will likely be able to "cash in" your public service at some point and double or triple your salary with a lobbying firm or policy consulting position. If we can demand and implement reforms that reduce the likelihood of getting rich from "public service," then, arguably more selfless individuals will be drawn toward serving. These reforms, in a way, make the decision to serve the public a financial sacrifice, in that members of Congress and congressional staff are effectively locking themselves out of a lobbying career indefinitely.

Campaign Finance Reform

To root out the power of secret money and the influence that lobbyists and their PACs have over elected officials, the only true solution is to remove private money from campaigns. Requiring all candidates to publicly finance their campaigns, made possible at the presidential level by the 1971 Federal Elections Campaign Act, would establish a level playing field for candidates and would deemphasize the importance of building a campaign war chest. Without the incentive to collect as much in private donations as possible, elected officials and their challengers would be tasked with managing their available funds as efficiently as possible.

Moreover, there is evidence that public financing of campaigns would attract a different type of legislator into the public forum, a legislator that is not solely focused on building and sustaining relationships with influential financial donors (Donnay & Ramsden, 1995). By requiring public financing of campaigns, we would effectively cap the total dollar amount that may be spent during an election cycle. Many countries such as the United Kingdom already have similar campaign finance restrictions in place. For instance, in the UK, parties are limited to spending about $30 million in the year before a major election (Castle, 2015). Televised election advertisements are banned and the campaign season is relatively short.

However, limiting the amount of money that candidates spend in an election would be almost completely undone if we continue to allow independent non-profits such as SuperPACs to continue to electioneer. A full eradication of private money from public elections would require a constitutional amendment to overturn the *Citizens United vs. FEC* ruling, admittedly a tall order.

Reforming Gift-Giving Laws

Currently, restrictions on gift-giving allow for a sizable number of loopholes and potential for exploitation by lobbying interests. To truly ensure that lobbyists are not buying favor with members of Congress or their staff, there must be more restrictive laws governing the interaction of elected officials and lobbyists. Specifically, we should consider banning all lobbyist-sponsored travel, gifts, and fundraisers, even those "that do not charge a cover fee" or "are open to the public." If an individual is a registered lobbyist, he or she must not be able to provide any type of financial contribution to members of Congress or their staff, including attendance at the same fundraising events or campaign contributions.

If an individual makes a living by lobbying members of Congress and their staff, it would seem to be a fundamental conflict of interest to allow these individuals to give financial contributions to the same elected officials they are trying to persuade. Simply, the current system allows for legalized bribery. Admittedly, policy reforms will place restrictions on personal freedoms such as prohibiting registered lobbyists from making personal campaign contributions to elected officials they have lobbied.

Forbidding members of Congress and their staff from benefitting or receiving any item or service of monetary value would potentially prevent some of the more egregious corrupting influences. For instance, the Motion Picture Association of America (MPAA) has long maintained a strong lobbying presence in D.C. and throughout the states, pressuring lawmakers and staff to adopt stringent anti-piracy laws and implement strong criminal penalties for copyright violations. Many of these sought-after policy reforms (e.g. SOPA, PIPA) entailed restricting Americans' rights to a free and open internet, authorizing corporations to monitor and patrol internet sites for copyright violations and to report offenders to government agencies, which would result in criminal charges and government censorship of the offending website. The MPAA regularly hosts "dinner and a movie" for members of Congress and their staff, whereby a large custom-built theater near the White House is used throughout the year to screen unreleased movies with complimentary drinks and dinner to congressmen and staff (Puzzanghera, 2007). These events qualify as exemptions under the gift-giving laws as the events are "widely attended" and technically "open to the public" (though the events are never publicized so "the public" is not in attendance). To reduce the corrupting influence of gift-giving, we should consider a full and complete ban on lobbyist or interest group sponsored events, travel, gifts, etc.

CONCLUSION

Does the U.S. Congress run cleaner in today's post-Abramoff era? Unlikely. Abramoff himself laments that most, if not all, of the unscrupulous activities that landed him in prison in the late 2000s are still going on in D.C. The biggest corrupting influences on America's national legislature, he argues, include the now largely accepted norm of leaving public service for the revolving door of K-Street, lucrative campaign finance deals in exchange for policy influence, and desirable all-expenses paid gifts made to officials and staffers still serving in office. Concurring with Abramoff, we argue that these three avenues hold the greatest potential for special interest influence over Congress. The question of corruption is, at its core, a question over policy. Addressing the issue of corruption will involve a discussion of the tradeoffs between the dual values of freedom, whereby any actor is free to petition government and to use their "speech" to influence policy, and equality, in which the voices of deep-pocketed actors do not drown out the voices and preferences of everyone else.

REFERENCES

Abramoff, J. (2011). *Capital punishment: The hard truth about Washington corruption from America's most notorious lobbyist*. Washington, DC: WND Books.

Auble, D. (2013). Lobbyists 2012: Out of the game or under the radar? Center for Responsive Politics. Retrieved from https://www.opensecrets.org/news/ 2013/03/lobbyists-2012-out-of-the-game-or-u/

Beckel, M. (2013). SuperPACs and the 2012 Presidential Election: What happened? What's in store? *Willamette Law Review, 49*, 655.

Birnbaum, J. H. (2008, April 1). "Wynn-Win" for K Street, loss for the public? *Washington Post*. Retrieved from http://www.washingtonpost.com/wp-dyn/content/article/2008/03/31/AR2008033102333.html

Burton, M. J., William, J. M., & Daniel, M. S. (2015). *Campaign Craft: The Strategies, Tactics, and Art of Political Campaign Management* (5th Ed.). Santa Barbara: Praeger.

Castle, S. (2015, May 4). Britain's campaign finance laws leave parties with idle money. *New York Times*. Retrieved from https://www.nytimes.com/2015/05/ 05/world/europe/britains-campaign-finance-laws-leave-parties-with-idle-money.html?_r=1.

Center for Responsive Politics. (n.d.) *The revolving door: Top Congressional Committees*. Retrieved from https://www.opensecrets.org/revolving/top.php?display=C.

Citizens United v. Federal Communications Commission. 558 U.S. 310 (2010).

Committee on Ethics. (2016). *Gift rule exceptions*. Retrieved from http://ethics.house.gov/gifts/gift-exceptions-0.

Committee on Ethics. (n.d.) *The House gift rule*. Retrieved from http://ethics.house.gov/gifts/house-gift-rule

Cowen, R. (2013, August 19). Lawmakers travel during recess on lobbyist-funded trips. *Huffington Post*. Retrieved from http://www.huffingtonpost.com/2013/ 08/19/lawmakers-travel-lobbyists_n_3780633.html?

Cox, G. W., & Mager, E. (1999). How much is majority status in the US congress worth? *American Political Science Review, 93*(2), 541–67.

Donnay, P. D., & Ramsden, Graham P. (1995). Public financing of legislative elections: Lessons from Minnesota. *Legislative Studies Quarterly, 20*(3), 351–64.

Eggen, D., & Farnam, T. W. (2011, October 27). Lobbyists playing key role in 2012 fund-raising. *Washington Post*. Retrieved from https://www.washingtonpost.com/politics/lobbyists-playing-key-role-in-2012fundraising/2011/10/24/gIQAUg0GMM_story.html?utm_term=.679c93e49251.

Goodwin, A., & Baccerellieri, E. (2016). "Number of registered lobbyists plunges as spending declines yet again." *Center for Responsive Politics*. Retrieved from https://www.opensecrets.org/news/2016/08/number-of-registered-lobbyists-plunges-as-spending-declines-yet-again/

Hasen, R. L. (2000). The surprisingly complex case for disclosure of contributions and expenditures funding Sham Issue Advocacy. *UCLA Law Review*, *48*, 265–268.

Kang, M. S. (2013). The year of the SuperPAC. *George Washington Law Review*, *81*(6), 1902–1927.

Kingdon, J. W. (1977). Models of legislative voting. *Journal of Politics*, *39*(3), 563–595.

Kirkpatrick, D. D., & Wilson, D. (2010, February 12). One grand deal too many costs lobbyist his job. *New York Times*. Retrieved from http://www.nytimes.com/2010/02/13/health/policy/13pharm.html

Klein, E. (2011, November 7). Jack Abramoff's guide to buying congressmen. *The Washington Post*. Retrieved from https://www.washingtonpost.com/blogs/ezra-klein/post/jack-abramoffs-guide-to-buying-congressmen/2011/08/25/ gIQAoXKLvM_blog.html

Magleby, D. B., & Nelson, C. J. (1990). *The money chase: Congressional campaign finance reform*. Washington D.C.: Brookings Institution Press.

Nasaw, D. (2009, April 7). US judge dismisses former Alaska senator's corruption conviction. *The Guardian*. Retrieved from https://www.theguardian.com/world/2009/apr/07/ted-stevens-corruption-dismissal-alaska

Puzzanghera, J. (2007, December 31). Courtship starts with free film screenings. *Los Angles Times*. Retrieved from http://articles.latimes.com/2007/dec/31/business/fi-mpaa31

Resnick, E. (2013, January 6). Jack Abramoff: Americans Believe the system is rigged against them. Retrieved from http://www.thelakewoodtimes.com/home/jack-abramoff-americans-believe-the-system-is-rigged-against-them

Schmidt, S., & Grimaldi, J. V. (2005, December 29). The fast rise and steep fall of Jack Abramoff. *Washington Post*. Retrieved from http://www.washingtonpost.com/wp-dyn/content/article/2005/12/28/AR2005122801588.html

Schouten, F. (n.d.). Door still revolving between capitol, lobbyists. *ABC News USA Today*. Retrieved from http://abcnews.go.com/Politics/story?id=7396717

Vidal, J. B., Draca, M., & Fons-Rosen, C. (2012). Revolving door lobbyists. *American Economic Review*, *102*(7), 3731–748.

Webber, A. (2011, March). *Open Government*. Retrieved from http://www.remappingdebate.org/category/topics/open-government/page/1/0

Wendland, J. (2005). Tom DeLay solicited donations with Skyboxes. *Political Affairs*. Retrieved from http://www.politicalaffairs.net/tom-delay-solicited-donations-with-skyboxes/

West, D. M. (2013). *Air wars: Television advertising and social media in election campaigns, 1952–2012* (6th Ed.). Washington, DC: CQ Press.

CHAPTER 4

CAMPAIGN CONTRIBUTIONS AND VOTE BUYING

Renee Prunty and Mandy Swartzendruber

ABSTRACT

There is a perception in the United States that campaign contributions equate with vote buying. Outright vote buying is illegal, but many citizens believe that loopholes in campaign contribution laws allow some to buy votes while perpetuating a façade of legitimacy. Both federal and state laws attempt to regulate campaign contributions, but many of those have been limited by the Supreme Court's ruling that campaign spending is considered free speech (Buckley vs. Valeo, 1976). Without the ability to limit campaign spending, the amount of money it takes to run a campaign, particularly a presidential campaign, has increased substantially. This had led to an increase in the use of bundling by presidential campaigns, with the winners often rewarding their bundlers. It has also led to an increase in outside independent organizations, known as Super PACs, with an unlimited ability to raise and spend money. This creates an additional problem as a small percentage of wealthy individuals constitute the vast majority of campaign contributors, leading to the perception that politicians cater to the elite. Whether a politician is affected by these factors or not is hard to prove, but it still leaves

Corruption, Accountability and Discretion
Public Policy and Governance, 61–83
doi:10.1108/S2053-769720170000029004

a perception by voters that their votes are less influential than large campaign contributors and there is always a risk that a vote has been bought.

Keywords: Bundling; campaign financing; *Citizens United*; lobbying; super PACs

INTRODUCTION

Under current campaign finance laws in the United States, it is believed that an elite few use loopholes in campaign contribution laws to buy votes of elected officials while perpetuating a façade of legitimacy, since outright vote buying is illegal. Both federal and state campaign finance laws attempt to regulate contributions minimizing the influence of special interests, but these attempts have been limited by the *Buckley vs. Valeo* (1976) Supreme Court holding that campaign spending is considered free speech. The inability to limit campaign spending has led to a substantial increase in the cost of campaigning, especially a presidential campaign. The cost of elections has led to more inventive ways of raising funds or promoting individual interests.

One of these is the increased use of bundling by presidential campaigns, with the winners often rewarding bundlers with administrative positions or White House visits. The expanded use of bundling was followed by expansion of the *Buckley* holding in *Citizens United vs. FEC* (2010), which led to an increase in independent organizations, known as Super PACs, and other dark money organizations, with an unlimited ability to raise and spend money to promote their agenda. The perception is based on the fact that a small percentage of wealthy individuals constitute the vast majority of campaign contributions. Therefore, this leads to a perception that politicians cater to the elite, particularly bundlers and interest groups, who are perceived to be buying votes in favor of their policies and initiatives. It is hard to prove if an elected official changes their vote or makes a decision based on these influences, but the perception by ordinary voters is that their votes are less influential. This is particularly true when large donors and special interests have the ear of elected officials to promote their own agendas and policy preferences in ways the ordinary citizens cannot.

HISTORY OF CAMPAIGN FINANCE LAWS AND CASES

The first campaign finance laws at the federal level were passed in 1867, which prevented federal officers from soliciting Navy Yard workers for contributions (Federal Election Commission [FEC], 2017). The next major piece of legislation was in 1907 when Congress passed the Tillman Act prohibiting contributions from corporations and national banks. This was furthered by the Taft-Hartley Act of 1947, which barred expenditures and contributions by corporations and labor unions in federal elections. During this period, there were also a number of pieces of legislation requiring various campaign disclosures; however, these were mostly ineffective. This became evident with the passage of the Federal Election Campaign Act [FECA] of 1971. The more stringent requirements to disclose campaign spending resulted in a substantial increase in reporting. According to the FEC (2017), in 1968, congressional members reported only $8.5 million in campaign spending, but the year after the law passed the amount reported jumped to $88.9 million.

Modern campaign finance laws are still based on the FECA of 1971. There were four major regulations in this law: limiting campaign spending, limiting campaign contributions, disclosure of campaign donors, and requirements for detailing campaign spending (52 U.S.C. § 30101). However, in *Buckley vs. Valeo* (1976), the United States Supreme Court removed some of these restrictions (424 U.S. 1). In a complicated *per curium* decision, the Court held that limitations on spending by campaigns, candidates, or independent groups, as well as contributions from the candidate, were unconstitutional violations of political expressions including rights to free speech and association. The Court upheld the requirements for disclosure of donors and campaign spending. Even though they believed these restrictions also infringed upon the First Amendment right to free speech, they believed it protected a vital interest of ensuring the process was fair. They further believed that "the sources of a candidate's financial support also alert the voter to the interests to which a candidate is most likely to be responsive and thus facilitate predictions of future performance in office" (*Ibid.* at 67). The limits on campaign contributions from individuals and PACs was also upheld. The case was heard by eight justices, of which there were five justices who agreed in part and dissented in part.

In addition to the restrictions on campaign financing, FECA as amended in 1974 created an option for federal funding of presidential campaigns still used today. If a candidate accepts federal funding, then they are obligated to limit their receipt and expenditure of private funds, including how much they can spend in each state. Under the Presidential Election Campaign Fund Act, citizens can donate $3 of their federal taxes to a U.S. Treasury fund for presidential elections. The system has separate rules for the primary and general campaigns. Presidential candidates may elect to receive matching contributions during the primary. Only individual contributions are matched up to $250. By taking the matching funds, the candidate is limited in how the money can be spent, how much they can spend, and where they can spend it. The limit with inflation was set at $45.6 million in 2012. In the general election, Republican and Democratic nominees are eligible for a grant to cover all campaign expenses, but can no longer accept or spend personal or campaign funds. The amount adjusted for inflation, was $91.2 million in 2012. Third party candidates may be eligible for funds after the election if they can get five percent of the popular vote (FEC, 2017). Table 1 which was originally created using FEC data shows the individual contribution limits for elections.

The 1974 amendment also established the Federal Election Commission [FEC] as an independent organization and gave it jurisdiction to ensure compliance with the new regulations. FECA not only increased federal regulations on campaign contributions, it also eliminated prohibitions on contributions from corporations and labor unions. FECA allowed for separate segregated funds now known as Political Action Committees [PACs] that could use treasury funds to operate and solicit funds for federal races (FEC, 2017). Over the past 45 years, *Buckley* has been the presiding rule of law on campaign finance reforms as Congress and most states have attempted to pass additional campaign finance reforms. Stricter restrictions, particularly on disclosure, have been passed mainly at the state and local levels, with all 50 states mandating disclosure of contributions in some form (National Conference for State Legislators [NCSL], 2015). The most recent attempts at reform at the federal level targeted soft money and issue ads with the Bipartisan Campaign Reform Act of 2002, which further amended FECA.

Table 1.   Individual Contribution Limits on Donations[***](FEC, 2017).

- **To Candidates/Campaigns:** $2,700 per election per candidate in federal elections[*]
- **To PACs:** $5,000 per calendar year to a federal candidate
- **To State and Local Parties:** $10,000 annually
- **To National Party:** $33,900 limit annually[**]

Notes: A donor may also give up to $50 cash to a candidate whenever they choose.
[*]Primaries, general elections, and runoffs are all considered separate elections.
[**]Contributions are separately applied to the Senate and House Committees and National Committee.
[***]All amounts are contribution limits for 2017–2018 federal elections from FEC.gov.

In 2010, the U.S. Supreme Court once again made waves in the area of campaign finance with their five to four decision in *Citizens United vs. FEC* (558 U.S. 310). This case overruled previous Supreme Court decisions. It completely overruled *Austin vs. Michigan Chamber of Congress* (1990) and partially overturned *McConnell vs. FEC* (2003). The holding that political speech could be banned based on the speaker's identity as a corporate entity was overturned. They reiterated the decision in *Buckley* that spending money to promote political speech is considered a fundamental right protected by the First Amendment and extended this right to corporate and other organizational entities. However, once again the Court upheld the disclosure requirements as promoting a fundamental interest in providing valuable information to the electorate. They also held that limits on corporations' direct contributions to campaigns were constitutional. This decision, while sparking outrage from many particularly since it was decided along an ideological divide, has prompted many states to act. Many states have enacted heightened disclosure laws requiring corporations or other independent groups to disclose donors. The NCSL tracks state campaign finance laws and reported that in "2015–2016, many states made administrative and procedural changes to their campaign finance laws" with many states focusing on disclosure of contributions for non-candidate groups (2016; para. 1).

Despite the current campaign finance laws there still seems to be a consensus that more needs to be done, but there is no consensus on what to do. The business of political elections has overshadowed the need for functioning government. Voters must regain trust in the election process so that their representatives can operate effectively. Susman, in an article examining the relationship between Congress and lobbyists, criticized the efforts made to reform the system stating, "Both Congress and the lobbying profession seem to be developing two-dimensional solutions to three-dimensional problems" (2008; p. 11). The continuing challenge of increasing voter confidence is hampered by the increasing cost of campaigning that has outpaced public financing.

THE COST OF RUNNING A CAMPAIGN

The cost of running an election at every level has increased substantially over the past few decades. It now costs more to run for election at all levels of government, even when taking into consideration inflation. Major congressional races can cost tens of millions of dollars. These numbers have grown progressively higher since *Citizens United*. Even judicial elections which historically have garnered little attention have seen record levels of spending over the past two decades. Presidential elections have always been the costliest since they run national campaigns, but the campaigns of 2008 and 2012 saw presidential donations and spending double with each election.

In the late 1820s, Andrew Jackson became the first president to hire a staff to raise money and in that election voter turnout nearly doubled (Morgan, 2013). This success drastically increased the cost of presidential campaigns, which in turn led to government jobs going to donors, an issue still debated today. Another substantial increase came in the 1960s, when Lyndon B. Johnson ran an attack ad, marking the beginning of the now common ad wars. By late 2015 and into early spring 2016, the cost of television advertising by candidates during the 2016 election was expected to reach $4.4 billion with the estimated total cost of all political ads reaching $6 billion (James, 2015; Overby, 2015). However, by early fall 2016, it appeared that the cost of ads by candidates would stay below $3 billion as Donald Trump relied heavily on free media attention (Ballhaus, 2016). While television ads are the costliest part of a campaign, candidates also need funds for public appearances, travel, and support staff.

The other reason for the increase in presidential fundraising and spending is due to candidates opting out of federal funding, which is the only way to limit campaign spending. Fundraising generally starts a year before the primary elections begin. A candidate can choose to limit fundraising and receive a matching amount from the federal government, or if a candidate chooses not to accept federal funding, then there are no limits on spending or requirements to spread the money across the country. In the 2000 primaries, George W. Bush raised his own money totaling nearly $100 million, which was over twice what he could have raised with the federal matching funds. In 2004, both Bush and Kerry opted to not use federal funding for the primaries with Bush raising nearly $300 million and Kerry just over $250 million (Center for Responsive Politics, 2017). Both amounts were well over the $37.3 million they could have raised and spent if they had accepted matching funds (FEC, 2017). Both candidates did accept federal funding in the general election of $74.6 million, which meant they could not spend any campaign money after accepting their party's nomination (Center for Responsive Politics, 2017).

The trend of not using matching funds in the primaries has continued since 2000, with recent candidates opting out of federal funding in the general election as well. In 2008, candidate Obama was the first candidate since 1972 to turn down federal funding, $84 million, in the general election. Instead, he raised nearly $1 billion and spent over $732 million (Gilson, 2012). His opponent John McCain did not have the same ability to raise money and had to accept federal funding, which limited him to $84 million for the entire general election. Obama raised $66 million in the month of September alone. As a result of this election, both Republicans and Democrats set a target of raising $1 billion for the 2012 election. Both were successful. Over $2.6 billion was spent on the 2012 presidential race when parties and all non-outside groups in the presidential election were included. That does not take into account the over $500 million that was spent by outside groups on the presidential election (Center for Responsive Politics, 2017). Had either candidate chosen to use federal funding they would have been limited to $45.6 million for the primaries and $91.2 million for the general election, roughly 15% of what each candidate raised and spent (FEC, 2017).

While the presidential election costs are hard to fathom, campaign costs have increased in all types of elections, including elections that previously had very little campaign financing such as judicial and local elections. The Center for Responsive Politics, a group that reports on campaign financing and spending, estimated that all of the elections in 2012 cost a total of $6.3 billion. This is up nearly a billion dollars from just four years earlier. The decision in *Citizens United* helped create this considerable increase in campaign spending as independent organizations now contribute large amounts of money, not directly to the candidates, but often advocating for or against them. In 2008, independent expenditures for all presidential candidates, including in the primary, was just over $233 million. However, after the decision in *Citizens United* in 2010, the 2012 election saw over $650 million from independent expenditures, which is nearly three times as much as the 2008 election (Center for Responsive Politics, 2017).

The 2016 presidential race seems to be an anomaly when it comes to campaign funding. Both general election candidates Clinton and Trump were viewed unfavorably and were not able to raise the same amount of money as previous candidates. Although Hillary Clinton was able to raise almost twice as much as Donald Trump, it was not to the same levels Barack Obama had reached in 2008 or 2012. Donald Trump raised money at a level similar to John McCain but his notoriety allowed him to take advantage of free publicity in a way previous candidates had not been able to do. This meant he did not have to raise or spend as much money as other presidential candidates. Hillary Clinton spent about $563 million and Donald Trump around $333 million. While this goes against the recent trend it is likely a bump in the road rather than a new downward trend (Center for Responsive Politics, 2017). This is particularly true given that a record $1.2 billion was spent campaigning for Clinton when parties and PACs are included (Fredericks, 2016).

Despite the lower numbers, neither candidate chose to accept federal funding in the primary or general election.

The cost of campaigning raises grave concerns because a small percentage of the population constitutes a large percentage of donors. Only a small percentage of the population donates amounts large enough to be itemized, over $200. In 2016, only 0.58% of the U.S. population donated over $200 and only 0.08% of the population donated over $2700. However, contributions over $200 made up 67.8% of all donations to candidates, parties, and independent organizations (Center for Responsive Politics, 2017). While the Supreme Court has upheld disclosure requirements in nearly every case, it is not always clear where all of the money is coming from, particularly when discussing other means of raising funds. There is still a large segment of campaign contributions and spending that is called "dark money." Many states are beginning to pass laws to change this but there are still areas where citizens are reliant on organizations who try to track it down to divulge the information. Reliance on campaigns volunteering information is the case when it comes to bundling.

EMERGING TREND IN CAMPAIGN FINANCING: BUNDLING

Campaigning in America has become so expensive that even the independently wealthy are forced to finance campaigns with donor money. To meet these costs, candidates court Super PACs, special interest groups, large donors, small donors, and the "bundlers." Bundlers are individuals counted on by the respective political parties or candidates to collect money from multiple "individual" donors and contribute those funds directly to campaigns. Credit for the funds goes to the bundler who solicited them. Often these are influential individuals who use their family, personal, or business connections to encourage donations.

Bundlers are those willing to make calls and persuade people to donate and are important in today's political system. It is cheaper for a federal candidate to buy a television ad than it is for a Super PAC so bundling of small donations can go further (Gilson, 2012). Once a socially connected person meets their personal contribution limit, they reach out to those in their circle to collect donations and then deliver them in a big bundle to the candidate. Bundling has been around for a while, but its increased use began with George W. Bush's campaign in 2000. His campaign gave the bundler a number that those he solicited would write on the check so the amount could be attributed to the correct person. They even gave names to levels of bundlers, "Pioneers" and "Rangers," which came with rewards like the ability to buy exclusive silver cufflinks or a belt buckle set. Notwithstanding the early success, the Bush campaign was able to almost double the number of reported bundlers for the 2004 re-election from 246 to 411 (Edsall, Cohen, & Grimaldi, 2004).

Disclosure of donors is only required by the FEC regulations when they are bundled by registered lobbyists. Candidates can choose to voluntarily disclose and most release the bundlers' names with a range like $100,000 or more. In 2008 both McCain and Obama agreed to disclose the identity of bundlers who raised greater than $50,000 but media outlets had to be tenacious to encourage both camps to provide the extensive lists (Luo, 2008). How much information the candidates choose to release is also up to the campaigns. In 2008, McCain disclosed bundlers' employers and occupations, while Obama did not. Watchdog groups such as the Center for Responsive Politics attempted to track down and include missing information (2017).

In 2012, Obama again released the names and donation ranges of his bundlers, but not the occupation or employer. Per the Center for Responsive Politics, 769 individuals oversaw the direction of at least $186,500,000 to the Democratic National Committee and Obama's re-election campaign in 2012. Based on their research, lawyers and law firms represented 184 of those bundlers and raised $43,750,000. In addition, the TV/Movies/Music industry bundlers raised $12,100,000 and made up 42 of those bundlers. Mitt Romney did not release the names of his bundlers, so only the names of registered lobbyists were released as required by law. There were 69 registered lobbyists identified with their bundling information and a total of $17,320,719. The Center for Responsive Politics identified 37 others who raised around the same amount by combing press reports (Center for Responsive Politics, 2017). In 2016, Hillary Clinton chose to release the names of bundlers who raised over $100,000. The Trump campaign has not released any bundler information. Clinton had 1,129 individuals oversee at least $112,300,000 with most money coming from the legal and economic sectors (Center for Responsive Politics, 2017). Even without the release of Republican bundlers, there is a clear trend toward the increased use of bundling to raise the large amounts of money needed to run a presidential campaign.

Because large wealthy families tend to be politically connected, family bundling has also been used to finance campaigns. In families like the Pritzkers, siblings support various candidates and bundle on their own. In others, like Robert McNair's family, the head of the family supports a campaign and the rest of the family follows suit (Pelosi, 2017). Most bundlers describe similar fundraising techniques that are tiered in terms of contribution levels.

Generally, there is a lower donation required to go to a reception with food and a speech; double that donation and there is a meet and greet and photo opportunity; triple that donation and you go to a roundtable with the candidate before the reception along with the other events.

Bundlers and large donors have varying expectations from the candidates. Some are involved so they can be made ambassadors or receive other positions in the Cabinet, or advisory positions. Some help for the ability to have the ear of the president or be invited to events. Nearly 40% of the Bush bundlers from 2000 were awarded an appointment or job following the election (Edsall, Cohen, & Grimaldi, 2004). After President Obama's 2008 campaign "nearly 200 of his biggest donors have landed plum government jobs and advisory posts, won federal contracts worth millions of dollars for their business interests or attended numerous elite White House meetings and social events" (Schulte, 2011; para. 4). The most notable 2008 bundler was Eric Holder who was appointed Attorney General. During Obama's second term he appointed 29 bundlers to ambassadorships all over the world. These bundlers raised more than $19.5 million (Zubak-Skees, 2014).

Alexandra Pelosi interviewed several elite individuals on both sides of the aisle for the documentary, *Meet the Donors*. Julian Robertson, a GOP mega-donor, noted that he had no expectations for a politician to enact policies that directly helped him but rather he sees his participation as noble, patriotic and an effort to get the best person as president (Pelosi, 2017). Bernard Schwartz, Clinton mega-donor, also said it is a patriotic act. When pressed as to whether he has undue influence he admitted that politicians were likely to hear him when he had a problem but that his influence had not directly improved his business (Pelosi, 2017).

This was echoed repeatedly by Republican and Democratic donors and bundlers alike. They were just contributing to the existing system in the best way they could with no expectation for special treatment. One donor, Hubbard, gave an example of an issue he wanted to discuss with a candidate – right to work policies and how he has advocated for them but did not always get his policies enacted (Pelosi, 2017). So perhaps there is no quid pro quo, but the average citizen cannot call a presidential candidate and argue for or against a major policy. These mega donors and bundlers can. And even if they cannot, they have multiple pictures with presidents in their offices, they are invited to all the major events – they receive perceived power from their increased social status that can also be leveraged on their behalves.

If one takes these bundlers at their word that they are simply doing their patriotic duty, it seems no harm would come from requiring all bundlers to be disclosed by presidential and congressional candidates. What is the justification for only requiring lobbyists to be disclosed? Is it that they represent special interest groups? Clearly, interest groups are involved in bundling as well. Although the logistics of policing everyone that collects contributions for every campaign would be overwhelming, setting a cap of say $50,000 could be tracked. But then would bundlers simply bundle up to $49,999? Until the cost of campaigning is lowered, the mechanisms for raising millions of dollars will be difficult to change as they remain necessary.

INTEREST GROUPS AND THEIR INFLUENCE

Many contend that both parties exist in a constant battle for election and re-election. This battle extends beyond the two parties as interests on both sides vie for political power. This has led to a situation where politics is a continuous campaign, with the number and type of groups entering the battle continuing to increase. Interests can select from a number of legally defined groups each with its own advantages and disadvantages:

- **501(c)(3)** – charities or non-profits not allowed to participate in the electoral process
- **501(c)(4)** – civic leagues and social welfare organizations that have some limits on how much they may participate in the electoral process
- **501(c)(5)** – labor unions can actively lobby Congress but may only contribute to political campaigns through PACs
- **501(c)(6)** – professional or trade organizations may actively lobby Congress but can also only contribute to the PACs
- **527s** – political groups that utilize issue advertisements to indirectly benefit or harm a candidate but do not donate to campaigns or advocate for/ against candidates
- **PACs** – political action committees accept contributions and donate directly to candidates with a current limit of $5000
- **SSFs** – separated, segregated funds are administered by corporations, membership organizations, labor unions, or trade associations and are only allowed to solicit funds from individuals who are associated with the sponsoring organization
- **Non-Connected Committees (including Super PACs)** – PACs not limited to corporations, unions, trade associations, or member organizations and able to solicit funds from the general public (FEC, 2017)

Most of these groups are involved in issue advocacy. Issue advocacy refers to the way interest groups spend donations to produce advertisements, which influence the way people think about a candidate by influencing the way they feel about specific issues. Around 527 groups, for example, can link candidates to their causes but they are not allowed to tell voters how to vote. This can be by inviting them to speak at a group event or by publicly rating candidates. Progressive interest groups will look at progressive issues and track how representatives vote. The more they vote for progressive policies, the higher their score. Conservative groups on the other hand, rate higher for those that vote for conservative policies. The NRA, for example, gives an actual letter grade like a report card to individuals so that members know which candidates share their viewpoint. A lack of sufficient public financing to pay for these lengthy and expensive campaigns has created a need for candidates to court the favor of advocacy groups that come through with donations or others who work outside the system altogether.

THE EFFECT OF *CITIZENS UNITED*: SUPER PACs AND DARK MONEY

Super PACs are the name for independent organizations or non-connected groups that have formed as a result of the *Citizens United vs. FEC* decision in 2010. They differ from their PAC counterparts and other legally defined groups, in that there are no limits to contributions that can be made to them or how they spend their money. The only restriction is that they are not allowed to directly contribute to or coordinate in any way with a candidate. They can spend their money arguing for or against a candidate on their own as long as they are not coordinating with the candidate's campaign. There is no limit to the amount of money they can use to promote or discourage voting for a particular candidate.

Unlike donors who contribute directly to political parties or campaigns, there are no disclosure requirements for 501(c)(4) and 501(c)(6) groups. The limited liability corporations or politically active nonprofits are not required to disclose their donors at the federal level and because of U.S. Supreme Court decisions, they can accept unlimited contributions from other organizations, corporations, and individuals which can then be used for television ads and other marketing options meant to influence voters. Because the public is kept in the dark about who is sponsoring these activities and their motives, this is referred to as "dark money." In 2004, this type of contribution was estimated at $6 million, in 2008 it jumped to $102 million, and following the *Citizens*

United decision in 2012, it tripled to $309 million. Although there are limits on what these groups can spend, they are generally not enforced, particularly after the *Citizens United* decision and the emergence of Super PACS (Center for Responsive Politics, 2017).

Dark money players such as limited liability companies (LLCs) and politically active nonprofits are allowed by the FEC to spend money on "independent expenditures" and "electioneering communications." This means that commercials, robo-calls, mailers, and ads can all be purchased as "outside spending" which is not made directly by the campaign and therefore not subject to the same rules as those coordinated by campaigns. This can be murky as the owners of LLCs can be hard to identify and the nonprofits allowed to engage in some political activity by the Internal Revenue Service (IRS) are not clearly held to a limit of how much political activity is acceptable (Center for Responsive Politics, 2017).

These groups can also contribute to Super PACs but they cannot give directly to campaigns. As previously discussed, while Super PACs do not give directly to campaigns, they can spend as much money as they want to advocate against or for a candidate, which creates another way of getting around the spending limits of 504 groups. While Super PACS are required to provide the names of the groups who donate, they do not have to share the identities of those groups' donors. For instance, if a donor contributes to a politically active nonprofit which then contributes to a Super PAC, the amount of the individual donation and name of the donor would not be revealed; only the group name will appear. There are rules that state the LLCs, Super PACs and politically active nonprofits are not allowed to coordinate spending with campaigns and the FEC is the enforcer of these rules. Per Ann M. Ravel, the commissioner at the FEC, "The likelihood of laws being enforced is slim" (Lichtblau, 2015; para. 2). Groups are often shifting from one type of group to another based on the different advantages or moving money between groups, which further complicates the process of monitoring and tracking funds.

This was demonstrated on the *Colbert Report* by host Stephen Colbert and Trevor Potter, a lawyer who has also been chairman and commissioner of the FEC and provided legal counsel to the John McCain and George H.W. Bush presidential campaigns. Colbert created a Super PAC, the Colbert Super PAC Shh!, for the purpose of demonstrating how Super PACs work. In one episode along with Jon Stewart, who he asked to run the Super PAC, Trevor Potter reveals the punishments for coordinating can be six-figure fines however those can be paid with Super PAC money (Colbert, 2012a). Finally, after several months of receiving money for the Super PAC, Colbert and Potter then demonstrated how easy it is to make the money disappear by creating a couple 501(c)(4) interest groups to funnel the money through until it is no longer trackable and essentially disappears (Colbert, 2012b). In the last three elections, upward of 30% of campaign spending was dark money (Center for Responsive Politics, 2017).

Democrats and Republicans believe that there is a need for campaign finance reform and there are many ways this reform could occur (*New York Times*, 2015). Congress could pass laws requiring more disclosure and force unions, politically active nonprofits, Super PACs, corporations and other groups to disclose individual donors and political contributions, but this means limiting their own ability to campaign. The last attempt, the DISCLOSE Act, died in the Senate in 2012 on a partisan vote of 51 Democrats favoring it and 44 Republicans opposed. It would have required corporate interest groups and politically active nonprofits to disclose donors giving over $10,000 (Riley, 2012).

The president could issue an executive order that requires federal contractors to reveal all their political contributions and could nominate tougher commissioners to the FEC and the SEC. The Federal Election Commission could better enforce the existing campaign finance laws as well as issue stricter disclosure requirements. The IRS could better define limits on political activities by politically active nonprofits. The SEC could issue rules forcing publicly traded corporations to disclose their political contributions. The FCC could require all groups to disclose their donors to buy radio and television ads. In 2016, over 160 Congressional Democrats sent a letter to the FCC chair that urged the agency to require the disclosure of actual donors behind the political ads (Eshoo, 2016). However, at the end of the day, the importance of funding campaigns and the aid offered by these outside groups makes changing the laws or regulations difficult and these groups always seem to find the loopholes left behind.

THE INFLUENCE OF LOBBYING AND LOBBYISTS

Super PACs are not the only entities protected by the First Amendment. Traditional lobbyists and some lobbying activities are also protected by the First Amendment right to petition the government. Susman (2008) explains that while lobbyists are often seen as the problem that needs to go away, the relationship between elected officials and lobbyists is necessary for our democratic system – particularly on complex issues with numerous competing sides. Lobbyists provide elected officials with information they may not otherwise have including counterarguments and potential consequences. In addition, he argues that "lobbyists help hold public officials accountable for their actions" (p. 12). The problem is reciprocity. Outright reciprocity is illegal.

Lobbyists cannot give large gifts or other gratuities directly to elected officials. However, there is an argument that the relationship between lobbyists and elected officials creates a feeling of reciprocity whether real or imagined by the public. This creates a feeling that those lobbying the government are getting more out of the government than those who do not have the means, knowledge, or connections. While the rules against lobbyists providing money, gifts, or favors continue to tighten, these same lobbyists or those they represent are still contributing to political campaigns. As a result, some argue the only way to eliminate the feeling of reciprocity is to create a system where all candidates use public financing for campaigns (Powell 2014; Susman, 2008).

Much like campaign financing, lobbying efforts are backed by large amounts of money. Between 2008 and 2016, the U.S. Chamber of Commerce spent $714,746,000 on lobbying (MapLight, 2017). This is a powerful group representing business interests in several key policy areas. They believe there is a need for tax and entitlement reform, so they lobby to have fewer regulations and simpler rules. They lobby to lower the business tax rate, shift to a territorial system of taxation, and allow capital investment. The U.S. Chamber also lobbies for coal, less regulation in energy projects, expanded nuclear energy, and greater access to oil and gas offshore and on federal lands. Other areas of policy focus include: reduced healthcare costs and taxes, support for the Trans-Pacific Partnership and the Transatlantic Trade and Investment Partnership, encouragement for school choice, reduced regulation to increase access to capital markets, and reduced litigation (U.S. Chamber of Commerce, 2017).

The National Association of Realtors spent the second largest lobbying amount at $313,597,000 during the same time frame. They advocated policies favorable to homeownership and real estate investment, credit and lending policies, access to flood insurance, commercial real estate finance and residential real estate finance like Federal Housing Administration (FHA) loans (National Association of Realtors, 2017). The U.S. Chamber of Commerce Institute for Legal Reform had the third highest expenditure at $237,790,000 focused on reducing the number of lawsuits. The rest of the top ten lobbying groups are as follows:

1. Apparel for All ($200,000,000)
2. General Electric ($188,370,000)
3. Pharmaceutical Research & Manufacturers of America ($177,500,520)
4. American Medical Association ($175,610,000)
5. American Hospital Association ($157,990,000)
6. Boeing ($154,187,000)
7. National Cable & Telecommunications Association ($147,160,000) (MapLight, 2017)

All together that is well over $2 billion spent by the top ten lobbying groups in the country.

Those opposed to lobbying make the case that the process itself has hurt our democracy. The debate over whether lobbyists are integral to democracy or hinder it by dissuading voters from participating in government is ongoing. Critics of restricting lobbying point out that it is a right for citizens to petition the government to redress grievances and restrictions impede that right. On the other hand, critics of lobbying advocate regulations to protect the political system and remove the perception that only special interests have access to those in power. Keep in mind lobbyists not only work for their organizations and interests, but they can also become bundlers for campaigns. Lobbyists are the most highly regulated group that contributes to and works to influence campaigns and elected officials, but that has not eliminated speculations that their efforts hurt the ordinary citizen and voter.

PUBLIC POLICY BASED ON CAMPAIGN CONTRIBUTIONS: REALITY OR PERCEPTION?

While PACs and other interest groups contribute and work to influence campaigns, under the current campaign finance laws and Supreme Court decisions, candidates running for office now appear to receive substantially more funds from individuals than from PACs. However, those numbers can be deceiving without digging a little deeper. The effect of individual contributions of ordinary citizens appears to be overshadowed by bundlers and outside organizations that find it more efficient to operate separately from campaigns. The current state of campaign financing and the increased influence of interest groups have many concerned about the public policy implications. There has always been a question about how much influence campaign contributors have over candidates who get elected, with the concern about the influence of a few superseding the influence of the many. This is the catalyst for campaign finance regulations, restrictions, and disclosures. Despite rhetoric to the contrary, many people donate to campaigns or promote candidates for office with the hope of receiving a benefit in return. The question is whether the benefit received is greater or different than it would have been without the contribution or from that of the ordinary voter and contributor.

Without an outright bribe or declared deal between a candidate and contributor to take a specific public policy stance, it is hard to prove a clear link between policy decisions and campaign funding. This is because citizens generally contribute to candidates who already share their world view.

Since outright bribes or perceived bribes are illegal and can (and have) landed lobbyists and elected officials in jail there is generally no clear paper trail linking a contribution to a specific public policy decision. Therefore, it is difficult to declare with absolute certainty that an elected official voted or acted in a particular way as a direct result of a specific campaign contributor. This has not stopped many people from continuing to note the anecdotal evidence, which suggests an undue influence by a powerful few on public policy decisions. One merely has to point to the small percentage of wealthy and powerful individuals who contribute a large majority of the campaign funding to arouse suspicion. The suspicions are furthered as these individuals receive positions in presidential administrations and private meetings with elected officials who are perceived to be working for themselves rather than the general public.

It seems that as campaign finance laws attempt to close one loophole, it often reveals an even larger one. For example, following the Bipartisan Campaign Reform Act to limit soft money, campaigns began to adapt by increasing their use of bundling to make up the difference (Edsall & Allen, 2003). Given the effectiveness of bundling, it could be argued that by leading the campaigns to adapt, the new law, in fact, helped campaigns increase their ability to raise funds as record campaign funds were raised in every election from 2000 to 2012. Bundling has the added bonus of allowing candidates to claim that they only raised funds from individuals, thereby avoiding being bought by interest groups attempting to influence public policy. For example, in 2008, President Obama took office declaring not to be beholden to interest groups since nearly all of his campaign contributions were from individuals. However, much of that "individual" money was contributed by bundlers who are seen as having the same influence as interest groups. The same was said of President George W. Bush although President Obama awarded his bundlers with administrative positions at a much higher rate than did his predecessor.

During his eight years in office President George W. Bush, who significantly expanded the use of bundling, gave administrative positions to 200 bundlers. President Obama appointed 200 bundlers to administrative positions by the end of his second year in office. This means President Obama had appointed nearly one-third of his bundlers to positions in the administration, but this number jumps substantially when looking at the top bundlers. Nearly 80% of President Obama's top bundlers, those raising over half a million dollars, were appointed to positions within the administration which leads to questions about public policy implications (Schulte, 2011). It is yet to be seen if President Trump will continue the trend since candidates are not legally obligated to disclose their bundlers and President Trump has so far not disclosed any bundlers. Although the speculation seems to be that he has rewarded his closest friends and allies who raised capital for his campaign and are likely to have their own agendas, it has not been proven.

Since 1883 with the passage of the Pendleton Act, political patronage has been illegal at the federal level. Political patronage first became popular with the populist President Andrew Jackson who rewarded campaign supporters with positions at all levels of government. Since 1883 this has been illegal however it does not mean that presidents cannot appoint supporters or friends to administrative positions. Most, but not all, positions have to be approved by the Senate which supposedly limits appointments to individuals with prior experience. Both Presidents Bush and Obama declared they made selections based on qualifications, not contributions. Not all positions such as ambassadors or other advisory positions require a specific set of skills or knowledge and these are generally the type of positions that are given to bundlers. However, some contributors have been appointed to more substantial Cabinet positions such as Eric Holder to Attorney General. This leaves the general public wondering if the president is creating public policy for the public or for special interests.

Being a donor does not guarantee a position in the White House, but as President Obama's White House spokesman Jay Carney stated at a 2014 press briefing, "being a donor does not get you a job in this administration nor does it preclude you from getting one" (U.S. Office of Press Secretary, 2014; First question from Scott, para. 4). A similar statement was given several times by the Obama administration when questioned about appointments, which echoed what the Bush administration had said and appears to be the stance of the Trump administration. Some may cry foul when bundlers or other contributors get positions in administrations, but as long as the candidates are qualified for these positions or the position requires no qualifications, then there is not much that can be done. Presidents often rely on the notion that this is how things have always been done, but the stakes and money have never been this high (Edsall & Allen, 2003; Schulte, 2011). While it is easy to focus on those who get positions in a presidential administration as influencing public policy, it is equally as likely that those who do not get positions still wield an unequally large influence over administrative policies and decisions. There is always a question of whether public policy is based on special interests and an elite few rather than the general public or what is best for the country.

The bundlers and other large contributors who do not get positions in the administration still get access to the president in ways ordinary citizens cannot and the same can be said for other outside organizers who unofficially help presidents get elected. They can use these meetings to directly lobby for public policies that favor their positions or even further their financial gains. Even President Obama who lamented those outsiders influencing public policy decisions seemed to fall into the same patterns as his predecessors. When then Senator Obama formally announced his presidential run on February 10, 2007, he called out "the cynics, the lobbyists, the special interests" he believed had "turned our government into a game only they can afford to play...They write the checks and you get stuck with the bill, they get the access while you get to write a letter, they think they own this government, but we're here today to take it back." However, once in office he was just as prone to accept visits and calls from large contributors as any other president. During his first term, "campaign bundlers and their family members account for more than 3,000 White House meetings and visits. Half of them raised $200,000 or more" (Schulte, 2011; para. 11).

This influence is not limited to bundlers. Leaders of outside organizations and interest groups, because of their impact on elections, have the same access and ability to influence public policy but it is easier to track bundlers if they have been identified by the campaign. President Trump also ran on the idea of "draining the swamp" and vowed during his campaign to remove special interests from politics (Arnsdorf, Dawsey, & Lippman, 2016; para. 1) As his cabinet and ancillary appointments are filled, it remains to be seen if this is the case. His appointments of former head of Exxon-Mobil, Rex Tillerson to Secretary of State and Steven Mnuchin, former head of Goldman Sachs, to Treasury Secretary have already raised some eyebrows about the public policy implications of these appointments. It appears at least, that the influential few are once again in the best positions to create public policies that benefit themselves and not the general public.

When the discussion turns to Congress it becomes more difficult to draw conclusions as there are 535 members and each has their own stance on how they deal with and are affected by interests. These differences become even more extensive when the discussion is taken to state legislatures. Lynda Powell did an extensive review of *The Influence of Campaign Contributions in State Legislatures* and found that "most members are ethical, and many want to be – but even members with the best intentions may compromise their beliefs when faced with the need to raise large amounts of money to win a competitive election or to hold or win a leadership post" (2012, p. 203). Even when setting the highest ethical standards elected officials are faced with competing against others who are more willing to blur the line of ethical fundraising. And with the cost of campaigns increasing, elected officials who plan to run for re-election must start thinking about fundraising often from the moment they enter office. This means taking meetings with donors, particularly donors with large amounts of cash to contribute to the next campaign, once they get into office and leaving themselves vulnerable to public policy influences. This was one of the main reasons for adding the federal funding of presidential campaigns, however, with the recent trend of rejecting public funds in both the primary and general elections, there is an opening for increased policy influence by large donors that have become necessary to run a successful campaign.

CONCLUSIONS

While meetings are not clear indications of policy manipulation, those with the ear of the president and other elected officials are more likely than those without to be able to influence public policy focus, regulations, and changes. There is no direct evidence that those contributing more to campaigns have a greater influence on policy, but most on the outside looking in find it hard to believe that they do not. In a follow-up article, Powell (2014) highlights that trying to connect public policy influence directly to roll call votes in legislatures is nearly impossible. Further, she explains that likely the influence by donors or interest groups takes place much earlier in the legislative process. It is more likely that they will influence public policy during the writing of the bill, the markup process, or even putting pressure to quietly kill a bill they do not want to see passed. Powell focuses on state legislatures and finds that the specific state institutions themselves have the greatest impact on the ability of interests to influence public policy than does the nature of politics alone. She also notes that some states have tried term limits to reduce the influence of special interests with mixed results, concluding that the best solution appears to be an improved public financing system that levels the playing field (2014). Given the Supreme Court's decisions on campaign spending as a fundamental right to free speech, a comprehensive and mandatory public financing system is not likely to occur without a constitutional amendment and given the difficulty in passing mere campaign finance reform bills, an amendment seems like a steep uphill battle. Therefore, until that time, public policy will be at least perceived to be, if not actually in fact, influenced by an elite few.

Money is perceived to influence decisions, therefore the amount of money being spent on elections and lobbying elected officials leads many to perceive that public policy is catering to the elite few rather than the general public. The billions of dollars spent by lobbying interests, Super PACS, and campaigns creates a perception that these elites are buying the votes of public officials. The perception is furthered as campaign bundlers and special interests are awarded administrative positions and special meetings with elected officials. Many citizens find it hard to believe that the shaping of public policy decisions is not the driving force behind those seeking the positions and meetings. Both parties agree there needs to be reform, although there is little agreement on which course of action is the best. Public financing appears to be the only way to limit spending, therefore perception is not likely to change until there is some form of mandatory public financing that assures the public that elected officials are creating public policy based on the general good and not based on who helped them get elected or more importantly who can help them get re-elected. Until such an amendment is approved, Congress and state legislatures should pass laws requiring more disclosure of individual contributions to unions, politically active nonprofits, Super PACs, corporations and other groups they pass their money onto, and executive administrations should enforce the policies in place.

REFERENCES

Arnsdorf, I., Dawsey, J., & Lippman, D. (2016, December 22). Will "Drain the Swamp" Be Trump's first broken promise? *Politico*. Retrieved from http://www.politico.com/story/2016/12/trump-drain-swamp-promise-232938

Austin v. Michigan Chamber of Congress, 484 U.S. 652 (1990).

Ballhaus, R. (2016, September 29). Political TV advertising is forecast to fall this election season: Drop comes as Donald Trump limits purchases of TV ads. *The Wall Street Journal*. Retrieved from https://www.wsj.com/articles/political-tv-advertising-is-forecast-to-fall-this-election-season-1475176575

Buckley v. Valeo, 424 U.S. 1 (1976).

Center for Responsive Politics (2017). Retrieved from www.opensecrets.org

Citizens United v. Federal Election Commission, 558 U.S. 310 (2010)

Colbert, S. (Host). (2012a, January 17). Colbert super PAC – Not coordinating with Stephen Colbert [Television series clip]. In *The Colbert Report, Season 8, Episode 45*. New York, NY: Comedy Central. Retrieved from http://www.cc.com/video-clips/3pwzi5/the-daily-show-with-jon-stewart-colbert-super-pac—not-coordinating-with-stephen-colbert

Colbert, S. (Host). (2012b, November 12). Colbert super PAC shh! – Secret second 501C4 - Trevor Potter [Television series clip]. In *The Colbert Report, Season 9, Episode 23*. New York, NY: Comedy Central. Retrieved from http://www.cc.com/video-clips/66y7dx/the-colbert-report-colbert-super-pac-shh—secret-second-501c4—trevor-potter

Edsall, T. B., & Allen, M. (2003, July 14). Bush "Bundlers" take fundraising to new level. *The Washington Post*. Retrieved from https://www.washingtonpost.com/archive/politics/2003/07/14/bush-bundlers-take-fundraising-to-new-level/21a00a3b-9012-4502-8178-437eb668bd88/?utm_term=.c79ec3ab0e06

Edsall, T. B., Cohen, S., & Grimaldi, J. V. (2004, May 16). Pioneers fill war chest, then capitalize. *The Washington Post*, p. A01.

Eshoo, A. G. (2016, January 20). Yarmuth, Eshoo to FCC: Unmask secret sponsors of political ads. *Congresswoman Anna G. Eshoo, California's 18th Congressional District*. Retrieved from   https://eshoo.house.gov/issues/yarmuth-eshoo-to-fcc-unmask-secret-sponsors-of-political-ads/

Federal Election Commission [FEC]. (2017). http://www.fec.gov/

Federal Election Commission v. Wisconsin Right to Life, 551 U.S. 449 (2007)

Federal Election Campaign Act of 1971, 52 U.S.C. § 30101.

Fredericks, B. (2016, December 9). *Hillary Clinton's losing campaign cost a record $1.2 billion. New York Post*. Retrieved from nypost.com/2016/12/09/hillary-clintons-losing-campaign-cost-a-record-1-2b

Gilson, D. (2012, February 20). The crazy cost of becoming President from Lincoln to Obama. *Mother Jones*. Retrieved from http://www.motherjones.com/mojo/2012/02/historic-price-cost-presidential-elections

James, M. (2015, November 8). Political ad spending estimated at 6 billion in 2016. *Los Angeles Times*. Retrieved from latimes.com/entertainment/enveleope/cotown/la-et-ct-political-ad-spending-6-billion-dollars-in-2016-20151117-story.html

Lichtblau, E. (2015, May 2). F.E.C. Can't curb 2019 election abuse, commissioner chief says. *New York Times*. Retrieved from https://www.nytimes.com/2015/05/03/us/politics/fec-cant-curb-2016-election-abuse-commission-chief-says.html?_r=0

Luo, M. (2008, July 10). Lax on its list of "bundlers," the Obama campaign names. *The Caucus*. Retrieved from https://thecaucus.blogs.nytimes.com/2008/07/10/lax-on-its-list-of-bundlers-the-obama-campaign-names-names/

MapLight. (2017, February 2). US Chamber of Commerce lobbying. *MapLight*. Retrieved from maplight.org/us-congress/lobbying

McConnell v. Federal Election Commission [FEC], 540 U.S. 93 (2003)

Morgan, A. (2013, July 21). US Campaign finance. *Jurist*. Retrieved from jurist.org/feature/2013/07/us-campaign-finance-1.php

National Association of Realtors. (2017, February 15). Federal Political Advocacy. *National Association of Realtors*. Retrieved from nar.realtor/political-advocacy/federal-political-advocacy

National Conference for State Legislatures [NCSL]. (2015, July 17). Disclosure and reporting requirements. *National Conference for State Legislatures*. Retrieved from http://www.ncsl.org/research/elections-and-campaigns/disclosure-and-reporting-requirements.aspx

National Conference for State Legislatures [NCSL]. (2016, July 21). 2015 and 2016 campaign finance enactments. *National Conference for State Legislatures*. Retrieved from http://www.ncsl.org/research/elections-and-campaigns/2015-and-2016-campaign-finance-enactments.aspx

New York Times. (2015, June 2). Americans views on money in politics. *New York Times*. Retrieved from https://www.nytimes.com/interactive/2015/06/02/us/politics/money-in-politics-poll.html?_r=0

Obama, B. (2007, February 10). *Senator Barack Obama campaign announcement*. Retrieved from https://www.c-span.org/video/?196594-1/senator-barack-obama-campaign-announcement

Overby, P. (20015, July 22). Political TV Advertising Expected to Cost $4.4 Billion in 2016. *NPR*. Retrieved from npr.org/2015/07/22/425377057/political-tv-advertising-expected-to-cost-4-4-billion-in-2016

Pelosi, A. (Director). (2017). *Meet the donors: Does money talk?* [Motion Picture]. United States: HBO.

Powell, L. W. (2012). *The influence of campaign contributions in state legislatures: The effects of institutions and politics.* Ann Arbor: University of Michigan.

Powell, L. W. (2014). The influence of campaign contributions on the legislative process. *Duke Journal of Constitutional Law & Public Policy, 9*(1), 75–100.

Riley, T. (2012, July 16). DISCLOSE Act blocked in the Senate. *Bill Moyers & Company.* Retrieved from billmoyers.com/2012/07/16/senate-readies-to-vote-on-the-disclose-act

Schulte, F. (2011, July 15). Obama rewards big bundlers with jobs, commissions, stimulus money, government contracts, and more. *Center for Public Integrity.* Retrieved from https://www.publicintegrity.org/2011/06/15/4880/obama-rewards-big-bundlers-jobs-commissions-stimulus-money-government-contracts-and

Susman, T. M. (2008). Private ethics, public conduct: An essay on ethical lobbying, campaign contributions, reciprocity, and the public good. *Stanford Law & Policy Review, 19*(1), 10–22.

U.S. Chamber of Commerce. (2017, February 7). *Taxes.* US Chamber of Commerce. Retrieved from uschamber.com/taxes

U.S. Office of the Press Secretary (Producer). (2014, February 12). *Press briefing by Press Secretary Jay Carney, 2/12/2014.* [Interview transcript]. Retrieved from http://www.presidency.ucsb.edu/ws/index.php?pid=104696

Zubak-Skees, M. B. (2014, February 7). Wanna be ambassador to Argentina? *Slate.* Retrieved from http://www.slate.com/articles/news_and_politics/politics/2014/02/map_of_ambassador_posts_given_to_obama_s_top_fundraisers_noah_bryson_mamet.html

CHAPTER 5

DO CONTRIBUTIONS TO JUDICIAL CAMPAIGNS CREATE THE APPEARANCE OF CORRUPTION?

Thomas E. McClure

ABSTRACT

Opinion polls show that contributions to judicial candidates create an appearance of corruption. This perception damages the institutional legitimacy of the courts. This chapter explores the relationship between integrity ratings of Illinois trial judges and campaign contributions. Specifically, it examines the Illinois State Bar Association judicial poll integrity scores of 253 elected judges seated in 101 Illinois counties during 1994–2012. Regression analysis reveals that judicial candidates' integrity scores declined as (a) the amount of attorney contributions increased; (b) the number of reported attorney contributors enlarged; and (c) the number of large attorney contributors grew. This chapter also discusses the efficacy and limitations of four policies meant to diminish the appearance of corruption: recusal and disqualification rules; anonymous contributions; public financing; and the elimination of the election of judges. Although a

Corruption, Accountability and Discretion
Public Policy and Governance, 85–105
Copyright © 2017 by Emerald Publishing Limited
doi:10.1108/S2053-769720170000029005

radical solution, the policy of abolishing judicial elections is more likely to
overcome the appearance of corruption than the other reforms.

Keywords: Attorneys; campaign contributions; courts; judges; judicial
elections; judicial integrity

INTRODUCTION

For over two centuries, policymakers have grappled with the proper balance
between judicial independence and public accountability in selecting judges.
If judges have absolute independence without any degree of accountability
to the electorate, some argue that litigants are subject to the court's arbitrary
whims. Conversely, judges dependent on campaign contributions to obtain
and secure office may cater to their contributors' interests rather than to the
rule of law. Under either extreme, parties coming to court have no assurance
of receiving a fair hearing before an impartial adjudicator.

Nearly 80% of the states require judges to face the voters to remain in
office. Exorbitant amounts of money are spent on these elections. Most everyone agrees that a judicial system is flawed if it produces judges who are
beholden to their financiers. Likewise, the system is also dysfunctional if
the courts appear to be unfair even though there is no proof of actual bias.
Judges must appear to have integrity.

This chapter argues that campaign contributions made to judicial candidates create an appearance of corruption, a perception that is damaging
to the institutional legitimacy of the courts. Next, the chapter presents an
empirical analysis demonstrating that increased attorney campaign contributions correspond to lower integrity scores for individual judges on the judicial bar poll. Finally, the chapter reviews and critiques key policy measures
designed to address the appearance of corruption stemming from attorney
contributions to candidates for judgeships.

CAMPAIGN CONTRIBUTIONS CREATE AN
APPEARANCE OF CORRUPTION

There is an appearance of corruption in state courts in which judges are
elected. In Dincer and Johnston's (2014) survey, state politics journalists identified 31 of the 50 U.S. states in which they perceived some level of judicial

corruption. The majority of the states in which corruption was perceived to be "not at all common" select their judges through merit selection (Dincer & Johnston, 2014). Respondents in the 2013 Transparency International's Global Corruption Barometer rated the United States judiciary 3.3 on a 5-point scale, where 1 means "not at all corrupt" and 5 means "extremely corrupt" (Transparency International, 2013, 38).

Many scholars believe contributions to judicial campaigns create the impression of improper influence (Aulet, 2011; Banner, 1988; Bonneau, 2005; Jackson & Riddlesperger, 1991; Susman, 2010; Ware, 2014). In the 2000s, judicial elections cost $200 million in direct campaign contributions, up from $60 million in the previous decade (Redish & Aronoff, 2014). Lawyers are one of the largest groups of contributors to judges' campaigns (Bonneau, 2007; Grannis, 1987; Nicholson & Weiss, 1986). When attorney and litigant contributors appear before judges that received their contributions, observers often draw "sinister conclusions" (Greene, 2010, p. 928–929). Indeed, Carrington (1998, p. 91) commented that "the contributions look a little like bribes or shake-downs related to the outcomes of past or future lawsuits." In other words, attorney campaign contributions create an appearance of corruption.

A clear majority of the public believe lawyers are purchasing influence when they donate money to judicial campaigns (Fisher, 2010; Greene, 2010; Pozen, 2008). This is reflected in a plethora of opinion polls. A 2011 survey of North Carolina voters showed that 94% thought campaign donations have some effect on judicial decisions, with 43% of the group indicating such contributions greatly influenced rulings (North Carolina Voters for Clean Elections, n.d.). A poll conducted by USA Today/Gallup in 2009 found that nearly 90% of those surveyed identified the influence of campaign contributions on judges' rulings as a problem, and 52% characterized it as a "major problem" (Biskupic, 2009). A 2013 national survey revealed that 87% of the respondents believed campaign contributions had some or a great deal of influence on judges' decisions and only two percent thought contributions had no effect (Brennan Center for Justice, 2013a). "Almost 9 in 10 Americans believe that campaign cash is affecting courtroom decisions. They're worried that justice is for sale." according to the Executive Director of Justice at Stake, a national organization focused exclusively on keeping courts fair and impartial (Brennan Center for Justice, 2013b, n.p.).

Polling of the legal community reveals similar concerns. In two surveys of the Texas bar, over three-quarters of responding attorneys indicated that judicial campaign contributions significantly affect decision-making (Swisher, 2011). A 2002 written poll of 2,428 state court judges revealed that 46% believed campaign contributions influenced their decisions in some respect (Greenberg Quinlan Rosner Research, Inc., 2002).

There is empirical evidence suggesting a basis for this perception. Although some studies fail to establish a connection between donations and judicial outcomes (Bonneau & Cann, 2009; Cann, Bonneau, & Boyea, 2012; Rotunda, 2004; Williams & Ditslear, 2007), most scholars have found a correlation between campaign contributions and high court rulings (Miller & Curry, 2013; Swisher, 2011). For instance, studies have found a statistically significant relationship between contributions and state supreme court decisions in Ohio tort decisions (Waltenburg & Lopeman, 2000); Texas commercial case rulings (McCall, 2003; McCall & McCall, 2007); Michigan government regulation and economic distribution cases (McLeod, 2008); Alabama arbitration cases (Ware, 1999); and Georgia decisions in general (Cann, 2007).

A nationwide study of more than 21,000 published state Supreme Court cases during the period 1995 to 1998 found a strong relationship between campaign contributions and judges' decisions (Shepherd, 2009). Contributions from groups representing business, labor, medicine, insurance companies, and lawyers were associated with favorable decisions for those interest groups. Using the same database, Kang & Shepherd (2011) found that every dollar of direct contributions from business groups is related to an increase in the probability that a state supreme court judge will vote for business litigants.

Gibson conducted several studies that measured the effect of judicial campaign contributions on public perception of impartiality and the legitimacy of the courts. Gibson (2008) created an experimental "vignette" presenting citizens with various election scenarios involving candidates for the Kentucky Supreme Court. He found that the perception of impartiality was reduced if a subject was aware of a judge's receipt of campaign contributions. He reaffirmed this finding in a representative national survey (Gibson, 2009). Gibson and Caldeira (2013) applied a similar methodological approach to measure the effect of recusals on West Virginia citizens' perception of impartiality and legitimacy. Again, the experimental vignettes showed that judicial campaign contributions reduced the perception of impartiality. They also found that contributions offered but rejected by the candidate have similar effects to contributions offered and accepted.

The appearance of corruption delegitimizes the courts. The apparent bias of the bench is as bad as actual bias (Rothman, 2009). The public's belief that judges are influenced by campaign contributions is itself damaging to the judicial system (Goodman, 2012). Confidence in the courts depends upon the litigants' impression that their cases are decided by an impartial bench (Benesh, 2006). Lawyer and litigant campaign contributions threaten judicial independence due to "the reality of undue influence and the appearance of impropriety" (Chemerinsky, 1998, p. 134). Thus, the mere perception of impropriety creates problems for the courts even if no *quid pro quo* exchanges take place (Cann, 2007; Schotland, 1985). As Barnhizer (2001, p. 366) stated:

> Even if judicial corruption through decisions that favor special interests is not empirically demonstrable, the public's perception will be that judicial decision-making favors special interests to which the judge is obligated through financial or other campaign support. The implications are quite serious. Without a widely held public perception of judicial fairness the members of political societies distrust their political institutions and lack the will to cooperate with others. If this distrust continues too long and becomes too intense and pervasive the social glue is not strong enough to prevent a weakening or even disintegration of the political system.

In summary, even if a causal relationship between contributions and court decisions cannot be proven, there is an appearance of corruption arising from knowledge of monetary donations to judicial campaigns. This perception is harmful to the legitimacy of the courts.

ATTORNEY CONTRIBUTIONS AND A REDUCED PERCEPTION OF IMPARTIALITY

If campaign contributions to judicial candidates create the general appearance of corruption, it seems rational to infer that the reputation of the individual judges receiving such donations would likewise suffer. To test the validity of this inference, this research examines the integrity scores of Illinois Circuit Court Judges ("circuit judges") who faced their initial retention election during the period 1994 through 2012 considering the contributions attorneys made to their campaigns. Circuit judges are trial judges that are first elected in a partisan election for a six-year-term. Thereafter, they run in non-partisan general elections for retention.

This study examines two sets of circuit judges. The first consists of 253 downstate and collar county circuit judges in Illinois. The second set, a subset of the first group, consists of 84 circuit judges that did not face an opponent in either the primary or general election when they first ran for office. This subset was isolated to eliminate judges who were perceived as lacking integrity because of their tactics in a contested election. One would expect that judicial candidates would be more likely to "act like politicians" in a contested race. On the other hand, judges running unopposed need not campaign at all and therefore would not need to engage in extensive political activity.

Illinois election law requires all campaign committees receiving contributions more than a meager amount to regularly report donations to the Illinois State Board of Elections. Reports identify the contributors giving $150 or more during a reporting period along with the respective amounts of their donations. Using the lawyer search tool found on the Illinois Attorney Registration & Disciplinary Commission's website, attorney donors were identified.

The Illinois State Bar Association [ISBA] regularly conducts a judicial advisory poll of attorneys to evaluate judges seated in all of Illinois except Cook County (the county in which Chicago is located). The ISBA administers the poll in the year a judge's current term of office concludes. Lawyers assess each judge on several qualifications, including integrity. An attorney casts a "yes" vote if he or she believes the judge possesses a particular trait. The ISBA publishes tabulation summaries showing the percentage of "yes" votes each judge received in all categories.

This chapter's analyses are designed to test three hypotheses. First, it is hypothesized that as a judicial candidate's campaign contributions from attorneys increase, their perceived integrity decreases. Second, it is theorized that as the number of reported attorney campaign contributors increases, a judicial candidate's perceived integrity declines. The final hypothesis is that a judicial candidate's perceived integrity will decrease as the number of large attorney judicial campaign contributors increases.

Data

This chapter looked at the 1994–2012 ISBA advisory bar poll integrity ratings for 253 circuit judges as well as the subgroup of 84 circuit judges that never faced opponents when they ran for office. In both instances, the research compared the scores they garnered when they were running for their first retention election to campaign contributions received when they were running for their initial term on the bench. Control variables were constructed based on biographical information found in Sullivan's Judicial Directory.

With some exceptions, there is little variation between the demographic characteristics of the 253 judges based on the amount of attorney contributions they received. Table 1 presents comparisons of the circuit judges at the time of their first retention election, arranged by groupings of total attorney contributions. Judges receiving more than $5,000 in attorney donations were more likely to have received their undergraduate degree from a school other than an Illinois public university, engaged in civic activities, and joined local

Table 1. Characteristics of Illinois Circuit Court Judges (Outside of Cook County) Seeking Initial Reselection by Total Attorney Campaign Contributions (1994–2012) N = 253.

	Total Attorney Contributions to Campaign		
	None N = 89	$1–5,000 N = 83	$5,001+ N = 81
Demographic traits			
Male	87% (77)	89% (74)	80% (65)
Average age	53	52	54
IL public university bachelor's degree	51% (45)	52% (43)	37% (30)
Bar association memberships			
ABA	35% (31)	24% (20)	27% (22)
ISBA	81% (72)	77% (64)	99% (80)
Local bar	45% (40)	49% (41)	61% (49)
Prior experience			
Average years as licensed attorney	26	25	27
Prosecutor	55% (49)	46% (38)	48% (39)
Public defender	17% (15)	17% (14)	15% (12)
Private practice	82% (73)	90% (75)	85% (69)
Judicial Law Clerk	2% (2)	1% (1)	5% (4)
Elective office	98% (87)	22% (18)	99% (80)
Civic Involvement	39% (35)	36% (30)	99% (80)
Republican	64% (56)	58% (48)	67% (55)

and state bar associations. Judges receiving either no attorney contributions or more than $5,000 were significantly more likely to have held elective office than were judges who received modest amounts of lawyer donations.

Contributions to judicial campaigns greatly differ. Table 2 displays the amounts attorneys donated to the judges' campaign committees. Over one-third of all of the judges studied received no attorney contributions, whereas two jurists received over $100,000 each from the bar. Judicial campaigns received an average of $7,938 in lawyer contributions with a median amount of $1,250. The highest amount received by a single campaign was $359,000.

More than half of the judges that did not have electoral opponents reported no attorney contributions. Three-quarters of this subgroup received less than $5,000 from lawyers, and ten percent received more than $20,000. The largest total amount of attorney donations reported by a single uncontested judicial campaign was $65,350.

Table 2.   Total Attorney Campaign Contributions to Illinois Circuit Court
Judges (Outside of Cook County) (1994–2012).

Donation Amount	Entire Group of Judges N = 253	Judges Without Electoral Competition N = 84
$0	35% (89)	55% (46)
$1–1,000	12% (31)	8% (7)
$1,001–5,000	20% (52)	4% (11)
$5,001–10,000	13% (32)	7% (6)
$10,001–15,000	7% (19)	6% (5)
$15,001–20,000	2% (6)	2% (2)
$20,001–25,000	2% (6)	2% (2)
$25,001–50,000	5% (12)	2% (2)
$50,001–75,000	2% (4)	4% (3)
$75,001–100,000	0% (0)	0% (0)
$100,001+	1% (2)	0% (0)

Variables

The dependent variable is the ISBA advisory bar poll integrity score ("**integrity**"). This rating is the percentage of "yes" votes cast by attorneys in answer to the ballot question, "[W]ill the candidate [a]dhere to the high standards of integrity and ethical conduct required of the office?" The lowest integrity score received for any judge was 48.17, and the lowest score of a judge facing no opposition was 71.30. Members of both groups attained a 100% rating.

Three independent variables were used to test the hypotheses. **Total attorney contributions** are the total contributions made by attorneys to a judge's campaign committee when the judge initially ran for office in primary and general elections. **Number of attorney contributors** is the number of lawyers reported that gave $150 or more when the judge first sought office in primary and general elections. **Number of attorney large contributors** is the number of attorneys that reportedly donated $1,000 or more when the judge initially ran for office in primary and general elections. Twelve control variables were employed which are described in Table 3.

To test the hypotheses, linear regression was used to analyze bar poll integrity scores that the circuit court judges received when they were evaluated at the end of their first term. Each poll was conducted six years after the judges' first election. At the time of the poll, they were candidates in a retention election.

Table 3. Control Variables.

Non-binary variables
Average poll score – mean of a judge's ISBA bar poll scores in the categories of impartiality, legal ability, temperament, court management, and health
Years as attorney – number of years between the judge's Illinois bar admission and the year of the bar poll
Dummy variables
Male – judge's gender
IL public university – judge graduated from an Illinois public university
Tier 1 law school – judge graduated from one of the top fifty law schools listed in US News and World Report 2017 rankings
Career prosecutor – prior employment as a career prosecutor
Prosecutor – prior employment as a prosecutor, but not necessarily as a career prosecutor
Public defender (never prosecutor) – prior employment as a public defender, but never as a prosecutor
Private practice – prior employment in the private practice of law
Elected office – prior service in an elected public office
Civic involvement – membership in a community organization open to non-lawyers
ISBA membership – membership in Illinois State Bar Association

First Study Group Results – All judges: As expected, regression analyses of the 253-judge group revealed an inverse relationship between total attorney contributions received and integrity scores. This relationship is statistically significant under the three scenarios tested: total contributions, number of attorneys contributing $150 or more, and number of attorneys donating at least $1,000. Thus, increased lawyer contributions are associated with a decreased perception of integrity. All models also showed a positive relationship between **integrity** and **average bar poll score.** The analyses are presented in Table 4.

Second Study Group Results – Judges without opponents: In the subgroup of unopposed judges, regression analyses also demonstrated the presence of a negative relationship between total attorney contributions and integrity scores. This relationship is statistically significant under the three scenarios tested. The models revealed a positive relationship between **integrity** and **average bar poll score** and **ISBA membership. Integrity** and past experience as a **prosecutor** were inversely related. The analyses are presented in Table 5.

There are two likely explanations for these findings. First, the judges that received low integrity ratings were known to be recipients of lawyer campaign contributions. Thus, the bar poll voters inferred a relationship between campaign cash and unethical behavior. This view is especially fitting when an unopposed judicial candidate's receipt of thousands of dollars is known. This explanation corresponds with the public's perception that judicial campaign donations affect decision-making (Brennan Center for Justice, 2013b; Greenberg Quinlan Rosner Research, Inc., 2002; Swisher, 2011).

Table 4. Predicting Integrity Scores of Judges Facing Electoral Opponents: Attorney Campaign Contributions.

Variable	Total Attorney Contributions Coefficient (S.E.)	Number of $150 + Attorney Contributors Coefficient (S.E.)	Number of $1,000 + Attorney Contributors Coefficient (S.E)
Total Attorney Contributions	−1.9* (0.1)	—	—
Number of $150 + Contributors	—	−0.0***(0.0)	—
Number of $1,000 + Contributors	—	—	−0.1**(0.0)
Average Poll Score (without integrity)	0.8*** (0.0)	0.8*** (0.0)	0.8*** (0.0)
Years as Attorney	0.0 (0.0)	0.0 (0.0)	0.0 (0.0)
Male	−0.5 (0.6)	−0.6 (0.6)	−0.5 (0.6)
IL Public University	−0.1 (0.4)	−0.2 (0.4)	−0.1 (0.4)
Tier 1 Law School	−0.4 (0.5)	−0.5 (0.5)	−0.4 (0.5)
Career Prosecutor	1.0 (1.6)	1.1 (1.6)	1.0 (1.6)
Prosecutor	−0.6 (0.5)	−0.6 (0.5)	−0.6 (0.6)
Public Defender (never prosecutor)	−0.8 (1.0)	−0.9 (0.9)	−0.8 (1.0)
Private Practice	0.1 (0.8)	−0.0 (0.7)	0.0 (0.8)
Elective Office	0.5 (0.6)	0.2 (0.6)	0.4 (0.6)
Civic Involvement	0.0 (0.4)	0.2 (0.4)	0.1 (0.4)
ISBA Membership	0.5 (0.5)	0.3 (0.5)	0.5 (0.5)
Constant	18.5*** (3.5)	18.7*** (3.4)	18.7*** (3.5)
R Square	0.711	0.728	0.714
Adjusted R Square	0.695	0.712	0.698

Notes: $p < 0.05$; ** $p < 0.01$; *** $p < 0.001$ N = 253

Table 5. Predicting Integrity Scores of Judges without Electoral Opponents: Attorney Campaign Contributions.

Variable	Total Attorney Contributions Coefficient (S.E)	Number of $150 + Attorney Contributors Coefficient (S.E.)	Number of $1,000 + Attorney Contributors Coefficient (S.E.)
Total Attorney Contributions	−7.9**	—	—
	(0.1)		
Number of $150 + Contributors	—	−0.1**	—
		(0.0)	
Number of $1,000 + Contributors	—	—	−0.2*
			(0.1)
Average Poll Score (without integrity)	0.7***	0.1***	0.7***
	(0.0)	(0.1)	(0.1)
Years as Attorney	0.0	0.0	0.0
	(0.1)	(0.1)	(0.1)
Male	0.5	0.5	0.8
	(1.2)	(1.2)	(1.2)
IL Public University	−0.1	−0.3	0.0
	(0.8)	(0.8)	(0.8)
Tier 1 Law School	−1.3	−1.3	−1.4
	(0.8)	(0.8)	(0.8)
Career Prosecutor	2.2	1.7	2.2
	(2.1)	(2.1)	(2.1)
Prosecutor	−2.3*	−1.0*	−2.4*
	(0.9)	(0.9)	(0.9)
Public Defender (never prosecutor)	1.0	0.7	1.1
	(2.0)	(2.0)	(2.1)
Private Practice	−0.6	−0.2	−0.4
	(1.3)	(1.3)	(1.3)
Elective Office	1.6	1.6	1.7
	(1.1)	(1.1)	(1.1)
Civic Involvement	0.6	0.8	0.7
	(0.7)	(0.8)	(0.8)
ISBA Membership	2.7*	2.4*	3.0*
	(1.2)	(1.2)	(1.2)
Constant	25.8***	25.5***	24.5***
	(1.2)	(6.7)	(6.8)
R Square	0.741	0.743	0.732
Adjusted R Square	0.690	0.694	0.680

Notes: * $p < 0.05$; ** $p < 0.01$; *** $p < 0.001$ N = 84

An alternative rationale is that bar poll voters witnessed unethical behavior. In other words, attorneys rated judges as lacking integrity when the lawyers witnessed a want of integrity. As regards the authority of the courts, it makes no difference which explanation is true. The perception of corruption is as damaging to institutional legitimacy as actual corruption.

POLICY IMPLICATIONS: HOW DO WE ELIMINATE THE APPEARANCE OF CORRUPTION?

Legal observers have proposed several options to reduce the appearance of corruption stemming from campaign contributions. To eliminate the perception of corruption, a remedy must convince the public that the measure prevents a judge from presiding over cases in which a known meaningful donor appears as either a lawyer or a party. This chapter discusses the benefits and limitations of four key proposals: recusal and disqualification rules, anonymous contributions, public financing; and the elimination of judicial elections.

Recusal and Disqualification Rules

First, state canons of judicial conduct recusal rules can be drafted to limit, or even forbid, a campaign contributor from appearing before a judge. Recusal is the process of disqualifying a judge from a hearing because of bias or a conflict of interest. All state judicial standards of conduct are based on the Model Code of Judicial Conduct (American Bar Association [ABA] Center for Professional Responsibility, 2010). Under the model code, judges must disqualify themselves in any proceeding in which the judge's impartiality might reasonably be questioned ("Rule 2.11, Disqualification," 2010).

Most states do not require recusal simply because a lawyer appearing before a judge was a campaign contributor. The Illinois approach is typical. Illinois Supreme Court Rule 63 (2017) provides, in pertinent part, as follows:

(C)(1) A judge shall disqualify himself or herself in a proceeding in which the judge's impartiality might reasonably be questioned, including but not limited to instances where:

(a) the judge has a personal bias or prejudice concerning a party or a party's lawyer, or personal knowledge of disputed evidentiary facts concerning the proceeding.

Unfortunately, judges have a great deal of discretion in applying this standard. Different judges may reach opposite conclusions. Although an argument could be made that campaign contributions inherently create a bias in favor of the contributor thereby requiring recusal, the ethical rules are not interpreted in this manner. Courts tend not to recuse themselves for a number of reasons. First, most judges believe they have a duty to sit on a case (Miller & Curry, 2013). Moreover, judges' unconscious bias impacts their rulings on recusal so they are unable to objectively conclude they are biased (Bam, 2010).

Since 2009, over 20% of the states supreme courts have amended their judicial codes or adopted comments to the code to provide more guidance on disqualification of judges assigned to hear cases of their campaign donors (NCSC Center for Judicial Ethics, 2016). For instance, in 2012 North Dakota adopted a comment to Rule 2.11 stating:

> The fact that a lawyer in a proceeding, or a litigant, contributed to the judge's campaign, or publicly supported the judge in the judge's election does not of itself disqualify the judge. However, the size of contributions, the degree of involvement in the campaign, the timing of the campaign and proceeding, the issues involved in the proceeding, and other factors known to the judge may raise questions as to the judge's impartiality ... (NCSC Center for Judicial Ethics, 2016, 8).

Other state supreme courts adopting similar disqualification rules include Arkansas, Georgia, Iowa, Michigan, Missouri, New Mexico, Oklahoma, Pennsylvania, Tennessee, and Washington (NCSC Center for Judicial Ethics, 2016). These rules give more guidance as to when a judge should be recused when a campaign contributor is before the court. However, it is doubtful whether the new rules will change public perception. Indeed, recusal remains discretionary and judges may continue to decide cases of some of their contributors. Gibson and Caldeira's (2013) study demonstrated that while recusal helps to restore the perception of impartiality, public confidence levels do not return to as high of a level existing before it was known that the judicial candidate received contributions.

The ABA modified its model code to include a disqualification rule that specifically triggers recusal once a party or attorney's contribution reaches a certain dollar amount. Rule 2.11 (A)(4) ("Disqualification," 2010) provides:

> The judge knows or learns by means of a timely motion that a party, a party's lawyer, or the law firm of a party's lawyer has within the previous [insert number] year[s] made aggregate* contributions* to the judge's campaign in an amount that is greater than [$[insert amount] for an individual or $[insert amount] for an entity] [is reasonable and appropriate for an individual or an entity].

This rule is tantamount to the imposition of a campaign contribution ceiling on attorneys.

Only a few states have taken this approach. In Arizona, a judge must recuse herself if a party or attorney made contributions exceeding $840 in the previous four years (NCSC Center for Judicial Ethics, 2016). California judges are disqualified from a case if the judge received $1,500 from a party or lawyer in the preceding or upcoming election years (NCSC Center for Judicial Ethics, 2016). Utah judges must disqualify themselves if a party, a party's lawyer, or a party's lawyer's law firm has within the previous three years made aggregate contributions to the judge's retention in an amount exceeding $50 (NCSC Center for Judicial Ethics, 2016). Some states adopted variations of the required recusal approach. For instance, New York judges do not disqualify themselves. Rather court administrators must not assign a case to a judge when a party, attorney, or attorney's firm has contributed $2,500 to the judge's campaign during a two-year period (NCSC Center for Judicial Ethics, 2016). There is no automatic recusal in Mississippi. Instead, a party *may* file a motion to recuse a judge when an opposing party or the party's attorney contributed more than $1,000 to the trial court judge or more than $2,000 to a judge sitting in a higher court (NCSC Center for Judicial Ethics, 2016).

The disqualification rule that triggers recusal once contributions reach a specific amount overcomes the primary objection to typical recusal rules. However, it appears this reform will not be adopted nationwide. The Wisconsin and Nevada supreme courts recently rejected recommendations to adopt specific contribution recusal trigger rules (NCSC Center for Judicial Ethics, 2016). Likewise, the ISBA's Special Committee on Judicial Disqualification Standards (n.d., 32) rejected proposing a rule requiring recusals when contributions reach a certain amount because such a rule lends credence to the belief "that campaign contributions buy influence."

Moreover, there are serious objections to disqualification rules setting contribution ceilings. Several scholars argue that lawyers who do not want a judge to hear their case will donate to the judge as a "forum shopping" strategy (Bopp & Woudenberg, 2010). If lawyers make strategic donations to bad judges and refrain from contributing to judges they respect, then inferior judges will be likely to wage stronger campaigns than their better regarded colleagues. Thus, good judges may ultimately be the ones harmed most by restrictions placed upon lawyer contributions (ISBA's Special Committee on Judicial Disqualification Standards, n.d.).

More problematic is the fact that lawyers may simply change their method of contribution. Instead of making direct donations, attorneys will shift to political action committees (Miller & Curry, 2013) or make independent expenditures on behalf of the candidate. Even if attorneys' overall contribution levels decline, the appearance of corruption would not be reduced. As stated in the ISBA special report:

> [D]ecreased participation in the electoral process by lawyers would create a void. That void would likely be filled by individuals and organizations not governed by the ethics code applicable to lawyers whose partisan interests and money would likely commandeer judicial elections (ISBA's Special Committee on Judicial Disqualification Standards, n.d., p. 26–27).

Anonymous Contributions to Judicial Campaigns

A second approach to reducing the appearance of judicial corruption is anonymous contributions to campaigns. Advocates argue that judges would not be in a position to show favoritism to their supporters if they do not know their identities (Bam, 2011). Under this approach, attorneys would mail their contributions to a trust fund which in turn would pass the money to campaign committees without revealing its sources (Bam, 2011; Siciliano, 1991). This plan was proposed in Dade County, Florida and in Detroit, Michigan. The Dade County plan was discontinued after two election cycles and the Detroit plan was never put into effect due to problems with the Internal Revenue Service (Siciliano, 1991). This reform appears to be based on the naïve assumption that attorneys do not expect recognition for their contributions.

Public Campaign Finance

A third proposed approach is public financing of judicial campaigns (Bam, 2011). Currently, two states have permanent public financing programs for judicial elections. In New Mexico, appellate court candidates are eligible to receive public funding if they limit their campaign spending to the amount of money provided through the program, and to decline contributions from other sources (Justice at Stake, n.d.). West Virginia appellate judge candidates qualify for campaign funding if they receive a specified number of small donations from citizens across the state (Justice at Stake, n.d.). Wisconsin and North Carolina both discontinued their judicial election public financing systems (Justice at Stake, n.d.). Hazelton, Montgomery, and Nyhan's (2016) empirical analyses of the public financing system for North Carolina Supreme Court Justices found that justices who accepted public funds became less favorable to attorney contributors. They concluded that public financing reduced the influence donors had on the justices. Despite this conclusion, public financing of judicial elections has its shortfalls. The cost of this scheme makes it a viable option in only less populous states (Schotland, 2009). More critically, public funding does not eliminate independent expenditures and might actually encourage them (Schotland, 2009).

Elimination of Judicial Elections

The option most likely to eliminate the perception of corruption is the replacement of judicial elections with alternative methods of selection and reselection. Without having to face voters, judicial candidates would not have to raise campaign funds and therefore, would not hear cases involving contribution contributors. Hence, the abolition of the election of judges will prevent the perception of corruption before it can even begin.

The major argument for state court elections is that they provide judicial accountability through democracy. Several judicial scholars assert that elected judges take public sentiment into account when they decide cases. For instance, in a series of studies Hall found that state supreme court justices alter their behavior to cater to the preferences of those who decide whether to keep them in office (Hall, 1987, 1992, 1995; Hall & Brace, 1989). There is persuasive evidence that regardless of how safe their seats are, elected judges often fear voters (Brace & Hall, 1990). Not surprisingly, Brace & Hall (1997) found that judges chosen through non-competitive methods exhibit weaker links to the electoral public.

Opponents of judicial elections offer a different perspective. If all three branches of the government are democratically elected, they maintain that there is no institution to safeguard constitutional rights (Weiner, 1996). Another challenge posed by elections is the prospect that judges will render decisions to further their interest in being re-elected rather than to disburse justice in an unbiased manner. Two studies suggest that the awareness of a forthcoming election may affect impartial decision-making. Brooks & Raphael (2003) analyzed detailed historical data on all murders recorded by the Chicago police from 1870 to 1930. They found that defendants found guilty of murder were 15% more likely to be sentenced to death when the sentence was imposed in the judge's election year. Huber & Gordon (2004) examined 22,095 Pennsylvania criminal cases and found that elected trial judges became more punitive in sentencing as their re-election to office approached. The authors attributed at least 1,818 to 2,705 years of incarceration to the electoral dynamic.

Despite the fact that most citizens believe the elected judiciary appears corrupt due to campaign contributions, there is no momentum to change the status quo. The public wants judicial elections. The vast majority of states choose their judges through elections. Judges in 39 states are required to participate in judicial elections to remain in office. Ninety percent of state court judges are elected (Bopp & Woudenberg, 2010). It is, therefore, highly improbable that states will eliminate their elected judiciaries.

Hence, the only action available to end electing judges is a ruling by the United States Supreme Court that judicial elections are unconstitutional. One decision addresses the effect of judicial campaign contributions on litigants' right to due process. In *Caperton vs. A.T. Massey Coal Co.* (2009), the Court held that the 14th amendment due process clause requires a state Supreme Court justice to recuse himself due to the sizeable amount spent by the defendant's CEO to support the justice's election. In addition to contributing the $1,000 maximum amount to the candidate's campaign, the CEO contributed nearly $2.5 million to a political organization and $500,000 in independent expenditures. Although the Supreme Court found no proof of actual bias, it determined there was a risk of actual bias in light of the contributions' relative size in comparison to the total amount of money contributed to the campaign, the total amount spent in the election, and the apparent effect the contributions had on the outcome of the election. The Court stated that not every campaign contribution by an attorney or litigant required a judge's recusal but rather its decision addresses an extreme and extraordinary situation.

While *Caperton* does not stand for the proposition that judicial campaign contributions *per se* create the risk of actual bias, several scholars argue that *Caperton* reasoning can be applied to establish that judicial elections create a risk of actual bias thereby violating due process. For instance, Redish & Aronoff (2014) argue that judges' prospect of losing their positions due to voter reaction to unpopular decisions creates the risk of actual bias. These scholars propose replacing judicial re-election with either life tenure or term limits.

As stated by Sandberg-Zakian (2011, p. 220):

> If, as *Caperton* holds, a judge who may be biased is constitutionally barred from hearing a case, then are elected judiciaries unconstitutional? After all, a judge is biased when she weighs an especially improper consideration, and personal-affinity considerations such as future career prospects are paradigmatically improper. *Caperton* does more than just pose this question. The Court's reasoning, if truly taken seriously, answers in the affirmative. Yes, that reasoning suggests that judicial elections do indeed offend the Due Process Clause.

Even though *Caperton* supports the elimination of judicial elections, such a court ruling flies in the face of widespread state practices and would likely be vigorously opposed.

CONCLUSION

Campaign contributions to judicial candidates create the appearance of corruption. Public opinion polls demonstrate the pervasiveness of this perception. An empirical analysis of bar poll integrity ratings demonstrates that the bar's perception of individual judges' integrity declines as campaign contributions from attorneys increases. While there are a number of policies available to potentially reverse the adverse effect caused by campaign contributions, only the radical reform of abolishing judicial elections can erase this taint on the reputation of state judiciaries.

REFERENCES

American Bar Association, Center for Professional Responsibility. (2010). *Model Code of Judicial Conduct*. Retrieved from http://www.americanbar.org/groups/professional_responsibility/publications/model_code_of_judicial_conduct.html
Aulet, K. J. (2011). It's not who you hire you but who can fire you: The case against retention elections. *Columbia Journal of Law & Social Problems, 44*(4), 589–615.
Bam, D. (2010). Understanding *Caperton*: Judicial disqualification under the due process clause. *McGeorge Law Review, 42* (1), 65–83.
Bam, D. (2011). Making appearances matter: Recusal and the appearance of bias. *Brigham Young University Law Review, 2011* (4), 943–1004.
Banner, S. (1988). Disqualifying elected judges from cases involving campaign contributors. *Stanford Law Review, 40*(2), 449–490.
Barnhizer, D. (2001). 'On the make': Campaign funding and the corrupting of the American judiciary. *Catholic University Law Review, 50*(2), 361–427.
Benesh, S. C. (2006). Understanding public confidence in American courts. *Journal of Politics, 68*(3), 697–707.
Biskupic. J. (2009, February 16). Supreme Court case with the feel of a best seller. *USA Today,* Retrieved from http://usatoday30.usatoday.com/news/washington/2009-02-16-grisham-court_N.htm
Bonneau, C. W. (2005). What price justice(s)? Understanding campaign spending in state supreme court elections. *State Politics & Policy Quarterly, 5*(2), 107–125.
Bonneau, C. W. (2007). Campaign fundraising in state supreme court elections. *Social Science Quarterly, 88*(1), 68–85.
Bonneau, C. W., & Cann, D. M. (2009). The effect of campaign contributions on judicial decision-making (unpublished manuscript). (February 4), Retrieved from http://papers.ssrn.com/sol3/papers.cfm?abstract_id=1337668
Bopp, J., & Woudenberg, A. Y. (2010). Extreme facts, extraordinary case: The *sui generis* recusal test of *Caperton v. Massey. Syracuse Law Review, 60*(2), 305–335.
Brace, P. R., and Hall, M. G. (1997). The interplay of preferences, case facts, context, and rules in the politics of judicial choice. *The Journal of Politics, 59*(4), 1206–1231.

Brennan Center for Justice. (2013a). *Justice at Stake/Brennan Center National Poll, 10/22–10/24*. [Data file]. Retrieved from http://www.justiceatstake.org/file.cfm/media/news/toplines337_B2D51323DC5D0.pdf

Brennan Center for Justice. (2013b). *New poll: Vast majority of voters fear campaign cash skews judges' decisions*. Retrieved from https://www.brennancenter.org/press-release/new-poll-vast-majority-voters-fear-campaign-cash-skews-judges-decisions

Brooks, R. R. W., & Raphael, S. (2002). Life terms or death sentences: The uneasy relationship between judicial elections and capital punishment. *The Journal of Criminal Law & Criminology*, *92*(3), 609–639.

Cann, D. (2007). Justice for sale? Campaign contributions and judicial decision-making. *State Politics & Policy Quarterly*, *7*(3), 281–297.

Cann, D. M., Bonneau. C.W., & Boyea. B.D. (2012). Campaign contributions and judicial decisions in partisan and nonpartisan elections. In Kevin T. McGuire (Ed.), *New Directions in Judicial Politics* (pp. 38–52). New York, NY: Routledge.

Caperton v. A.T. Massey Coal Co., 556 U.S. 868 (2009).

Carrington, P. (1998). Judicial independence and democratic accountability in highest state courts. *Law & Contemporary Problems*, *61*(3), 79–126.

Chemerinsky, E. (1998). Preserving an independent judiciary: The need for contribution and expenditure limits in judicial elections. *Chicago-Kent Law Review*, *74*(1), 133–149.

Dincer, O., & Johnston, M. (2014, December 1). Measuring illegal and legal corruption in American states: Some results from the Edmond J. Safra Center for Ethics Corruption in America Survey. *Edmond J. Safra Working Papers*, *58*. Retrieved from http://ethics.harvard.edu/blog/measuring-illegal-and-legal-corruption-american-states-some-results-safra

Fisher, K. R. (2010). Selva oscura: Judicial campaign contributions, disqualification, and due process. *Duquesne Law Review*, *48*, 767–838.

Gibson, J. L. (2008). Challenges to the impartiality of state high courts: Legitimacy theory and "new-style" judicial campaigns. *American Political Science Review*, *102*(1), 59–75.

Gibson, J. L. (2009). 'New-style' judicial campaigns and the legitimacy of state high courts. *The Journal of Politics*, *71*(4), 1285–1304.

Gibson, J. L., & Caldeira, G. (2013). Judicial impartiality, campaign contributions, and recusals: Results from a national survey. *Journal of Empirical Legal Studies*, *10*(1), 76–103.

Goodman, S. J. (2012). The danger inherent in the public perception that justice is for sale. *Drake Law Review*, *60*(3), 807–826.

Grannis, M. A. (1987). Safeguarding the litigant's constitutional right to a fair and impartial forum: A due process approach to improprieties arising from judicial campaign contributions from lawyers. *Michigan Law Review*, *86*(2), 382–419.

Greene, N. L. (2010). How great is America's tolerance for judicial bias? An inquiry into the Supreme Court's decisions in *Caperton* and *Citizens United*, their implications for judicial elections, and their effect on the rule of law in the United States. *West Virginia Law Review*, *112*(3), 873–945.

Greenberg Quinlan Rosner Research, Inc., (2002, January 2). *Justice at Stake-National Surveys of American Voters and State Judges*. Retrieved from http://www.justiceatstake.org/media/cms/JASJudgesSurveyResults_EA8838C0504A5.pdf

Hall, M. G. (1987). Constituent influences in state supreme courts: Conceptual notes and a case study. *Journal of Politics*, *49*(4), 1117–1124.

Hall, M. G. (1992). Electoral politics and strategic voting in state supreme courts. *Journal of Politics*, *54*(02), 427–446.

Hall, M. G. (1995). Justices as representatives: Elections and judicial politics in the American states. *American Politics Quarterly*, *23*(4), 485–503.

Hall, M.G., & Brace, P. (1989). Order in the courts: A neo-institutional approach to judicial consensus. *The Western Politics Quarterly*, *42*(3), 391–407.

Hazelton, M. L., Montgomery, J. M., & Nyhan, B. (2016). Does public financing affect judicial behavior? Evidence from the North Carolina Supreme Court. *American Politics Research*, *44*(4), 587–617.

Huber, G. A., & Gordon, S.C. (2004). Accountability and coercion: Is justice blind when it runs for office? *American Journal of Political Science*, *48*(2), 247–263.

Illinois State Bar Association's Special Committee on Judicial Disqualification Standards. (n.d.) *Report and recommendations of the Illinois State Bar Association's Special Committee on Judicial Disqualification Standards*. Retrieved from https://www. isba.org/sites/default/files/committees/judicialdisqualification/Report%20 and%20Recommendations%20of%20the%20ISBA's%20Special%20Committee% 20on%20Judicial%20Disqualification%20Standards.pdf

Illinois Supreme Court Rule 63 (2017).

Jackson, D. W., Riddlesperger, Jr, J. W. (1991). Money and politics in judicial elections: The 1988 election of the chief justice of the Texas Supreme Court. *Judicature*, *74*(4), 184–189.

Justice at Stake. (n.d.) *Public financing*. Retrieved March 29, 2017 from http://www.justiceatsta ke.org/issues/state_court_issues/public-financing/

Kang, M. S., & Shepherd, J. M. (2011). The partisan price of justice: An empirical analysis of campaign contributions and judicial decisions. *New York University Law Review*, *86*(1), 69–130.

McCall, M. (2003). The politics of judicial elections: The influence of campaign contributions on the voting patterns of Texas Supreme Court justices, 1994–1997. *Politics and Policy*, *31*(2), 314–343.

McCall, M. M., & McCall, M. A. (2007). Campaign contributions, judicial decisions and the Texas Supreme Court. *Judicature0 90*(5), 214–225.

McLeod, A. (2008). Bidding for Justice: A case study about the effect of campaign contributions on judicial decision. *University of Detroit Mercy Law Review*, *85*(3), 385–406.

Miller, B., & Curry, B. (2013). The effect of per se recusal rules on donor behavior in judicial elections. *Justice System Journal*, *34*(2), 125–151.

NCSC Center for Judicial Ethics. (2016, November). *Judicial disqualification based on campaign contributions*. Retrieved from http://www.ncsc.org/~/media/Files/PDF/Topics/Center%20 for%20Judicial%20Ethics/Disqualificationcontributions.ashx

Nicholson, M., & Weiss, B. S. (1986). Funding judicial campaigns in the Circuit Court of Cook County. *Judicature*, *70*(1), 17–26.

North Carolina Voters for Clean Elections (n.d.), *94% believe campaign contributions have some sway on a judge's decision*. Retrieved from http://www.ncvce.org/content/94-beleive-cam-paign-contributions-have-some-sway-judges-decision

Pozen, D. (2008). The irony of judicial elections. *Columbia Law Review*, *108*(2), 265–330.

Redish, M. H., & Aronoff, J. (2014). The real constitutional problem with state judicial selection: Due process judicial retention and the dangers of popular constitutionalism. *William & Mary Law review*, *56*(1), 1–58.

Rothman, R. L. (2009). Judicial campaign contributions: How much is too much? *Litigation*, *35*(2), 1–46.

Rotunda, R. D. (2004). Judicial impartiality and judicial campaign contributions: Evaluating the data. *Engage: The Journal of the Federalist Society's Practice Groups*, *5*(1), 122–127.

Rule 2.11, Disqualification. (2010). in American Bar Association, Center for Professional Responsibility. *Model Code of Judicial Conduct*. Retrieved from http://www.americanbar. org/groups/professional_responsibility/publications/model_code_of_judicial_conduct/ model_code_of_judicial_conduct_canon_2/rule2_11disqualification.html

Sandberg-Zakian, E. (2011). Rethinking "bias": Judicial elections and the due process clause after *Caperton v. A.T. Massey Coal Co. Arkansas Law Review*, *64*(1), 178–220.

Schotland, R. A. (1985). Elective judges' campaign financing: Are state judges' robes the emperor's clothes of American democracy. *Journal of Law and Politics*, *2*(1), 57.

Schotland, R. A. (2009). A plea for reality. *Missouri Law Review*, *704*(3), 507–529.

Shepherd, J. M. (2009). Money, politics, and impartial justice. *Duke Law Journal*, *58*(4), 623–685.

Siciliano, B. A. (1991). Attorney contributions in judicial campaigns: Creating the appearance of impropriety. *Hofstra Law Review*, *20*(1), 217–227.

Susman, T. M. (2011). Reciprocity, denial, and the appearance of impropriety: Why self-recusal cannot remedy the influence of campaign contributions on judges' decisions. *Journal of Law and Politics*, *26*(3), 359–384.

Swisher, K. (2011). Legal ethics and campaign contributions: The professional responsibility to pay for justice. *Georgetown Journal of Legal Ethics*, *24*(2), 225–280.

Transparency International. (2013). *Global Corruption Barometer, 2013*. Retrieved from https://www.transparency.org/gcb2013/report

Waltenburg, E., & Lopeman, C. (2000). Tort decisions and campaign dollars. *Politics and Policy*, *28*(2), 241–263.

Ware, S. J. (1999). Money, politics and judicial decisions: A case study of arbitration law in Alabama. *Journal of Law & Politics*, *15*(645), 645–685.

Ware, S. J. (2014). Judicial elections, judicial impartiality and legitimate judicial lawmaking: Williams-Yulee v. The Florida Bar. *Vanderbilt Law Review En Banc*, *68*, 59–81.

Wiener, S. D. (1996). Popular justice: State judicial elections and procedural due process. *Harvard Civil Rights-Civil Liberties Law Review*, *31*(1), 167–221.

Williams, M. S., & Ditslear, C.A. (2007). Bidding for justice: The influence of attorneys' contributions on state supreme courts. *Justice System Journal*, *28*(2), 135–156.

CHAPTER 6

MEDIA COVERAGE OF CORRUPTION AND SCANDAL IN THE 2016 PRESIDENTIAL ELECTION: FANTASY THEMES OF CROOKED HILLARY AND CORRUPT BUSINESSMAN TRUMP

John P. McHale

ABSTRACT

This chapter explores the media coverage of the 2016 Presidential campaign and reveals the corruption fantasy themes that emerged. Media coverage of corruption can uniquely affect voter attitudes and public policy formulation and implementation, as revealed in previous scholarship on media coverage of corruption. By tracing the competing narratives offered in media coverage utilizing the constant comparative method, the dramatic characters, Crooked Hillary and Corrupt Businessman Trump, are identified and their storylines are explicated. Analysis reveals these dramatic fantasy themes chained through social media, evincing and promoting the narratives that drove media coverage of our political leaders and public policy results.

Corruption, Accountability and Discretion
Public Policy and Governance, 107–123
doi:10.1108/S2053-769720170000029006

The chapter illustrates that the narratives involving corruption were promi-
nent and negative, further indicating that the media's obsession with scandal
contributed to and supported the narratives that portrayed both candidates
as corrupt, adding pollution to the 2016 U.S. political environment.

Keywords: Hillary Clinton; corruption; Presidential campaign;
political media; Donald Trump

INTRODUCTION

In this chapter, we introduce the importance of the 2016 presidential elections to the direction of public policy and governance and outline existing
literature that looked at portrayal of corruption in the media. It discusses
the implications of media coverage on public policy and governance and
helps scholars understand how the media covers political corruption as well
as media coverage of candidate responses to accusations of corruption. The
media covered corruption in the 2016 presidential election extensively, contributing to a cynical democratic environment in which voters have less trust
both in elected officials and the media.

This chapter uses a triangulation of methodological approaches to study
this phenomenon including explication of narrative themes amplified and
articulated by media coverage of political corruption in the 2016 U.S. presidential election. A dramaturgical approach was applied to the media coverage of corruption during the campaign to identify the narratives presented
by the media. Results suggests that the media coverage of corruption in
the 2016 presidential campaign was rife with fantasy themes of Crooked
Hillary and Corrupt Businessman Trump. Media coverage of corruption in
the 2016 presidential election was prominent, as voters faced the unpleas-
ant task of choosing between Crooked Hillary and Corrupt Businessman
Trump.

These results have important implications for governance, as the election
of a U.S. President is seismic in its importance to governance and public
policy. In the first one hundred days in office, Trump initiated as well as
withdrew several notable executive orders with deep public policy impact
across a range of issues including immigration, environmental regulation,
and health care. Looming changes in budget priorities will have deep impact
on public policy and the governing direction of the federal government.

Media coverage of corruption and scandal in political campaigns can likewise have impacts on public policy and governance. This coverage may have strong influence on U.S. voters and important consequences for the U.S. political system.

DOMESTIC CORRUPTION, SCANDAL, AND THE MEDIA

In the U.S. context, scholars Welch & Hibbing (1997) explored the effect of discussion of corruption in congressional races. The authors studied the effects of charges of corruption on voting behavior in congressional elections between 1982-1990. Welch & Hibbing (1997) noted "evidence from 1968 to 1978 indicated that [corruption] charges generally produced a decline in vote share of between 6% and 11% depending upon the nature of the charge. Moral violations were the most consequential for candidates and conflict of interest the least" (p. 226). Thus, there have been periods in which corruption charges, and presumably media coverage of those charges, have become more frequent and have had more importance in congressional races. A limitation of the transferability of these findings is that these scholars focused on corruption charges as identified in the *Congressional Quarterly* rather than the media reports of those findings. The authors assert that there is no proof of correlation between local media coverage of charges leveled at candidates in the *Congressional Quarterly*, but recognize this limitation of their work. In addition, the studies in this area have a heavy incumbency focus, inapplicable in the case of the 2016 campaign, unless one would characterize Clinton as a career politician and government official. Nevertheless, this work is important for our inquiry as it indicates a relationship between corruption and the outcomes of elections.

A study from the Harvard Shorenstein Center indicated the media coverage of the 2016 Presidential campaign was negative in tone. This included heavy emphasis on discussion of both major party campaigns (Patterson, 2016). Media coverage of the presidential race was negative in at least 64% of the coverage every week. When horserace coverage was excluded, the media coverage of both Trump and Clinton, individually, was 87% negative. Of import for our discussion, 17% of the coverage was on controversy such as charges of corruption. This negative tone of presidential media coverage has increased over the last 56 years. Patterson's (2016) typology of the coverage illustrates journalist's role in the controversy:

> To journalists, the real issues of presidential politics are not the candidates' policy com-
> mitments but instead the controversies that ensnare them. The 2016 campaign fit the
> pattern to a tee. Everything from Clinton's emails to Trump's taxes was grist for the media
> mill. They accounted for 17% of the coverage—one in every six news reports (p. 9).

Patterson (2016) found that 91% of the discussion of controversies was negative. Patterson did not differentiate the personal controversies from those dealing particularly with corruption, but much of the media coverage of controversies was charges about governmental or business corruption. Patterson suggested the negative tone of media coverage creates a cynicism about politics that obfuscates coverage of issues and disheartens voters. Patterson (2016) concluded highly critical of decisions made by media gatekeepers. In whole, the research suggests that corruption captures the attention of the American people. However, the media also plays an important role in influencing how the American people perceive corruption.

FANTASY THEME ANALYSIS

This chapter utilizes Symbolic Convergence Theory as an analytic lens through which to examine the fantasy themes perpetuated by the media in its coverage of the 2016 presidential election. Benoit, Kluykovski, McHale, & Airne (2001) used a similar framework in their analysis of political cartoons in the Clinton-Lewinsky-Starr affair, which critically informs this analysis. This chapter uses Ernest Bormann's Symbolic Convergence Theory (SCT) and fantasy theme analysis (1972) as a theoretical perspective in this portion of the chapter. (See Appendix A.) Bormann's (1973) fantasy theme analysis is a tool to understand public discourse. Bormann, Cragan, & Shields (1994) wrote "if asked what SCT and fantasy theme analysis do that is different, we reply that fantasy analysis…provides a clear technical vocabulary for the general analysis of imaginative language" (p. 276). Media coverage of the Trump-Clinton race was certainly filled with imaginative language and imagery. For example, Trump and supporters were chanting "lock her up" while gesturing as if in handcuffs. These rhetorical visions take dramatic form, and include such elements as "characters, scenarios, scenes, etc." (Cragan & Shields, 1981, p. 1). Characters in the rhetorical vision can take on the personae of villain, hero, or victim, among other arch-typical identities. Fantasy theme analysis is an excellent tool to understand the dramaturgical assumptions that form the fantasy themes presented by the mass media driven to greater or lesser extent by the statements and actions of the candidates.

Sample

This chapter sought saturation on exposure to media coverage of the campaign and the major events in the campaign process. It involved at least 20 hours of television coverage per week for eight weeks of the campaign. (See Appendix B.) This extensive sample, time, and effort committed to immersion in the media environment during the 2016 presidential campaign provided conceptual saturation. This saturation enabled the identification of dominant fantasy themes in media coverage of corruption.

Method

The method of constant comparison was used as an organizing procedure of fantasy themes that emerged from media coverage of corruption in the 2016 presidential campaign. The method of constant comparative method (Glaser & Strauss, 1967) is based on the assumptions of grounded theory, which permits the development "of a complex theory that corresponds closely to the data, since the constant comparisons force the analyst to consider much diversity in the data" (Glaser & Strauss, 1967, pp. 113–114). (See Appendix C.)

Next, this chapter articulates the fantasy themes that emerged from analysis. The dramaturgical visions are negative, as the themes sought were about corruption. The chapter first outlined the fantasy themes related to Trump as Corrupt Businessman, then turns to the fantasy themes that portrayed Crooked Hillary.

TRUMP AS CORRUPT BUSINESSMAN

Media coverage of corruption in the campaign supported fantasy themes that also presented Trump as a Corrupt Businessman. Trump's refusal to make his tax returns public fed the fantasy theme of Trump as a Corrupt Businessman. For instance, in the presidential debates and subsequent coverage of those debates, Clinton's attacks on Trump's failure to release his tax records was prominent. Trump's lack of financial transparency fed coverage of his potentially corrupt business practices.

Media coverage of other Trump business ventures contributed to a portrayal of Trump as a Corrupt Businessman. Media coverage revealed that Trump has hired undocumented workers from Eastern Europe and had, it was suggested, failed to provide the requisite recompense. In other cases, the media covered instances in which Trump had failed to pay contractors after work had been completed. Another controversy covered by the media was controversy surrounding Trump University.

There was a constant battle over this storyline or dramaturgical fantasy chain. Trump claimed he had received a small loan of one million dollars from his father. Clinton, in one debate, asserted it was a 14 million dollar loan. Media coverage of Clinton's statements and discussion by media pundits fed the storyline that Trump is a shady businessperson.

Corrupt ties to Russia were an issue raised in media coverage of the Trump campaign, although not extensively emphasized. During the Republican convention, there was discussion of Trump's contribution to the Republican Party platform. CNN noted Paul Manafort, Trump's campaign manager, requested opposition to Russian presence in the Ukraine be removed from the party platform (Frank & Pagliery, 2017). It was the only issue in the platform where the Trump campaign expressed interest. Trump's ties to Russia resurfaced in much of the media coverage of the Trump campaign. These ties were covered less before the election than after. Nevertheless, media coverage of the Trump campaign did feed fantasy themes depicting Trump as a Corrupt Businessman with dubious ties to Russia.

Corruption was a major theme in the rhetoric of both parties during the 2016 Democratic and Republican conventions. One issue related to ethical questions arose when Donald Trump's wife Melania seemed to plagiarize a speech given by Michelle Obama. This reinforced the fantasy theme that Trump and his campaign lacked ethical standards, supporting the narrative of Trump as Corrupt Businessman.

Another significant source of controversy for Trump that was not related to corruption *per se* was coverage that offered a fantasy theme of Trump as misogynistic and lascivious. Of note was the notorious "grab them by the genitalia" recording from 2005. Media coverage supplied portrayals that posited Trump was a sexual creep, inappropriately touching and talking about women. Media coverage offered reports of many women making such claims. His involvement/ownership with beauty contests and, by his own admission, the use of the prerogative to enter dressing rooms and ogle for his pleasure. While this discussion is distasteful and disgraceful, it is not about corruption, and thus, not as germane to our focus as others.

There were hints of a fantasy theme of Trump as reformer that emerged in the media coverage of the campaign. Trump was going to "drain the swamp." With that narrative, Trump needed his bad guy, and he found her in crooked Hillary. Trump the reformer was going to lock her up. Corrupt Businessman

Trump often stumbled over reformer Trump, so this reforming hero was often overshadowed in media coverage.

The media's coverage of Trump was extremely negative (Patterson, 2016), despite this glimmer of positivity rooted in the negative. Trump's coverage was negative two to one on positive weeks, ten to one on the most negative weeks (Patterson, 2016). Overall, media coverage of Trump and corruption did offer material for constructing fantasy theme chains of Trump as Corrupt Businessman.

CROOKED HILLARY FANTASY THEME

There were several fantasy themes that constituted the dramaturgical conceptualization of the corruption committed by Clinton. Crooked Hillary was a central theme repeatedly used by Trump and amplified by the media. Crooked Hillary was a dominant theme of the campaign coverage. Under this fantasy theme, Clinton and her husband would do anything to get and maintain power, including cheating, lying, hiding incriminating evidence (emails), catering to the whims of Wall Street, and, in the most extreme fantasy themes of the Crooked Hillary narrative offered from fake news sources, murder.

Clinton's email troubles were a lightning rod for the fantasy theme of Crooked Hillary. When the media covered the Director of the FBI's announcement of the inquiry into more Clinton emails nine days before the election, this fed the fantasy themes of Clinton as corrupt politician. The chaining themes supplied by media coverage not only found fault in her use of a private server for government business (a violation of State Department policy), but also for potentially lying about emails and intentionally destroying email evidence. The prominent discussion of corruption themes related to Clinton's email contributed to the fantasy theme as Crooked Hillary. Berney (2016) aptly identified this Crooked Hillary cycle:

> If you start with the assumption that Clinton is corrupt, then of course Comey's letter is the biggest story of the election. After all, even if the FBI hasn't reviewed the emails (the agency only just obtained a warrant to do so), there must be something in them: They're emails, and we know there's something wrong with Clinton's emails, because we keep hearing about how her emails are connected to some grave scandal (n.p.).

The media threw continual fuel on the email scandal in the last two weeks of the campaign. Much if not most of that coverage was simply about how media attention on the scandal was hurting Hillary's campaign.

For example, during the Republican convention, General Mike Flynn led the crowd in the chant, "Lock her up" during Flynn's campaign speech, and this was broadcast by all outlets. Flynn is the former national security advisor under Trump and currently under investigation for collusion between Trump's campaign and the Russian government. Flynn's participation in and encouragement of that chanting and the media airing the spectacle reified the fantasy theme of Crooked Hillary as a criminal.

Revelations about collusion between the Clinton campaign and the Democratic National Committee was a source of themes that fed this Crooked Hillary narrative. Media coverage of the campaign disclosed emails between the Clinton campaign and the DNC that suggested conspiracy against Bernie Sander's campaign in the primaries. This issue of corruption in politics was brought to the fore with WikiLeaks' leak of emails between the Clinton campaign and the Democratic National Committee members, which revealed collusion in the effort to thwart the Sanders campaign. When Wasserman-Schultz resigned as DNC chair, it seemed that collusion solidified as a fantasy theme of Crooked Hillary.

Another feature of the Crooked Hillary narrative is her relationship with large banks. In the first debate, Trump challenged Clinton to release transcripts of her paid speeches to Goldman Sachs. In addition, media coverage of charges related to foreign contributions to the Clinton Foundation were spun by Trump advocates as potential sources of corruption and, possibly, even as the result of corruption while Clinton served as Secretary of State. These issues featured in media coverage contributed to the Crooked Hillary narrative.

Interestingly, fake news as well as traditional media forms contributed to these themes. Fake news may reflect the fantasy theme already held. When applying the concepts of selective reception, perception, and retention, fake news stories would go viral because it was consistent and supportive of the Crooked Hillary theme.

Media coverage featured the Crooked Hillary theme prominently and more often than Corrupt Businessman Trump. Patterson (2016) suggested the media attacks on Clinton were more focused than on Trump. Clinton's controversies also got more attention (19% to 15%), according to Patterson (2016). The coverage of Clinton's controversies often centered around her campaign and the tone of that coverage was ten times more negative than positive (91% negative and 9% positive). When the media discussed Clinton scandals, the coverage was 19-to-1 negative. Other studies corroborated these trends. For example, according to the Tyndall Report, which tracks the composition of the nightly news programs for the three major networks ABC's *World News Tonight*, *CBS Evening News* and *NBC Nightly News*, "Combined, the three network newscasts have slotted 100 minutes so far this year for reporting on Hillary Clinton's emails while she served as secretary of state, but just 32 minutes for *all issues coverage*" (Boehlert, 2016, n.p.). This negative media coverage of Clinton was filled with fantasy themes of her as a corrupt politician. Corruption discussion was prominent, as Patterson (2016) explained:

> Clinton's badgering had a laser-like focus. She was alleged to be scandal-prone. Clinton's alleged scandals accounted for 16% of her coverage—four times the amount of press attention paid to Trump's treatment of women and sixteen times the amount of news coverage given to Clinton's most heavily covered policy position (p. 89).

Clinton and corruption were dominant themes in media contribution to the fantasy themes used to frame the two major party candidates in the 2016 election.

This study conducted analyses of Twitter communication in traditional battleground counties in Ohio and Wisconsin with the NUVI social media analytics program to see if these fantasy themes chained into this social media realm. NUVI is a real-time monitoring, analytics, and data visualization platform for social media. With NUVI one can study social conversations on the web. The platform allows scholars to instantly see what people are saying about political candidates across the Internet. The monitors used explored tweets contained the in key counties in the election (hillary, clinton, trump, donald, @HillaryClinton, @realDonaldTrump, @GovGaryJohnson, "Gary Johnson," @DrJillStein, "Jill Stein"). These collections of public Twitter data were built using these key terms and were geographically targeted. Each monitor is a little different, but the search for Hamilton county (Cincinnati, OH) used a 16.9-mile radius. Again, the size of each county varied.

Analysis of social media use supported the presence of these fantasy themes. Micro-analysis of Twitter messages from Hamilton County, Ohio between Oct. 8 and 10, 2016, revealed negative conversations included the concepts of "leaked,""rapist,"and "rape."While 30% of the messages were negative and 26% were positive. Many of the fantasy themes identified in the study were present in the Hamilton County tweets: "Warren Buffet avoids taxes like me: Nope."

Social media was used by the campaigns, and these messages chained the fantasy themes of corruption. For example, Vice-presidential candidate Mike Pence's October tweet reified the fantasy theme of Crooked Hillary: "Ohio knows we need to win on Election Day to stop @HillaryClinton's tidal wave of corruption and job-killing policies." This is certainly consistent with the Crooked Hillary fantasy themes supported by media coverage.

An analysis of the social media from Hamilton County, Ohio between November 6 and 9, 2016, revealed that negative conversations included the words racism, racist, and hate. This micro-analysis also revealed the discussion on social media was 24% negative and 38% positive.

Social media messages also supported the fantasy theme of Trump as Corrupt Businessman. When studying this period, in Hamilton County, one of the tweets most retweeted (8,845 times) was from Democratic leader Eric Holder: "Be afraid of any candidate who says he will order the DOJ/FBI to act on his command. This is dangerous/so is @realDonald Trump-he's not qualified." Likewise, this brought out fantasy themes of Clinton as corrupt. One respondent to Holder's tweet replied, "Mr. Holder you are part of the reason Clinton needs to go to jail."

An analysis of twitter communication between Oct. 1 and Nov. 7, 2016, in Brown County, WI, another barometer area, revealed that negative conversations included concepts of "rigged," "lobbying," and "such a nasty woman." Coverage was 22% positive and 29% negative. Themes of corruption were ubiquitous in the social media interaction in Brown County. Corruption themes were prevalent although much of the negative communication was about personal characteristics or communicative practices (i.e. "Block @realDonaldTrump and #GOP – and make America progressive again."). Trump as enemy of corruption was also a theme that emerged in the social media. Italians for Trump on Oct. 17th tweeted, "@realDonaldTrump unveils plans to clean up corruption including ban on all exec. branch officials lobbying for 5 years after leaving office." The message was retweeted at least 300 times.

There was a massive increase in social media communication of FBI investigation of Clinton's emails, particularly on October 28. An indicative example of tweets passed through Brown County: "FBI has just told Congress that it is reopening the Clinton email case." Clinton's emails seemed a major corruption controversy in social media communication during the campaign, especially after the FBI discussed continuing investigations 11 days before the election. Thus, the fantasy themes identified in media coverage did not stop there, but were extended in social media. The stories of Crooked Hillary and Corrupt Businessman Trump chained in social media.

IMPACT OF MEDIA COVERAGE OF CORRUPTION IN THE 2016 CAMPAIGN

The media coverage of corruption during the 2016 campaign has had and will continue to have great impact on governance and public policy. As chief executive, the President is responsible for implementation of all federal policy, and the disposition of the president toward policy has massive impact on the direction, implementation, or enforcement of many federal policies. If the fantasy theme of Crooked Hillary had not been stoked by FBI Director James Comey's announcement of further FBI email investigations on Oct. 29, our federal government might have a completely different set of public policy and governmental priorities. It is even possible that if Comey had reified the fantasy theme of Trump as Corrupt Businessman by announcing, at the same time, that the FBI was engaged in continuing investigation of ties between the Trump campaign and the Russians, the direction of national public policy could be different.

The media coverage of the Hillary Clinton email server misuse as Secretary of State increased awareness of State Department guidelines of acceptable email protocol. This increased media scrutiny undoubtedly raised awareness for State Department personnel, thus improving the execution of public policy.

The media coverage of corruption in the 2016 presidential campaign may have an impact on how the political parties conduct themselves, particularly the Democratic Party. In the discussions leading to the choice of a new DNC chairperson, the candidate for the party chair position discussed how confidentiality can no longer be assumed for any electronic communication between party officials (Marans, 2017). Rep. Keith Ellison (D-Minn.) said, "We have got to communicate to every staff member that what you write in an email could well end up being a headline. And so you have got to be scrupulously fair to everyone because you might not think anyone is watching, but probably someone is" (Marans, 2017). The scandal-ridden campaigns of 2016 will likely make party officials and anyone in government more careful about how they communicate via email.

Overall, the media coverage of the 2016 presidential campaign was obviously negative. This is a general trend of media coverage of political candidates: it has grown more negative. Sabato, Stencel, & Lichter (2000) suggested there might be positive effects of media discussion of corruption. The benefits, however, seems to pale to insignificance when compared to the corrosive effect the focus on the negative may have on our political environment:

> But the cost of today's politics-by-scandal outweigh any remedial benefits. With public trust of politicians near all-time lows, confidence in the media is no higher, and participants on both sides say the emphasis on scandal is reducing voter turnout, distracting from important policy debates and discouraging the best politicians and best journalists (p. xvi).

The public evaluation of our potential governmental officials has become a very nasty process. In 2016, our nation may have hit a new low.

CONCLUSION

This chapter introduced the importance of the 2016 presidential elections on the direction of public policy and governance and outlined existing literature that looked at portrayal of corruption in the media. The media covered corruption in the 2016 presidential election extensively, contributing to a cynical democratic environment in which voters distrust both elected officials and the media. The voters could choose between Crooked Hillary or Corrupt Businessman Trump and hold their noses as they wondered if this is really the best of the bad bunch.

REFERENCES

Bales, R. F. (1950). *Interaction process analysis: A method for the study of small groups.* Cambridge, MA: Addison-Wesley.

Benoit, P. J. (1997). *Telling the success story: Acclaiming and disclaiming discourse.* Albany, NY: State University of New York Press.

Benoit, W. L., Kluykovski, A. A., McHale, J. P., & Airne, D. (2001). A fantasy theme analysis of political cartoons in the Clinton-Lewinsky-Starr affair. *Critical Studies in Media Communication, 18,* 377–395. Retrieved from http://www.tandfonline.com/doi/pdf/10.1080/07393180128097?needAccess=true

Benoit, W. L., & McHale, J. P. (2003). Presidential candidates' television spots and personal qualities. *Southern Communication Journal, 68,* 319–334.

Berney, J. (2016, Oct. 31). How the Hillary outrage cycle took over the media. *Rolling Stone.* Retrieved from http://www.rollingstone.com/politics/features/how-the-hillary-clinton-outrage-cycle-took-over-the-media-w447574

Boehlert, E. (2016, Oct. 26). Study confirms network evening newscasts have abandoned policy coverage for the 2016 campaign. *Media Matters for America.* Retrieved from https://mediamatters.org/blog/2016/10/26/study-confirms-network-evening-newscasts-have-abandoned-policy-coverage-2016-campaign/214120

Bormann, E. G. (1972). Fantasy theme and rhetorical vision: The rhetorical criticism of social reality. *Quarterly Journal of Speech, 58,* 396–407. Retrieved from http://web.b.ebscohost.com/ehost/pdfviewer/pdfviewer?sid=c2e987d2-77c3-4921-9b86-be257f46a73e%40sessionmgr101&vid=1&hid=116

Bormann, E. G. (1973). The Eagleton affair: A fantasy theme analysis. *Quarterly Journal of Speech, 59,* 143–159. Retrieved from http://web.b.ebscohost.com/ehost/pdfviewer/pdfviewer?sid=aea490cd-3ce1-40f9-90ed-47f94f24438a%40sessionmgr104&vid=1&hid=116

Bormann, E. G. (1977). Fetching good out of evil: A rhetorical use of calamity. *Quarterly Journal of Speech*, *63*, 130–139. Retrieved from http://web.a.ebscohost.com/ehost/pdfviewer/pdfviewer?sid=ec4775fd-bd2a-4c18-85c5-caeedcfb4ccb%40sessionmgr4008&vid=1&hid=4101

Bormann, E. G. (1980). *Communication theory*. New York: Holt, Rinehart, & Winston.

Bormann, E. G. (1982a). A fantasy theme analysis of the television coverage of the hostage release and the Reagan inaugural. *Quarterly Journal of Speech*, *68*, 133–145. Retrieved from http://web.a.ebscohost.com/ehost/pdfviewer/pdfviewer?sid=4667fc31-5a1e-4983-b671-8ee1346ef469%40sessionmgr4007&vid=1&hid=4101

Bormann, E. G. (1982b). Fantasy and rhetorical vision: Ten years later. *Quarterly Journal of Speech*, *68*, 288–305. Retrieved from http://web.b.ebscohost.com/ehost/detail/detail?sid=d61650a3-239b-47aa-8368-5ec3e5bb7769%40sessionmgr102&vid=0&hid=116&bdata=JnNpdGU9ZWhvc3QtbGl2ZSZzY29wZT1zaXRl#AN=9993326&db=cms

Bormann, E. G. (1983a). Rhetoric as a way of knowing: Ernest Bormann and fantasy theme analysis. In J. L. Golden, G. F. Berquist, & W. E. Coleman (Eds.), *Rhetoric of western thought* (3/e, pp. 431–449). Dubuque, IA: Kendall/Hunt.

Bormann, E. G. (1983b). The symbolic convergence theory of communication and the creation, raising, and sustaining of public consciousness. In J. I. Sisco (Ed.), *The Jensen lectures: Contemporary communication studies* (pp. 71–90). Tampa, FL: Department of Communication, University of South Florida.

Bormann, E. G. (1985a). Symbolic convergence theory: A communication formulation based on homo narrans. *Journal of Communication*, *35*, 128–138. Retrieved from http://onlinelibrary.wiley.com/wol1/doi/10.1111/j.1460-2466.1985.tb02977.x/

Bormann, E. G. (1985b). *The force of fantasy: Restoring the American dream*. Carbondale: Southern Illinois University Press.

Bormann, E. G. (1986). Symbolic convergence theory and communication in group decision making. In R. Y. Hirokawa & M. S. Poole (Eds.), *Communication and group decision making* (pp. 219–236). Beverly Hills: Sage.

Bormann, E. G., Cragan, J. F., & Shields, D. C. (1994). In defense of symbolic convergence theory: A look at the theory and its criticisms after two decades. *Communication Theory*, *4*, 259–294. Retrieved from http://onlinelibrary.wiley.com/wol1/doi/10.1111/j.1468-2885.1994.tb00093.x/

Bormann, E. G., Koester, J., & Bennett, J. (1978). Political cartoons and salient rhetorical fantasies: An empirical analysis of the '76 presidential campaign. *Communication Monographs*, *45*, 312–329. Retrieved from http://web.a.ebscohost.com/ehost/pdfviewer/pdfviewer?sid=0b4faced-2234-4854-834a-8e568458ba23%40sessionmgr4008&vid=2&hid=4207

Bormann, E. G., Kroll, B. S., Watters, K., & McFarland, D. (1984). Rhetorical visions of committed voters in the 1980 presidential campaign: Fantasy theme analysis of a large sample survey. *Critical Studies in Mass Communication*, *1*, 287–310.

Cragan, J. F. (1981). The origins and nature of the cold war rhetorical vision, 19461972: A partial history. In J. F. Cragan & D. C. Shields (Eds.), *Applied communication research: A dramatistic approach* (pp. 47–66). Prospect Heights, IL: Waveland Press.

Cragan, J. F., & Shields, D. C. (1995). *Symbolic theories in applied communication research: Bormann, Burke, and Fisher*. Cresskill, NJ: Hampton Press.

Cragan, J. F., & Shields, D. C. (Eds.). (1981). *Applied communication research: A dramatistic approach*. Prospect Heights, IL: Waveland Press.

Fairhurst, G. T. (1993). The leader-member exchange patterns of women leaders in industry: A discourse analysis. *Communication Monographs, 60*, 321–351. Retrieved from http:// web.b.ebscohost.com/ehost/pdfviewer/pdfviewer?sid=be7256cd-5da1-45bf-9696-3112b2a8f758%40sessionmgr120&vid=1&hid=115

Frank, T., & Pagliery, P. (2017, April 14). Paul Manafort's two big issues: His finances and Ukraine. *CNN*. Retrieved from http://www.cnn.com/2017/04/14/politics/manafort-finances-ukraine-connection/

Giglioli, P. P. (1996). Political corruption and the media: The Tangentopoli affair. *International social science journal, 48*(149), 381–394. Retrieved from http://web.b.ebscohost.com/ehost/detail/detail?sid=c90c8bc5-7488-45a3-b060-138bc19958fb%40sessionmgr104&vid=0&hid=115&bdata=JnNpdGU9ZWhvc3QtbGl2ZSZzY29wZT1zaXRl#AN=9702026890&db=sih

Glaser, B. G., & Strauss, A. L. (1967). *The discovery of grounded theory: Strategies for qualitative research.* Chicago: Aldine/Atherton.

Lange, J. I. (1993). The logic of competing information campaigns: Conflict over old growth and the spotted owl. *Communication Monographs, 60*, 239–257. Retrieved from http:// web.a.ebscohost.com/ehost/pdfviewer/pdfviewer?sid=e1b92f34-a7ed-4622-a033-9a9a8a89c50e%40sessionmgr4007&vid=1&hid=4207

McHale, J. P. (2004). *Communicating for change: Strategies of social and political advocates.* Lanham, MD: Rowman & Littlefield.

Marans. (2017, Jan. 19). The DNC candidates get that the party messed up the 2016 primary. *The Huffington Post, 120*. Retrieved from http://www.huffingtonpost.com/entry/dnc-candidates-2016-primary_us_58813c6ce4b096b4a230d341?sh0ivh54e9jc92j4i

Patterson, T. E. (2016, Dec. 7). News coverage of the 2016 General Election: How the press failed the voters. *Harvard Kennedy School Shorenstein Center on Media, Politics, and Public Policy.* Retrieved from https://shorensteincenter.org/news-coverage-2016-general-election/

Sabato, L., Stencel, M., & Lichter, S. R. (2000). *Peepshow: Media and politics in an age of scandal.* Rowman & Littlefield.

Welch, S., & Hibbing, J. R. (1997). The effects of charges of corruption on voting behavior in congressional elections, 1982-1990. *The Journal of Politics, 59*(1), 226–239. Retrieved from http://www.jstor.org/stable/2998224?seq=1#page_scan_tab_contents

APPENDIX A: FANTASY THEME ANALYSIS

Fantasy theme analysis and the concept of rhetorical vision developed out of the study of small group activity. While at Harvard, Bales (1950) identified the development of fantasy themes within the communication of small groups. Some groups could formulate fantasy themes, or mental pictures of the future completion of a project. When the views of the group members were in alignment, a symbolic convergence was achieved, and the vision was shared. When this occurred, members of the group experienced heightened emotionalism, an increased commitment to the group and the vision, and higher levels of motivation for action.

Bormann (1972, 1973, 1977, 1980, 1982a, 1982b, 1983a, 1983b, 1985a, 1985b, 1986) further developed Bales' ideas and applied them to the criticism of rhetoric in a dramatist approach, as did Cragan (1981) and Cragan & Shields (1995). There are several critical assumptions that should guide critics who utilize fantasy theme analysis. Cragan & Shields (1995) outlined six assumptions of symbolic convergence theory (SCT), the theoretical basis of fantasy theme criticism. SCT assumes that "Meaning, emotion, and motive for action are in the manifest content of a message" (p. 31), that "reality is created symbolically" (p. 32), "fantasy theme chaining creates symbolic convergence that is dramatistic in form" (p. 32), "fantasy Theme Analysis (Bormann, 1972) is the basic method to capture symbolic reality" (p. 33), "fantasy themes occur in and chain out from all discourse" (p. 33), and the final assumption of SCT, as suggested by Cragan & Shields, is "At least three master analogues – righteous, social, and pragmatic – compete as alternative explanations of symbolic reality" (p. 34). These assumptions influence the study of media coverage of the 2016 presidential campaign through fantasy theme analysis.

Fantasy theme criticism entails multiple levels of analysis (Cragan & Shields, 1995). The fantasy theme consists of a shared vision regarding a specific issue. Fantasy types are a more abstract conceptualization. Fantasy types supply archetypal structure, form, and players for specific fantasy themes.

Another analytic level recognized by Cragan & Shields (1995) is rhetorical vision. A rhetorical vision may entail several fantasy themes to form a unified field of perception of aspects of symbolic reality. Cragan & Shields (1995) defined rhetorical vision as "a complete drama that catches up large groups of people into a common symbolic reality" (p. 39). Rhetorical visions are fantasy theme clusters that can be used as a lens through which shared visions of social reality are articulated and identified by rhetorical critics.

Effective articulation of a rhetorical vision reveals a greater or lesser fantasy theme artistry (Cragan & Shields, 1981). Rhetorical vision-reality links can strengthen a rhetorical vision, in which examples of reality are referenced. This is important for critical analysis of the 2016 presidential campaign drama. A master analogue is often implied in a rhetorical vision, which may provide normative standards of right and wrong, and this element was be identified in media coverage of corruption in the 2016 campaign.

APPENDIX B: MEDIA COVERAGE SAMPLE

This sample, composed of over 20 hours of media coverage of the 2016 campaign a week for eight weeks, focused on Fox (The O'Reilly Factor,

Megyn Kelly & Sean Hannity were consistently consumed), CNN (Anderson Cooper, Wolf Blitzer, & their coverage team), and MSNBC (Rachel Maddow, Chris Matthews).

The media consumption intensified during events of import to the campaign. The researcher spent at least four hours a day consuming coverage of the political conventions and watched and re-watched all three debates, consuming around three hours of consumption of the analysis from Fox, CNN, and MSNBC per debate. The researcher also consumed CBS coverage of the conventions and debates when offered as well. YouTube augmented repeated consumption of the debates and key speeches from the conventions.

The method utilized a system of commercial announcement avoidance to diversify emersion. While the researchers' predilections certainly influenced news consumption, he consciously sought out countervailing coverage to seek a synthesis of understanding of the media discussion of corruption in this campaign.

During eight weeks preceding the presidential election the researcher read the online offering of the local newspaper daily. He read the university newspaper twice a week. He also spent 30 minutes a day consuming the *New York Times* and Huffington post's mobile apps.

Social media consumption was also a part of his attempt to submerge himself in the media landscape to achieve saturation. A half hour a day was spent on Facebook. With over 800 Facebook friends, feeds became dominated by media posts, legitimate and fake. An additional source of immersion was television talk shows, in particular *The Late Show with Stephen Colbert*. Also, the researcher was a consistent albeit disappointed viewer of *The Daily Show* with Trevor Noah. He also consumed almost all of *Saturday Night Live*'s satirical takes on the campaign, and comedy on corruption.

APPENDIX C: CONSTANT COMPARATIVE METHOD

Several communicative areas have been studied using constant comparative method including political cartoons (Benoit, Kluykovski, McHale, & Airne, D., 2001), social activist communication (McHale, 2004), personal qualities of presidential candidates (Benoit & McHale, 2003), acclaiming and disclaiming discourse (Benoit, 1997), dissemination of other types of messages through the mass media (Lange, 1993), and leader-member exchange patterns of female business leaders. (Fairhurst, 1993). Because the goal of this analysis is to draw out the fantasy themes on corruption manifest in the media coverage of the 2016 presidential election, this method is used to develop categories of fantasy themes that emerged from media of corruption in the campaign. This method derived categories *from the media coverage itself* rather than imposing preconceptions onto it. Thus, the best answer to how the media covered corruption in the 2016 presidential campaign was to develop a set of categories from immersion in the media landscape during the campaign.

One theme was scrutinized at a time. The research began by tentatively creating a category to encompass the first theme followed by a second theme. If the theme of corruption was distinct from the first theme, a second provisional category for that theme was created. The research examined the remaining themes, one at a time, and established tentative categories for each utterance that appeared to address a distinctive discussion of corruption. When a new theme appeared to be like one previously categorized, it was tentatively placed in the same category as the one considered earlier. Thus, one rule followed was to contrast the themes in one category with the themes assigned to other categories to be sure that they seemed different, to ensure that the categories would be mutually exclusive. A second rule was to compare the themes tentatively assigned to the same category to each other to make sure they fit together. Eventually, classified every excerpt was classified into one of the categories so the typology would be exhaustive for the emerging fantasy theme chains.

Groups of themes began to emerge. Some themes solidified some categories and dispersed others, consistent with the assumption that the constant comparative method is continually reflexive.

PART III

POLICY ISSUES

CHAPTER 7

CRIME, INJUSTICE, AND POLITICS

Cara E. Rabe-Hemp, Philip Mulvey and
Morgan Foster

ABSTRACT

Issues of crime, justice, and incarceration play a crucial role in electoral politics. Recent Gallup polls reveal that nearly half of Americans view crime as an extremely serious or very serious problem. Such polls also reveal that Americans have little confidence in the criminal justice system. These issues have been exacerbated recently by the deaths of several young Black men including Michael Brown in Ferguson, Missouri, Eric Garner in Staten Island, New York, and Laquan McDonald in Chicago, Illinois, which brought national attention to the strained relationships between local law enforcement agencies and the communities that they are sworn to serve and protect. Ironically, this concern coincides with a U.S. crime rate that has dropped steadily for more than a decade. Why is the American public increasingly concerned with crime if crime rates are steadily dropping? This chapter explores the role of crime, politics, and media imagery in the making of criminal justice policy. We argue that crime is one of the most enduring political issues of this century and that, in turn, politicians have played a fundamental role in constructing criminal justice policies.

Corruption, Accountability and Discretion
Public Policy and Governance, 127–141
Copyright © 2017 by Emerald Publishing Limited
doi:10.1108/S2053-769720170000029007

The implications for public governance and policymaking are many, as criminal justice policies rely on the public perception of officials as legitimate and just. Scandal and corruption reduce the legitimacy of public officials and lead to public questions about the discretionary decision-making of criminal justice actors as well as the disproportionate consequences in the criminal justice system for poor and minority communities.

Keywords: Crime; framing; incarceration; political elites

INTRODUCTION

"Get tough!" This has been the crime moniker of politicians over the past several decades. The belief is that the current criminal justice system is too soft on criminals to deter them from offending. In response, politicians have authored get-tough policies to deter crime, such as the War on Drugs, zero-tolerance policing, and mandatory sentencing. The get-tough movement has been wildly successful in the United States (U.S.) at imposing harsher punishments on individuals. Today, the U.S. has the highest incarceration rate in the world. When compared with other industrialized nations, like Canada and England, the U.S. has similar punishments for crimes such as robbery and murder, but when you look at less serious offenses, (e.g. property crime, drugs, and public order crimes) the U.S. has much harsher penalties (Walker, 2011). Our prisons are vastly overcrowded. The past four decades have seen a 500% increase in incarceration, resulting in an annual 80-billion-dollar corrections budget (Mauer, 2014). Police departments across the nation have also adopted a get-tough ideology by utilizing paramilitary practices and strategies to tackle crime problems in American neighborhoods (Human Rights Watch, 2000).

Here is where the problem lies: social science research consistently refutes the effectiveness of get-tough policies, arguing instead that severity of punishment has little to do with deterrence. Further, there is considerable evidence that these practices have disproportionately affected already marginalized, poor and minority communities. For example, in 2000, the Humans Right Watch published "Punishment and Prejudice: Racial Disparities in the War on Drugs," arguing that the War on Drugs was overwhelmingly a war against Black Americans. The publicity surrounding these practices have called into question the legitimacy of criminal justice actors. This is important because the criminal justice system emphatically relies on the community to prevent, investigate, and solve crimes. Citizens who believe in the legitimacy of criminal justice actors are more likely to cooperate with them, increasing the criminal justice system's effectiveness. The reverse is also true. Citizens who perceive the criminal justice system as unfair or corrupt are less likely to cooperate, reducing the legitimacy and effectiveness of criminal justice agencies. Why do politicians continue to argue that we need to get tough on crime even though experts argue against the effectiveness of this agenda? This chapter explores the question by examining the role politicians play in constructing and framing crime policies and the consequences and legacy of the get-tough crime agenda.

THE ORIGINS OF LAW AND ORDER IN THE NATIONAL POLITICAL DISCOURSE

Crime is one of the most enduring political issues of this century and politicians have played a fundamental role in constructing crime policy in the United States. While crime is a concern of American citizens today, it has not always been this way. Before the 1960s, crime played much less of a prominent role in the list of concerns of American citizens (Beckett, 1997; Rosch, 1985). In fact, before the 1964 presidential election, politicians rarely focused on the topic. On the advice of strategists in 1964, Barry Goldwater was the first presidential candidate to make crime a central issue in his presidential campaign, hoping to appeal to white suburban voters by highlighting issues of social unrest during the era (Baker, 1983; Marion, 2010; Rosch, 1985). Although Goldwater was ultimately unsuccessful in his presidential campaign, his rhetoric around law and order remained.

The turbulence of the 1960s, including multiple high-profile assassinations of American leaders, societal unrest surrounding the Vietnam War and the civil rights movement, coupled with rising violent crime rates, made crime a poignant issue among voters during this era (Marion, 2010). Rosch (1985) astutely pointed out that many of Americans' fears about crime during the era were actually about public disorder, "…civil rights, demonstrations, urban riots, and anti-war protests. While little of this disorder had to do with the rise of murder, assault, rape and burglary, it contributed to people's fear that crime was rising" (p. 33). In 1968, for the first time, crime became the number one domestic policy issue of concern for American citizens, illustrated by a Gallup poll finding that 81% of respondents believed that "law and order has broken down in this country" (Edsall & Edsall, 1992, p. 38).

Richard Nixon seized upon these changing concerns of the American public during the 1968 presidential election, arguing that the problems facing the nation regarding crime and criminal justice were largely a result of liberal social policies of earlier administrations (Marion, 2010). Nixon made law and order politics a core theme to his election campaign. Additionally, he promised to do something "about crime in the streets" as part of his political narrative (Rosch, 1985, p. 20). To help win the presidential election, conservative republicans targeted the southern states in what they referred to as "The Southern Strategy." In this political calculation, Nixon and his advisors focused on disenfranchised white voters living in the south who largely resented the progress that had been made by minorities in the civil rights era (Alexander, 2012). As noted by Alexander (2012), "The racialized nature of this imagery became a crucial resource for conservatives, who succeeded in using law and order rhetoric in their effort to mobilize the resentment of white working class voters, many of whom felt threatened by the progress of African Americans" (p. 46). The strategy ultimately proved successful as Nixon became president, and a voting block of working class, white voters in the southern states became republicans – helping to reconfigure the political map for generations to come.

From this point forward, ideological viewpoints of law and order, better known as the get-tough movement, became a critical piece in the U.S. politics of criminal justice. Ronald Reagan, George H.W. Bush, and Bill Clinton all used varying aspects of the get-tough narrative during their campaigns and subsequent presidential administrations. Reagan's criminal justice policy initiatives, and the focus on "The War on Drugs" during the 1980s, manifested from an emphasis on control over "bad people" who were responsible for their actions (Beckett & Sasson, 2004). George H.W. Bush famously ran months of advertisements against presidential frontrunner Michael Dukakis for being "soft on crime" that most scholars conclude was at least partially responsible for changing the outcome of the 1988 presidential election. In these political advertisements, Willie Horton, a Black man who had previously been convicted of murder was featured. Horton absconded from a weekend furlough program in Massachusetts and kidnapped a couple – stabbing the man, before sexually assaulting his fiancée. Dukakis was the Governor of the state of Massachusetts at the time and in the past, had been in favor of furlough programs as a rehabilitative tool for offenders (for reviews see Alexander, 2012; Beckett & Sasson, 2004; Marion, 2010).

It is important to note that although conservative Republican politicians are credited with originally championing the get-tough narrative in American politics, many Democrats have also supported these ideological viewpoints since the 1960s. Beckett & Sasson (2004) remarked that at first glance, it is difficult to understand why Democrats would also get behind aspects of law and order politics, but ultimately it was necessary to attract "swing voters" and Independents to which this more conservative ideology involving crime and criminal justice is particularly appealing. For example, Bill Clinton spoke of more anti-crime initiatives and agenda items than any of his predecessors since the 1960s (Marion & Farmer, 2004). Not wanting to make the same political missteps as Dukakis and other more liberal politicians, the Clinton administration was often supportive of the draconian policies with get-tough views on crime (Becket & Sasson, 2004; Marion, 2010). Clinton favored the death penalty, supported mandatory minimum and three strikes sentencing, and signed the 1994 crime bill to put 100,000 more police officers on the streets and provide billions of dollars in funding to prisons. Walker (2011, p. 30) addressed the ideological disconnect of some politicians noting, "the conservative/liberal dichotomy" has been blurred in the contemporary criminal justice system with some conservatives supporting liberal arguments and vice versa. In sum, although the liberal/conservative dichotomy is a helpful way to consider political aspects of criminal justice policy, some politicians from both ideologies have ascribed to get-tough policies, which have produced limited to no success in solving the crime problem.

FRAMEWORK: FRAMING POLITICS

In the U.S., political elites such as politicians can socially construct crime issues for the people in deciding what to feature (priming) and how to discuss the issue (framing). Priming encourages the public to use specific events or benchmarks in history to evaluate and make decisions, forming an agenda. For example, the more politicians and the media discuss certain topics, the more the public is going to think the topic is important (Scheufele & Tewksbury, 2007). Specific to crime, this is how political elites draw attention to crime as a social problem worthy of addressing through public policy.

In addition to defining what people pay attention to, political elites can also frame crime for the American people. Scheufele & Tewksbury (2007) argued that political elites characterize and portray specific events in a certain way to change how the intended audience understands it. The lens through which the audience receive these stories "is not neutral but evinces the power and point of view of the political and economic elites who operate and focus it. And the special genius of this system is to make the whole process seem so normal and natural that the very art of social construction is invisible" (Gamson, 1992, p. 373).

How does this work? Goffman (1974) argued that because individuals do not fully understand the world and struggle to understand their life experiences, they apply different schemas to interpret events meaningfully. Framing, then, is a schema of interpretation. Individuals take their personal and cultural experiences to set a mental frame of reference. It is important to note that political elites do not have the ability to mold or shape issues completely to their liking. Both the amount of public information available about an issue, as well as the public mood constrains elite framing strategies. The partisan political system in the U.S. guarantees that there are competing ways of framing and understanding crime. For every frame, there is a counter frame. For example, Karen Callaghan and Frauke Schnell, editors of the text, *Framing American Politics*, argued that the framing of issues in American politics is as old as politics in America, pointing to the "federalist" versus the "anti-federalist" frames in the battle to ratify the United States Constitution.

Politicians and the media have a symbiotic role in framing crime for the public. The media essentially shapes what the public believes about crime, and the public, in turn, influences the media's depiction of crime by watching (and increasing the ratings and advertisement dollars) topics that are of predominant interest to them. Crime is a particularly popular topic for the media both as news and as entertainment. Scholars have noted that crime is often featured more often in the broadcast news than any other topic (Beckett & Sasson, 2004; Dorfman & Schialdi, 2001). In addition, a multitude of television shows that revolve around crime, criminal justice, law enforcement, the courtroom, and the prison system are televised as entertainment daily (Mallicoat, 2014). Although Americans are besieged with media representations regarding crime and criminal justice, the depictions are often inaccurate or biased. For example, the most "celebrated cases" which are normally delineations of particularly unique and violent crime (e.g. The O.J. Simpson trial) dominate much of the news coverage, even though this type of crime is quite uncommon in comparison to non-violent misdemeanors that garner little media attention (Walker, 2011). Importantly, scholars have found that the way crime is displayed in the media can influence the public's beliefs about crime and criminal justice, and this can influence the public's anxieties about these topics (Surette, 2010).

The media also is an important political tool regarding crime and criminal justice policy as it serves as a significant "linkage institution" between the public and politicians (Marion, 2010). Politicians can learn about specific crime issues that are important to their constituents by hearing, watching, and reading about those issues in the media. In the same way, the public can consider politicians' viewpoints on crime and criminal justice by learning about those viewpoints in the media. This is so the public can make informed voting decisions. For example, what candidates say during the election is important as voters want to know what a president will do about crime if elected to office. These statements may influence voters choices in the election booth. As a result, the media serves as a critically important tool to connect politicians and the public regarding crime and criminal justice policy.

The problem, however, about addressing the media as a linkage institution occurs because crime and criminal justice issues are not always accurately displayed within the media. Beckett (1997) argued that the media can shape politician's views about crime and criminal justice by what is depicted. If the media emphasizes an issue that has little initial public concern, politicians may, in turn, focus on it assuming it is a pressing issue for their constituents. Beckett (1997) also supposed that politicians can shape public concern through the media regarding issues of crime and criminal justice. She evidenced this by pointing out that there was generally little public concern about law and order when Goldwater first focused on this topic in his 1964 presidential campaign, minimal public anxiety about drug abuse when Reagan implemented the fight on The War on Drugs, and crime was not the most significant concern of the American people when Clinton initiated the 1994 crime bill (Beckett, 1997, p. 25). It was only after each of these politicians and their subordinates discussed the issues repeatedly in the media that the public became overwhelmingly concerned with each of these policy issues. Thus, the media helped these politicians advance their political initiatives and garner political support from the public.

Why do politicians frame crime? Clearly, there is power in controlling how the American people think about crime. All media that is viewed is somehow filtered by importance, and the importance is determined by the politician (Scheufele, 1999). Beckett & Sasson (2004) argued that not only can politicians dominate the discussion regarding crime and the policies that address them, but can also utilize framing to align public issues with a given political party. They noted that the purpose of "get tough" political frames of crime was to reorient state policy around social control and realign the electorate towards the Republican party. These findings suggest that the framing of crime may have the added benefit of supporting partisan politics.

ELECTION 2016

Issues of crime, justice, and incarceration have played an important role in many modern elections. Perhaps this was no more evident than throughout the 2016 presidential campaign, where both Donald Trump and Hillary Clinton spoke at length about criminal justice policy and reform. Their commentary illustrates how the framing of crime can lead the American people to two divergent but definitive pictures of the criminal justice system. In his classic essay, Packer (1964) put forth two distinct models regarding the "criminal process" – crime control and due process. These diametrically opposed models capture the competing conservative and liberal values that inform the laws and institutions of criminal justice. Conservatives support the crime control model, which tends to paint criminal justice officials (e.g. police officers, probation and parole officers, attorneys, and judges) as the thin blue line between order and anarchy. Due to these high stakes, advocates of the crime control model are willing to excuse violations by criminal justice officials that lead to the control of crime. The model focuses on means to efficiently deal with crime. As part of the crime control model conservatives have reasoned that liberal judicial decisions (e.g. the Warren Supreme Court) altered the capability of the criminal justice system to fight crime in a negative way. In this argument, less focus should be placed on the rights of the offender, and stricter laws that punish individuals more quickly for not adhering to established regulations should be implemented (Marion, 2010).

By comparison, the due process model, embraced by many liberals, focuses on effectively handling crime. Advocates of the due process model argue that the stigma and loss of liberty that accompanies the criminal process makes the administration of the criminal justice system a potential risk to justice. Instead, they argue for fair treatment of the accused and the presumption of innocence, which safeguards the system against injustices. Liberals have traditionally supported theories focused on social conditions as the defining factors in crime – such as poverty and racial inequality (Beckett & Sasson, 2004). The premise of the liberal argument has been that providing individuals more opportunity for advancement (e.g. the 1960s welfare programs of the Great Society) through better access to services, employment opportunities, and racial justice would substantially improve social conditions for many Americans and thus lower crime (Beckett & Sasson, 2004; Marion, 2010).

These models were illustrated in the candidates' framings of crime and criminal justice in their 2016 nationally televised conventions. Donald Trump, a proponent of the crime control model, argued that get-tough crime strategies are the only way to establish order. In his speech at the Republican

National Convention, he referred to issues of crime in detail, "the crime and violence that today afflicts our nation" and "decades of progress made in bringing down crime are now being reversed" while also selectively noting that homicide had increased in America's most populous cities and our nation's capital. He linked this violence to killings of police officers, arguing it had "risen by almost 50% compared to this point last year" (CNN, 2016). His solutions centered on law and order, reciting that phrase several times:

> We have a situation where we have our inner cities, African-American, Hispanics, are living in hell because it's so dangerous. You walk down the street, you get shot. In Chicago, they've had thousands of shootings, thousands, since January first. Thousands of shootings. And I'm saying where is this? Is this war-torn country? What are we doing? And we had to stop the violence. We must bring back law and order.

Even Trump's use of credible experts revolved around the crime control model. He featured "the law-and-order mayor of New York," Rudolph W. Giuliani and self-described as "America's Toughest Sheriff" Joe Arpaio as law and order criminal justice officials. Each has a recognized public reputation and has established respect as a criminal justice official, enacting get-tough policies in their respective jurisdictions.

By comparison, Hillary Clinton, an advocate for the due process model, framed crime solutions in equality and justice. At the Democratic National Convention in Philadelphia, some of the *Mothers of the Movement* spoke in primetime about their unarmed children, who had each died violently at the hands of law enforcement or gun violence (Bradner & Scott, 2016). Hillary Clinton pleaded for criminal justice reform arguing that race and guns are driving forces behind the crime epidemic in America:

> Everyone should be respected by the law and everyone should respect the law. Right now, that's not the case in a lot of our neighborhoods. So, I have, ever since the first day of my campaign, called for criminal justice reform. I've laid out a platform that I think would begin to remedy some of the problems we have in the criminal justice system. But we also have to recognize in addition to the challenges that we face with policing there are so many good brave police officers who equally want reform. So, we have to bring communities together in order to begin working on that as a mutual goal. And we've got to get guns out of the hands of people who shouldn't have them (Presidential Debate, September 26, 2016).

Where Trump commonly played upon the theme of returning to law and order to make our cities safer during the 2016 presidential campaign, Clinton was often more nuanced in her approach. When multiple killings of unarmed Black men at the hands of law enforcement made front page news, as well as multiple police officers being the victims of shootings across the U.S.,

Clinton was quoted as stating, "Everyone should have respect for the law and be respected by the law" (MacCammon, 2016). Trump and Clinton were only the most recent in a long line of politicians who have discussed differing aspects of crime and criminal justice while running for public office. The viewpoints expressed in their conversations symbolize the contestation of how to understand crime policies and criminal justice in America.

THE REALITY OF CRIME 2016

There is some empirical evidence regarding crime, which supports statements made by the candidates. For example, Donald Trump emphasizing the murder rates in Chicago, and the discussion on gun crime by Hillary Clinton, highlight important policy considerations about violent crime in the United States. Firearms, specifically handguns, play a serious part in the crime problem. They are used in 70% of all homicides and 41% of all robberies committed each year (Federal Bureau of Investigation, 2011). The cost of gun violence in human lives is staggering. The most recent findings from the National Crime Victimization Survey show 467,321 persons were victims of a crime committed with a firearm in 2011 and 6,371 people died from gun-related homicides (Bureau of Justice Statistics, 2011).

The clear majority of gun-related violence occurs in impoverished, high crime, and predominately Black and Hispanic neighborhoods. Homicide is the leading cause of death among Black men, aged 15 to 24 (Centers for Disease Control and Prevention, 2014). These neighborhoods are plagued by poverty, violence, and neglect (Beckett & Sasson, 2004). In fact, almost 20% of children in the U.S. live in poverty, which is a rate two to three times higher than most other Western, industrialized nations. The gun violence in Chicago mirrors the connection between crime, race, and poverty in American cities. Black and Hispanic communities are more likely to be victimized by gun violence. In 2011, 75% of murder victims in Chicago were Black, 18% were Hispanic, and 4% were white (Chicago Police Department, 2011, pp. 37–39).

The candidates' solutions to this violence varied significantly. Donald Trump depicted the criminal justice system as soft on crime and promoted the solution of tougher criminal justice policies. By comparison, Hillary Clinton framed the origins of crime mired in inequality and poverty. Her solutions embodied social and economic welfare policies to improve these conditions. Regardless of the solutions, both agreed that the social construction of crime centered on themes of immigration, race, and guns. This is not a new construction.

In the United States, race has been intertwined with definitions of crime and deviance since the slavery era. Today, the causes and consequences of the intertwining of race and crime are contested. Drakulich (2015) found that people with racial biases favor frames of crime that support a punitive approach. This frame is described as seeing crime as a serious, increasing problem, preferring explanations based on individual explanations of criminal behavior, and elevated levels of anger and anxiety over the potential of becoming a crime victim. Drakulich's argument is that racial biases are hidden from view, framed instead in criminological concerns. It seems clear that crime is often framed with race and immigration, suggesting to the American people that people of color are more likely to commit crime. A recent Sentencing Project report confirmed that white Americans over-associate Blacks with criminality.

The same holds true for immigrants. Research has consistently found that "illegal" immigrants are no more likely to engage in crimes (excluding their illegal status in the country) than other groups (Lee & Martinez, 2009). Despite this fact, they are often seen as a crime-prone group (Wang, 2012). This perception may be because their illegal status in the country is perceived as a predisposition to crime (Brown, 2016). This perception is supported by political statements. In the 2016 political debate, Donald Trump was asked, "race has been a big issue in this campaign and one of you is going to have to bridge a very wide and bitter gap. So how do you heal the divide?" While not asked about immigration, in his response, Trump linked race, crime, and immigration, arguing: "We have gangs roaming the street and in many cases, they're illegally here, illegal immigrants. And they have guns and they shoot people. And we must be very strong and we have to be very vigilant (Presidential Debate, September 26, 2016)." These statements have important implications for policy as Americans "who associate crime with Blacks and Latinos are more likely to support punitive policies, including capital punishment and mandatory minimum sentencing, than whites with weaker racial associations of crime" (Sentencing Report, 2014, p. 3).

CONCLUSION

In closing, some may ask – why was crime and criminal justice even a political issue in the 2016 election? Crime is down. With a handful of exceptions (primarily in large cities in the U.S.), official statistics show that serious and violent crime has decreased nearly every year from 1994 through 2010. Recently, this has been a widely-debated topic, as some politicians (most notably Donald Trump), have argued that a dramatic increase in crime has occurred (Diamond & Landers, 2017). Although some major cities have undergone an increase in certain crimes recently, other cities have sustained their decades of crime decline. According to the U.S. Department of Justice, Bureau of Justice Statistics (2013), the overall violent crime rate for rape, sexual assault, robbery, aggravated assault and simple assault fell from 80 victimizations per 1,000 persons in 1994 to 19 per 1,000 in 2010. So, one thing is clear, crime does not need to be on the rise for the fear of crime to be relevant to Americans.

One answer as to why crime was an issue in the 2016 election given its historic low rates is that the American people do not perceive crime as down. In fact, most Americans believe there is more crime in the U.S. than there was a year ago, as is typical for this long-term Gallup trend. A recent Gallup poll revealed that 70% of Americans state that crime is worse compared to the previous year, and almost 60% of Americans state that crime in the U.S. is either an "extremely" or "very" serious problem (McCarthy, 2015). Likewise, scholars have noted that the public's fear of crime has fluctuated considerably over the last two decades, but generally, most Americans assume crime has increased in the United States. This is true despite most of the best statistics on crime in the United States illustrating an overall decline in crime during this same period (Marion & Oliver, 2012). This chapter makes clear that while crime rates tell us something about crime, that symbolic framing of crime is just as important to understanding how the public perceives crime.

IMPLICATIONS FOR PUBLIC POLICY

Today, the public has become increasingly skeptical of the consequences of the get-tough policies and the rising costs of the criminal justice complex, resulting is increasing questions regarding the legitimacy of the entire system. Scandal and corruption have reduced the legitimacy of public officials and led to public questions about the discretionary decision-making of criminal justice actors as well as the disproportionate consequences in the criminal justice system for poor and minority communities. In 2014, the police were involved in several well-publicized shootings including Eric Garner, Michael Brown, and John Crawford III. The public responded with outrage, resulting in protests, sit-ins, and the popularization of an international activist group,

Black Lives Matter. Sadly, from 2014 to 2016, violence between police and citizens of color has consistently made national headlines. In this contestation, there is an opportunity for change.

While historically the story of crime and crime control has been used to "get tougher" on street crime, we know that these findings are not supported by empirical evidence in the mainstream criminological research, which suggests that the severity of punishment has little to do with deterrence and that the U.S. criminal justice system is already hard on criminals. Further, these policies have resulted in the marginalization of minority and immigrant groups. Racial bias and fear of immigrants are intertwined with the crime problem in the U.S. by flavoring the preference Americans have for understanding crime problems, even in people who explicitly deny holding racial biases (Drakulich, 2015). We need to be clear that the get-tough policies of the past several decades have not worked to reduce crime. The legacy of the policies has created an imprisonment boom, resulting in deep racial divides and a criminal justice system that is lacking in legitimacy. We must abandon this rhetoric.

Future demographic voting trends suggest that utilizing race and crime dialogue may pose a challenge in framing criminal justice policy in the future. Jessica Autumn Brown (2016) found that "racially divisive appeals (RDA)" are rhetorical strategies intended to denigrate a particular minority by framing that group as a threat to the audience, advocating for restrictions against minorities and/or reassuring the audience of their privileged position. However, the white population is both aging and shrinking, which means both political parties must attract minority voters. This may present an opportunity to publicly disentangle crime and criminal justice, from race and immigration concerns.

Today, the socially constructed get tough on crime rhetoric can be contested and challenged. In addition to being a tool of oppression, it can also be used as a "tool of control and resistance" (Hayward, 2010, p. 5). To do so, politicians must begin to be transparent about the reality of crime. If "politicians prevailing mood is always that the world is going to hell in a handcart, and woe betide any political candidate who suggests otherwise" they will continue to argue for punitive crime policies, and the American people are left with an enduring fear of crime (Fogg, 2016, p. 1). Of course, no politician is going to argue that we need more crime, but given that politicians can shape the scope, explanations, and consequences of crime, they need to better use their discretion to frame crime problems in research rather than rhetoric. This is because there is power in framing crime and criminal justice policies for the American people.

REFERENCES

Alexander, M. (2012). The new Jim Crow: Mass incarceration in the age of colorblindness. New York: New Press.

American Presidency Project. (2016, September 26). Presidential Debates. Retrieved from http://www.presidency.ucsb.edu/ws/index.php?pid=118971

American Presidency Project. (2016, October 19). Presidential Debates. Retrieved from http://www.presidency.ucsb.edu/ws/index.php?pid=119039

Baker, L. (1938). *Miranda: Crime, law, and politics.* New York, NY: Atheneum.

Beckett, K. (1997). *Making crime pay.* New York, NY: Oxford University Press.

Beckett, K., & Sasson, T. (2004). *The Politics of Injustice* (2nd ed.). Thousand Oaks, CA: Sage.

Bradner, E., & Scott, E. (2016, July 26). Mothers of the movement makes case for Hillary Clinton. Retrieved from http://www.cnn.com/2016/07/26/politics/mothers-movement-dnc-hillary-clinton/index.html

Brown, J. A. (2016). Running on fear: Immigration, race and crime framing in contemporary GOP Presidential Debate discourse. *Critical Criminology, 24,* 315–331.

Bureau of Justice Statistics (2013). Nonfatal firearm violence, 1993–2011: Special tabulation from the Bureau of Justice Statistics' National Crime Victimization Survey.

Callaghan, K., & Schnell, F. (2005). *Framing American Politics.* Pittsburgh, PA: University of Pittsburgh Press.

CNN. (2016). Donald Trump's speech at the Republican convention, as prepared for delivery. Retrieved from http://www.cnn.com/2016/07/22/politics/donald-trump-rnc-speech-text/

Diamond, J., & Landers, E. (2017, February 28). Trump correctly cites rising crime rates in cities. Retrieved from http://www.cnn.com/2017/02/08/politics/donald-trump-murder-rate-cities/index.html

Dorfman, L., & Schiraldi, V. (2001). Off balance: Youth, crime, and race in the news. Retrieved from http://www.justicepolicy.org/uploads/justicepolicy/documents/off_balance.pdf

Drakulich, K. (2015). Explicit and hidden racial bias in the framing of social problems. *Social Problems, 62,* 391–418.

Edsall, T.B., & Edsall, M.D. (1992). Chain reaction: The impact of race, rights, and taxes on American politics. New York, NY: Norton.

Federal Bureau of Investigation. Crime in the United States, 2011. Retrieved from https://ucr.fbi.gov/crime-in-the-u.s/2011/crime-in-the-u.s.-2011

Fogg, A. (2013, April 24). Crime is falling: Now let's reduce fear of crime. Retrieved from https://www.theguardian.com/commentisfree/2013/apr/24/crime-falling-reduce-fear-crime

Gamson, W.A. (1992). *Talking Politics.* Cambridge,UK: Cambridge University Press.

Goffman, E. (1974). Frame analysis: An essay on the organization of experience Cambridge, MA: Harvard University Press.

Hayward, K. & Presdee, M. (2010). *Framing Crime: Cultural Criminology and the Image,* New York, NY: Routledge.

Health Equity - Men's Health. (2017, January 26). Retrieved from https://www.cdc.gov/men/lcod/2014/black/index.htm

Human Rights Watch (2000). United States punishment and prejudice: Racial disparities in the war on drugs. Retrieved from https://www.hrw.org/reports/2000/usa/

Lee, M. T., & Martinez, R. (2009). Immigration reduces crime: An emerging scholarly consensus. *Sociology of Crime, Law and Deviance, 13,* 3–16.

Maccammon, S. (2016, August 19). Hillary Clinton walks a fine line when she addresses the issue of policing. National Public Radio. Retrieved from http://www.npr.org/2016/08/19/490591320/hillary-clinton-walks-a-fine-line-when-she-addresses-the-issue-of-policing

Mallicoat, S.L., & Gardiner, C. (2014). *Criminal Justice Policy*. Thousand Oaks, CA: Sage Publications.

Marion, Nancy and Rick Farmer. (2004). A preliminary examination of Presidential anti-crime promises. *Criminal Justice Review*, 29:1, 173–195.

Marion, N.E. (2010). *The Politics of Disgrace*. Durham, North Carolina: Carolina Academic Press.

Mauer, M. (2014, May 22). Is the 'tough on crime' movement on its way out? Retrieved from http://www.msnbc.com/msnbc/sentencing-reform-the-end-tough-crime

McCarthy, J. (2014). Most Americans still see crime up over last year. Retrieved from http://www.gallup.com/poll/179546/americans-crime-last-year.aspx

MSNBC LIVE. (2016, July 8). Giuliani on shooting deaths of Dallas police. Retrieved from http://www.msnbc.com/msnbc-news/watch/giuliani-on-shooting-deaths-of-dallas-police-721347139887

Packer, H. L. (1964). Two models of the criminal process. *University of Pennsylvania Law Review*, *113*(1), 1–68.

Rosch, J. B. (1985). Crime as an issue in American politics. *The Politics of Crime and Justice*, Beverly Hills, CA: Sage, pp. 19–34.

Scheufele, D. A. (1999). Framing as a theory of media effects. *Journal of Communication*.

Scheufele, D. A., & Tewksbury, D. (2007). Framing, agenda setting, and priming: The evolution of three media effects models. *Journal of Communication*, *57*(1), 9–20.

Sentencing Project. (2014). Race and punishment: Racial perceptions of crime and support for punitive policies. Retrieved from http://www.sentencingproject.org/wp-content/uploads/2015/11/Race-and-Punishment.pdf

Surette, R. (2010). *Media, Crime, and Criminal Justice*. Boston, Massachusetts: Cengage.

Walker, S. (2011). *Sense and Nonsense about Crime and Drugs*. Boston, Massachusetts: Cengage.

Wang, X. (2012). Undocumented immigrants as perceived criminal threat: A test for the minority threat perspective. *Criminology*, *50*(3), 743–776.

CHAPTER 8

MAYORS' AND CITIZEN ATTITUDES TOWARD SEXUAL HARASSMENT IN POLICE DEPARTMENTS

Eric E. Otenyo and Earlene A. S. Camarillo

ABSTRACT

This essay explores the reactions within police departments toward sexual harassment scandals. The study describes and analyzes reported cases of sexual harassment and misconduct in police departments to discern citizen narratives and political consequences for elected officials. This assessment hypothesizes that political leadership is an essential element in establishing organizational cultures that combat sexual harassment in local governments. The article contributes to the knowledge about possible gaps in agenda setting, especially for a policy area in which knowledge and problem definitions continue to evolve.

Keywords: Organizational culture; police departments; power; sexual harassment; workplace policies

Corruption, Accountability and Discretion
Public Policy and Governance, 143–161
doi:10.1108/S2053-769720170000029009

INTRODUCTION

Sexual harassment has been illegal since the enactment of *Title VII* of the *Civil Rights Act of 1964*. Although illegal, reports of sexual harassment occur across the nation, unabated. As a matter of legal concern, sexual harassment is the unwelcome sexual advances, requests for sexual favors, and other verbal or physical conduct of a sexual nature (U.S. Equal Employment Opportunity Commission [EEOC], 1990). Harassment may occur in the form of submission to sex as a condition for employment, promotion, or additional benefits, work assignments and other work-related perks and employment decisions, known as the quid-pro-quo standard. By comparison, harassment may also include instances which cause an employee to feel uncomfortable and abused at the workplace, defined as a hostile workplace. These experiences can cause adverse individual health outcomes (Brown & Campbell, 1995; Lee & Greenlaw, 1995). Data show that far more women (40–80%) than men (5–15%) experience sexual harassment in their lifetime, which helps explain why studies on attitudes toward sexual harassment focus on women (Bauer & Green, 1996; Cowan, 2000; Crittenden, 2009; Dekker & Barling, 1998; Ellis, Barak, & Pinto, 1991; Herzog, 2007; Katz, Hannon, & Witten, 1996; Lonsway, Cortina, & Magley, 2008). However, even while sexual harassment is still prevalent in the workplace, generally speaking, cases of hostile work situations are often hard to prove because there must exist a traceable pattern of such behavior.

A huge challenge in addressing sexual harassment is that agency attitudes are compromised due to the difficulty in clearly defining and identifying sexual harassment (Menard et al., 2003; Quinn, 2002). Victims' responses are not always uniform, complicating policy interventions (Naff, 2001). The different responses and reactions to harassment make a one-size-fits-all policy intervention impractical. Similarly, lack of clarity has been linked to communication barriers (Dougherty et al., 1996). These variations may manifest in different organizational settings, including police departments and other local government organizations. Even though the lack of clarity in problem definition exists, the principles for managing sexual harassment can be extrapolated from a vast body of case law. Case law on sexual harassment establishes the contours of what one may construe to be national values and attitudes. The overriding national mindset is that sexual harassment is punishable by monetary fines, often decriminalizing all forms of sexual harassment because the accused can simply pay a fine without any professional consequences, allowing the perpetrator to continue on without any serious repercussions.

Although a few cases – such as *Faragher v. City of Boca Raton* (1998), *Burlington Industries, Inc. v. Ellerth* (1998), and *Henson V. Dundee* (1982) – are specific to municipalities and local governments, the political debates that inform the harassment scandals in local police departments are largely understudied, even while sexual harassment cases in police departments continue to be reported. This chapter is the first step toward developing an understanding of how this issue plays out in agenda setting at the local government level by discerning prevailing attitudes toward sexual harassment.

BACKGROUND

Literature on sexual harassment is broad and ever increasing. A CATO Institute (2010) study reveals that sexual violence by police (10% of cases) is second only to the use of excessive force (about 25% of cases) (Packman, 2010). Sexual misconduct ranks higher than incidents of DUI (Driving Under the Influence) and drugs, fraud and theft, false arrests, accountability, civil rights infractions, and numerous other categories of misconduct. A national level study on sexual misconduct among sworn law enforcement officers confirms the existence of oppressive organizational cultures across the nation. In many instances, the hidden crime is unreported (Stinson, Liederbach, Brewer, & Mathna, 2015). This highlights a major problem in police department training and socialization techniques which perpetuate sexist tendencies that may lead to sexual misconduct against citizens as well as harassment in the workplace. Research suggests that attitudes toward sexual harassment are driven by sexist beliefs harbored by the public, especially notions that some behaviors are acceptable in workplaces (Baker, 2007; MacKinnon, 1979). While attitudes vary by gender, age matters because younger adults may trivialize incidents of sexual behavior (Xenos & Smith, 2001).

Naff (2001) explains that sexual harassment at federal government offices is costly. She also develops a strong case for the need to have in place measures to prevent or eliminate harassment at the workplace. Importantly, she sees harassment as a key barrier to organizational development and a factor in lowered productivity. While recognizing the importance of enforcing the law, she situates the management of sexual harassment problems within managers' responsibilities to address issues of discrimination. Other scholars view sexual harassment as a component of unequal power relations

(Baugh, 1997; Hotelling, 1991; Katz, 2017; MacKinnon, 1979). The concept of power explains a host of challenges in the workplace, including bullying and sexual harassment. The structures seemingly favor those in positions of power to victimize their subordinates (Hajdin, 1997). Stolberg (2016) posits that sexual harassment persists in the workplace because of the disproportionately lower power base among women in organizations. From Congress to the courts and other arms of government, national attention to sexual harassment may grow only if we adjust hierarchical power structures that enhance stronger protections for women in the workplace.

According to democratic theory of organizations, power is a function of numbers. Perhaps the small number of women in policing is by itself one of the reasons why public awareness of sexual harassment in police departments has yet to receive much political traction. In 2001, women represented only 11.2% of the police force. In 2011, the number increased to just 12% of the over 700,000 police officers in the U.S. (Johnson, 2013). Currently, approximately 13% of employees in police departments are female (NPR, 2017). Rabe-Hemp (2008), among others, observed that the numerical disadvantages within police departments make it hard for women officers to combat aggressive masculine cultures within their police departments. Arguably, it is this subculture, inculcated in training programs, which defend existing definitions of sexual harassment within departments.

Democratic theory meshes well with feminist literature, which condemns sexual harassment for wearing down victims (Brodsky, 1976). Specific to administrative settings, Condit & Hutchinson (1997) call for changing administrative practices to embrace practices that are cognizant of feminist perspectives to liberate women from oppressive managerial practices and attitudes. The ultimate goal is to eradicate gender-specific roles and reject stereotypes such as those existing in some police departments. Recently, Hutchinson (2011) suggested that liberal feminist goals of participatory equality are not enough and that non-masculinist public administration is essential. Feminist theory helps us recognize that some male members of the police force extend acts of violence against female colleagues as a part of their identity. This sexist ideology is documented in influential scholarship including Kraska & Kappeler (1995) and Martin (1979; 1994). Sexist ideology undermines organizational performance at all levels of government and is a major component of police subcultures (Scarborough & Collins, 2002).

It follows, therefore, that there is a need for more gender parity in promotions and a move away from existing frameworks to reduce sexual harassment in police departments. Employing or promoting only a few women creates numerous problems, including an attempt to fit female officers into stereotypical roles such as "kid sister," "sex object, "mother," or "women's liberationist" (Seklecki & Paynich, 2007, pp. 19-20). Similarly, African American police officials in urban departments often get stigmatized into the supportive role of "outsiders" or "intruders" (Martin, 1994; Pogrebin, Dodge, & Chatman, 2000). As a result, many have been kept in "supportive roles" rather than in positions of authority and leadership.

Today, few police departments have women at the helm. Dick & Jankowicz (2001) regard the slow progression as a function of the way society constructs gender roles and how those social constructions intersect with societal expectations. Even though women, as a group, are as competent as men, they have not been promoted to the top positions in high enough numbers (Do et al., 2005; National Center for Women and Policing, 2003). Women's underrepresentation in high-ranking law enforcement positions is well documented, even while there are some who have "made it," including Cathy Lanier Washington D.C. police chief, Amtrak Police Department chief Polly Hanson, Valerie Parlave at the FBI, and Julia Pierson at the Secret Service (Johnson, 2013). Other examples include Jerri Williams who became the first woman police chief in Phoenix (Cassidy & Gardiner, 2016), and Cressida Dick who became the first female metropolitan police chief in London. Dick's appointment meant that for the first time "all three top policing jobs in the UK [were] held by women" (BBC, 2017, n.p.). Professor Dorothy Schulz, former police captain and author of *Breaking the Brass Ceiling: Women Police Chiefs and Their Paths to the Top* (2004) states that about three percent (and increasing) of police chiefs are women, but she does not think this number is sufficient to change organizational culture in many units (Schulz, 2004).

Since we know that power dynamics within police organizations are changing, albeit slowly, a unique opportunity exists for us to explore the political and governmental roles in creating change and disrupting existing stereotypes about women police officers. An exploration of how members of the public react to sexual harassment, especially through voting and the exertion of pressure on elected officials, can move the local government system toward a model for directing cultural change that opposes sexual harassment. The push for stronger actions against sexual harassment in police departments encourages fruitful discussions, particularly because law enforcement organizations epitomize masculine-based cultures (see *Sun Sentinel*, 2016), which are frequently at the heart of harassment.

METHODS OF INQUIRY

To explore these themes, this chapter focuses on sexual harassment at selected police units across the nation. Empirical data are documented in published archival resources, many of which are searchable through existing online databases. The cases are randomly selected for a qualitative content analysis and corroborated with data reported on *Access World News*, police websites, and in court cases. Where many of the cases are inconclusive, the intention is to capture arguments that speak to broad policy and governance concerns of the parties involved. This assessment uses qualitative data to understand organizational culture in the respective police departments. The analysis first considers qualitative evidence that sexual harassment, as an organizational problem, continues to exist and has not been resolved.

Is There a Problem and How Do We Know? Examples from Police Departments

Following complaints from multiple female police officers, Salt Lake City's Human Relations Department determined that sexual harassment had occurred in the police department. The Deputy Police Chief was sued on allegations that he had taken photographs of women in bikinis from the officer's phones and shared them with coworkers. The Mayor, Ralph Becker, issued an ultimatum to police chief to apologize or resign for not handling the harassment cases appropriately (Green & McDonald, 2015). At the heart of the plaintiff's complaints were accusations that the culture of the police department encouraged behaviors that were demeaning to female officers. Police chief Chris Burbank eventually resigned and the three female officers settled the suit for $85,000 each. The issue was one of the issues that cost the mayor re-election in 2015. Mayor Burbank lost his seat to Jackie Biskupski who asked all senior officials to resign.

Another example of a sexual harassment case filed against a police department involved Mountain View Police Department. In this particular instance, a female police dispatcher alleged that the police chief and other officers encouraged conduct that created a hostile workplace. The dispatcher alleged that the police chief personally made sexual advances toward her and was not sanctioned for his behaviors. After exhausting administrative remedies, her complaints were forwarded to the California Department of Fair Employment and Housing and also to the U.S. Equal Employment Opportunity Commission. According to Attorney James McManis, leadership was insensitive to the sexual harassment and reinforced an existing culture that allowed this behavior (Noack, 2016).

In another well-documented case, the New York Police Department was accused of failing to ensure a less-hostile culture toward female officers. According to Benjamin Weiser (2015), Lieutenant Alexander Rojas was accused of groping female officers, exposing himself, and making sexually explicit comments in the presence of female colleagues. Lieutenant Rojas was also accused of sending text messages with pictures of male genitalia making comments like "check me out" to one female colleague (Weiser, 2015, n.p.). New York City ultimately agreed to pay $1.25 million as a result.

Another case against the Phoenix Police department illustrates that contractors can also be affected by sexual harassment. Donna Tavilla sued a police officer in 2002 after she felt his "harassing and terrorizing sexual advances" (Ferraresi, 2009). Ms. Tavilla contended "that the sexual harassment behavior caused her emotional distress and threatened to hurt her family's contract with the city" (Ferraresi, 2009, n.p.).

While many cases were resolved in favor of the victim of the alleged harassment, not all cases were. For example, Kathy Durkin argued that she was sexually harassed and retaliated against for filing complaints during her police training. She asserted that she did not perform well during the training due to the hostile environment. In *Kathy Durkin v. City of Chicago* (2003), the court ruled against the plaintiff, asserting that the City of Chicago had provided a framework for handling sexual harassment cases. According to the city policy, any official who experiences sexual harassment has to report the incident to their supervisor or one above the supervisor within 180 days of the incident. "The supervisor who receives the complaint must then contact the Office of Professional Standards, obtain a complaint register number, and then report to the Internal Affairs Division," which investigates the allegations (FindLaw, 2016, n.p.). The court acknowledged that the behavior of police officers was uncontested, but it based its ruling on the grounds that the harasser was not in a supervisory position and that the victim was not denied training, as her deposition alleged.

The effects of sexual harassment vary in severity. In one case, Kelly Hespe claimed that unprofessional conduct resulted in her being diagnosed with post-traumatic stress disorder. Hespe claimed her perpetrator, Sergeant Breimon, had connections which discouraged her from pursuing charges. She claimed he "was always wanting to check to see if she was wearing underwear" (Wojciechowski, 2013, n.p.). He also sent her hurtful messages and even after complaining, the department's superiors did not stop the conduct (Wojciechowski, 2013).

The case involving officer Alice Valdez also illustrates the inaction of superiors to stop sexual harassment. Valdez indicated her superiors did nothing to end a culture that promoted a hostile workplace (*Las Vegas Sun*, 2013). Valdez accused her supervisor, Edward Rubio, for failing to document her complaints and stop the officers' misconduct (Whaley, 2013). Her claim led to an investigation, leading to the eventual firing of Sergeant Rubio.

In Gainesville, Florida, reports of sexual harassment by four female lieutenants led Gainesville Police Chief Tony Jones to ask retired Alachua Police Chief Joel DeCoursey Jr. to investigate. DeCoursey's report confirmed sexual harassment was rampant. Among the complaints was that Captain Brian Helmerson made crude jokes and comments about female officer's breasts and pulled female officers' ponytails. On one occasion, he grabbed a female officer's cell phone and when she asked him to return it, "he put the phone between his legs in his crotch area," and told her, "If you want it, come get it" (Swirko, 2015, n.p.). Further, it was alleged that Captain Helmerson commented that women "don't belong in law enforcement" (Swirko, 2015, n.p.).

A culture of exclusion was also evident in a case involving a female officer hired at Tolono Police Department. Officer Carrie Mathews filed a suit claiming that police chief Richard Raney and the Tolono Police Department violated her civil rights and sexually harassed her. Among the allegations, she asserted that Raney told other officers that "women don't belong in Tolono; they belong in Champaign, where they have backup" (*News-Gazette*, 2008, pp. A-7).

The final case discussed here illustrates how sexual harassment issues are not entirely gender specific. In Missouri, Kyle Brewer, a male city police officer, sued the St. Louis Police Department and three supervisors, alleging that he was sexually harassed and suffered from retaliation on behalf of the police chiefs after he submitted a complaint. The police supervisors asserted that the plaintiff, Brewer, was an excellent investigator but "he didn't fit in," an obvious reference to an organizational culture dynamic (Patrick, 2015, n.p.). Unlike the previously discussed cases, this case shows same-sex sexual harassment also poses a problem in police departments. We include it here to highlight that it is the organizational culture of these departments that is reportedly questionable.

The cases above represent only a few examples of the numerous cases that fit into the narrative of sexual harassment as a "silent epidemic," to use the words of Debra Katz (2017, n.p.). These cases help illustrate the complexities involved in combatting sexual harassment in modern American society and the link to organizational culture that perpetuates harassment in the workplace.

ATTITUDES TOWARD SEXUAL HARASSMENT: MAYORAL AND ADMINISTRATIVE RESPONSES

For governance and policy purposes, the discourse on sexual harassment within police departments has not been problematized as a crisis that would trigger political action and, therefore, greater presence in the policy stream. The evidence suggests the possibility that, with increased public interest and activism, election to office of mayor can be tied to their performance in ensuring safe working environments for key staff in critical organizations including police departments. Public actions observed in these cases match Beauvis' (1986) conclusions that public attitudes toward sexual harassment are complex and may not be reduced to a few characteristics. We offer a few additional explanatory variables using examples from the departments observed.

To begin, we share some thoughts on the dynamics of politics and governance within specific localities to help develop organizational and cultural profiles that inform the level of salience of the sexual harassment problem within local governments in general and police departments in particular. Some of these dynamics have ramifications beyond specific cities and are consistent with studies conducted in multiple jurisdictions and public organizations. In our analysis, we do not discount the diversity within local governments and police departments. We are aware that strong mayors in some municipal structures have greater potential for shaping public policy. This is opposed to small town mayors with limited political capital that may reduce sexual harassment to an administrative action as opposed to a legal or political action.

More specifically, when considering the reported cases of sexual harassment within New York City one cannot lose sight of the high degree of professionalism linked to successful policing. In the post 9/11 era, successive mayors have often noted that the city has one of the best police departments in the country. Being associated with sexual harassment implies a failure of leadership. Indeed, the association of any form of sexual misconduct can reduce a mayor's political currency. The best example of this perception is New York City mayoral hopeful Anthony Weiner's poor performance during the election primaries in 2013. In a widely-reported case, Weiner was separated from his wife for sexual misconduct, including exchanging lewd text messages and photos with another woman. According to Quinnipiac University polls, Democratic voters regarded Weiner as not having a "strong personal moral character" (*CBS New York*, 2013, n.p.). Based on this logic, a weak personal moral character could weaken his ability to lead in matters such as combatting sexual harassment in the city's police department. The morality discourse, to some degree, plays a role in mayoral elections and, if linked with sexual harassment within specific local government organizations, can set the tone within units such as in police departments where administrative policies have been set in motion to create an inclusive work environment.

Looking at Chicago, the city has a well-documented history of corruption, including links between some officials to the underworld of sex and immorality (Taylor, 2003; Vaughn & Otenyo, 2007). Because of Chicago's machine-type politics, which has been promoted by several mayors – including "Big Bill" Thompson who had an association with Al Capone and Richard J. Daley's patronage system – the link between morality and governance is very strong and has been at the center of governance discourses. As such, sexual harassment within the police department is considered a part of the larger moral condition in city management and within the governance structure.

As Mayor Richard M. Daley (son of former Mayor Richard J. Daley) understood, his political capital was enhanced by establishing mechanisms for dealing swiftly with cases of sexual harassment within the entire government operation. For example, in 2011 Mayor Daley forced out fire chief John Brooks who had been accused of sexual harassment (Dizikes, 2011). Mayor Daley's zero-tolerance policy on sexual harassment extended to the police department as part of his strategy for branding and building a workplace culture that promoted employee safety and reduced hostile activities. Although Brooks ultimately sued the city for violating his terms of employment and damaging his reputation, the mayor's actions sent clear political and symbolic messages to the electorate that sexual harassment has no place in the government.

For Phoenix, the appointment of the first female Police Chief symbolized a change in the power discourse by underscoring the system's readiness to more aggressively combat sexual harassment in one of the country's largest departments. Perhaps it should be noted that the political platform to promote a female Police Chief, Jeri Williams, in a "Red State" was based on the Phoenix's known leadership in cultural innovations concerning matters of city governance. Phoenix was an early pioneer in promoting efficiency through competition between public and private providers in selected services. The city is also the first in the nation to have female chiefs of both the fire department, Kara Kalkbrenner, and the police department at the same time (Cassidy & Gardiner, 2016). The appointment of a female leader reset the tone for the police department's interpersonal relations, further strengthening the change in attitudes toward women officers.

The constant need for female police officers to push for progressive consciousness and safe work environments manifest in a case involving a female officer who accused Wayne McDonald, a former aide to Denver Mayor Michael Hancock, for sexual harassment. Although McDonald was fired for sexual harassment, he denied the offense and filed a countersuit in the U.S. District Court claiming Mayor Hancock slandered his name (AP, 2013). The initial case resolved against McDonald, and although the City of Denver settled the countersuit by paying McDonald $200,000 as a "business decision," the publicity generated from the case was sufficient to rekindle the importance of combatting conditions that create hostility in the workplace (Mitchell, 2016, n.p.). This case demonstrates political leadership's commitment to organizational justice in city managerial structures and further illustrates that political will makes a difference in establishing organizational norms.

The political salience of sexual harassment within police departments may not rise to the top of the policy agenda stream, but if specifics of harassment garner national headlines, the chance of the issue becoming a major political issue increases exponentially. The case gets greater traction among the public, especially if the mayor is the subject of the case. This is evident in many cases. For example, in the Village of Alsip the city settled a lawsuit which alleged Mayor Patrick Kitching sexually harassed the treasurer in 2014 (Pratt, 2014). Similarly, Mayor John Norquist of Milwaukee was removed from office for sexual misconduct with staff in 2002 (Henry, 2013).

Perhaps the most widely recognized example occurred in San Diego where in 2013, the San Diego City Council voted out Mayor Bob Filner after numerous women accused him of workplace sexual harassment. At least 20 women accused Mayor Filner of acts such as slobbery kisses and unwanted verbal advances. The scandal cost the city over $8 million, including a special election to replace him. Again, the relevance of the mayor's moral failures was framed as leadership failure and a threat to efforts to change the police department's culture to be more accommodating for female officers. San Diego's response to the city government's reputation was swift. The new mayor, Kevin Faulconer, and his administration, working with the Department of Justice, performed management audits to restore public trust (Perry, 2014). The SDPD was reformed, and the city achieved further national attention, this time positively, through the appointment of a woman, Shelley Zimmerman, to police chief in 2014 (Perry, 2014). Chief Zimmerman was the first female chief in SDPD's history. Mayor Faulconer's office responded to public pressure to change attitudes with the police department which had been tainted by a culture of sexual harassment.

Our final illustrative example of leadership's role in sending signals of zero-tolerance for sexual harassment is evident in well-established literature. Spann (2001) reported that policies to reduce and manage cases of sexual harassment in the city of Madison, WI, were driven by the leadership's ability to respond to "currents of change in both the local community and the nation as a whole" (p. 54). Amidst resistance, the police chief promoted a female to rank of lieutenant in the early 1980s (Spann, 2001). In 1979, the city put in place aggressive policies to combat and prevent harassment in the entire organization. In the case of Madison, the mayor's management team in 1980 was responsible for enforcing the Madison Equal Opportunity Ordinance (Section 3.23) of the Madison General Ordinances. The mayor worked with advocacy groups like the City's Women's Issues Committee and the Minority Affairs Committee to promote a progressive agenda. Through the Mayor's Memorandum # 3-29, harassment was listed as a major violation of conditions and terms of work (Spann, 2001). Therefore, progress occurred through political action and leadership, inspired by public support.

LESSONS LEARNED AND IMPLICATIONS FOR GOVERNANCE AND POLICY MANAGEMENT

These case studies and reports lead us to sharpen the frameworks for explaining the current relative absence of a national mood of outrage within the discourse on sexual harassment in society. Perhaps the tipping point at which sexual harassment becomes a major governance problem is at hand, but the policy management to catapult intervention to the next level is yet to be realized. First, from a practical standpoint, variations across departments and local jurisdictions exist in the manner in which sexual harassment becomes a priority governance issue for attention. Although organizational actions against sexual harassment in police departments are largely aligned with federal policy prescriptions, the policy issue gains greater political traction if it receives national attention. In other words, the strength of impact on local governance and politics is positively associated with greater national attention, as was evident in San Diego, New York, and Chicago among other cases.

Second, the research reveals that framing of sexual harassment as an organizational rather than societal problem weakens the ability of advocates for change to create a "mood" or "movement" for change when thinking about workplace tranquility. Framing the issue in terms similar to the "culture wars" discourse is often clouded in partisan arguments and fails to move sexual harassment cases at the local level to a place where investment in non-partisan efforts are welcome. In other words, sexual harassment in police departments requires activism outside of partisan political argumentation.

Third, and associated with framing and concerns with problem definition, is that data on sexual harassment are often inaccurate, partly due to under-reporting, and even when available, sexual harassment, especially the quid-pro-quo type, is not framed as an issue of corruption in available databases. For example, conviction data from the U.S. Department of Justice shows that cities such as Chicago, New Orleans, Washington, DC, and New Jersey are among the most corrupt in the nation. However, we do not have data dis-aggregation to show the incidence of sexual harassment in respective police departments, making these data difficult to find. In many instances, the exist-ence of sexist ideologies in some police departments suggests reporting can be mishandled as is often the case with other sexual assault crimes. For example, in the case of the New Orleans Police Department, investigators reported that 90% of sex crime-related calls were mishandled (Weinreich, 2014). Of course, notwithstanding the reality that police departments are only a small part of city government.

Fourth, public attention to police brutality of minorities appears to attract greater governance space. While this is understandable, there is evidence that police shootings compete for attention with sexual assault and harassment cases within police departments (Moore, 2015). Some observers contend that police misconduct and aggressive policing with reference to minorities are ideologically similar issues that reinforce police masculine subcultures (Gross & Lavingston, 2002; Rudovsky, 2001; Scarborough & Collins, 2002). Therefore, consistent with discourses and narratives on externally aggressive and excessive use of force on minorities, sexual harassment in police depart-ments is an internally aggressive behavior integrated into police subcultures (Satzewich & Shaffir, 2009).

Perhaps complicating the over-policing narrative is that public confidence – defined as the extent of public trust in policing – is generally high among the more affluent members of society (Cao, Frank, & Cullen, 1996; Decker, 1981). This confidence perhaps leads to less scrutiny of internal mechanisms and workings within police departments. The message here is that democratic governance processes should go beyond trust and verify existing abnormali-ties in a holistic way.

Fifth, although policy guidelines from the federal government exist, each individual organization has established cultures that may be catalysts in shaping prevailing workplace behaviors. Here is where representativeness and inclusionary practices may help tilt the balance in favor of building a progressive organizational culture within police establishments. Still, one must acknowledge that organizational socialization seeks to encourage unit members to pursue goals that minimize personal values and instead enhance decision-making choices that favor organizational development efforts.

CONCLUSIONS AND WHERE DO WE GO FROM HERE?

Based on this preliminary analysis of the intersection between public officials and cases of sexual harassment in police departments, four main ideas emerge. First, sexual harassment in police departments is partly a function of organizational cultures that consign women to traditional occupations and weak societal political responses to change those cultures at the local level. Second, the framing of sexual harassment in male-dominated occupations, such as police departments, must be tackled through increased empowerment among female officers. One way this can be accomplished is by public policies that more strictly reprimand sexual harassment. For example, public policies that require automatic termination for repeat offenders or, at minimum, removal from leadership roles could be adopted. Additionally, these public policies need to inflict harsher professional penalties for people who are convicted, such as disqualification from future public offices. Third, politics in local governments should provide better local models for dealing with sexual harassment instead of overreliance on federally mandated standards and approaches. This would be the equivalent of compiling a registry for offenders within professional association membership lists. Such an approach would likely be harsher than current practices. Fourth, public attitudes are not strong enough to change political dynamics and strengthen policy actions against harassment. Still, this matter requires further research. By and large, federal case law and the EEOC are the source of the operating definitions of sexual harassment. Through federal court cases, local governments, including police units and divisions know what should be professional conduct in their units. Local situations sharpen our understanding and knowledge of sexual harassment not just as a barrier to workplace stability but as a societal problem.

In terms of accountability discourses, sexual harassment exists in all regions and there is no indication that cities have higher rates of professional misconduct as measured by the pervasiveness of sexual harassment cases. The lesson from the cases discussed is that even at the local level, mayors can pay a price for weak oversight of police and other departments. Perhaps, also, tougher and more public shaming of public officials found guilty of sexual harassment can contribute to workplace safety. In theory, political leaders should continue to promote the virtues of accountability in organizations where women and minority groups are underrepresented.

From a reform perspective, the issue has both administrative and political manifestations. Administratively, the responsibility of police organizations to change cultures and eliminate sexual harassment can be a huge part of the "measureable attributes" of chiefs of police and mayors. So, if sexual harassment is an issue of power differential, the task is to disentangle the implied powerlessness to understand the continuation of harassment within police departments across the nation. Knowing what works in terms of policy agenda setting contributes to finding enduring political solutions to sexual harassment and creates a stronger public policy to reduce the incidences of harassment.

REFERENCES

AP. (2013, May 14). Judge throws out lawsuit from Denver mayor's aide. *Denver Post*. Retrieved from http://www.gjsentinel.com/opinion/articles/judge-throws-out-lawsuit-from-denver-mayors-aide

Baugh, G. S. (1997). On the persistence of sexual harassment in the workplace. *Journal of Business Ethics, 16*, 899–908.

BBC. (2017, February 22). Cressida Dick appointed as first female Met Police chief. *BBC News*. Retrieved from http://www.bbc.com/news/uk-39055696

Beauvis, K. (1986). Workshops to combat sexual harassment: A case study of changing attitudes. *Signs, 12*(1), 130–145.

Brodsky, C. (1976). *The Harassed Worker*. Lexington, MA: Lexington Books.

Brown, J., & Campbell, E. A. (1995). Adverse impacts experienced by police officers following exposure to sex discrimination and sexual harassment. *Stress Medicine, 11*, 221–228.

Cao, L., Frank, J., & Cullen, F. T. (1996). Race, community context and confidence in the police. *American Journal of Police, XV*(1), 3–22.

Cassidy, M., & Gardiner, D. (2016, July 13). Phoenix makes history with the hire of female police chief. *AZ Central*. Retrieved from http://www.azcentral.com/story/news/local/phoenix/2016/07/13/jeri-williams-named-new-phoenix-police-chief/87043798/

CBS New York. (2013, July 29). Poll: Weiner drops to 4th place in wake of sexting scandal. *CBS Radio, Inc.* Retrieved from http://newyork.cbslocal.com/2013/07/29/weiner-staying-in-mayors-race-after-campaign-manager-quits/

Condit, D. M., & Hutchinson, J. R. (1997). Women in public administration: Extending the metaphor of the Emperor's New Clothes. *American Review of Public Administration, 27*(2), 181–197.

Cowan, G. (2000). Women's hostility toward women and rape and sexual harassment myths. *Violence Against Women, 6*(3), 238–246.

Crittenden, C. (2009). *Examining attitudes and perceptions of sexual harassment on a university campus: What role do myths and stereotypes play?* (Master's thesis). University of

Tennessee, Chattanooga. Retrieved from http://scholar.utc.edu/cgi/viewcontent.cgi?article= 1381&context=theses

Decker, S. (1981). Citizen attitudes toward the police: A review of past findings and suggestions for future policy. *Journal of Police Science and Administration, 9*, 80–87.

Dekker, I., & Barling, J. (1998). Personal and organizational predictors of workplace sexual harassment of women by men. *Journal of Occupational Health Psychology, 3*(1), 7–18.

Dick, P., & Janokwicz, D. (2001). A social constructionist account of police culture and its influence on the representation and progression of female officers: A repertory grid analysis in a UK police force. *Policing: An International Journal of Police Strategies & Management, 24*(2), 181–199. http://dx.doi.org/10.1108/13639510110390936

Dizikes, C. (2011, April 29). Former fire chief sues Daley, says he was forced out. *Chicago Tribune.* Retrieved from http://articles.chicagobreakingnews.com/2011-04-29/news/29488958_1_ sexual-harassment-raymond-orozco-brooks.

Do, M. L., Schmitt, W. J., Styles, J. L., Wang, H. C., Wincek, Z. J., & Zeddies, A. E. (2005, Spring). *Reducing sexual harassment and gender discrimination: Recommendations for the Mexico City police department.* Paper prepared for Public Affairs Workshop, International Issues. Robert M. La Follette School of Public Affairs. University of Wisconsin, Madison. Retrieved from https://www.lafollette.wisc.edu/images/publications/workshops/2005-mexicoharass.pdf

Dougherty, T., Turban, D. B., Olson, E. D., Dwyer, P. D., & Lapreze, M. W. (1996). Factors affecting perceptions of workplace sexual harassment. *Journal of Organizational Behavior, 17*(5 September), 489–501.

Ellis, S., Barak. A., & Pinto, A. (1991). Moderating effects of personal cognitions on experienced and perceived sexual harassment of women at the workplace. *Journal of Applied Social Psychology, 21*(16), 1320–1337.

Ferraresi, M. (2009, December 11). Phoenix to pay woman $600,000 in damages in police harassment lawsuit. *The Arizona Republic.* Retrieved from http://archive.azcentral.com/ community/phoenix/articles/2009/12/11/20091211phxtavilla1211.html

FindLaw (2016). *Durkin v. City of Chicago* (2003, August 22). U.S. Court of Appeals, 7th Circuit. No. 02-2358. Retrieved from http://caselaw.findlaw.com/us-7th-circuit/1410835. html

Green, M., & McDonald, M. (2015, September). Women suing Salt Lake City, police department and superior officers over sexual harassment case. *Fox 13 News.* Retrieved from http://fox13now.com/2015/09/04/women-suing-salt-lake-city-police-department-and-superior-officers-over-sexual-harassment-case/

Gross, S. R., & Lavingston, D. (2002). Racial profiling under attack. *Columbia Law Review, 102*(5), 1413–1438. Retrieved from http://repository.law.umich.edu/cgi/viewcontent.cgi?article= 2588&context=articles

Hajdin, M. (1997). Why the fight against sexual harassment is misguided. In L. LeMoncheck & M. Hajdin (Eds.), *Sexual harassment: A debate* (pp. 97–164). Lanham, MD: Rowman and Littlefield Publishers.

Henry, C. (2013, March 21). Lawyer who represented woman who brought down mayor being disciplined. *ABC WISN.* Retrieved from http://www.wisn.com/article/lawyer-who-represented-woman-who-brought-down-former-mayor-being-disciplined/6314423

Herzog, S. (2007). An empirical test of feminist theory and research: The effect of heterogeneous gender-role attitudes on perceptions of intimate partner violence. *Feminist Criminology, 2*(3), 223–244.

Hotelling, K. (1991). Sexual harassment: A problem shielded by silence. *Journal of Counseling and Development, 69*(July/August), 497–501.

Hutchinson, J. R. (2011). Feminist theories and their application to public administration. In J. M. D'Agostino & H. Levine (Eds.), *Women in public administration: Theory and practice* (pp. 3–14). Sudbury, MA: Jones & Bartlett.

Johnson, K. (2013, August 13). Women move into law enforcement's highest ranks. *USA Today*. Retrieved from http://www.usatoday.com/story/news/nation/2013/08/13/women-law-enforcement-police-dea-secret-service/2635407/

Katz, D. (2017, March 2). Sexual harassment at work. *National Public Radio (NPR)*. Retrieved from http://www.npr.org/podcasts/510316/1a

Katz, R. C., Hannon, R., & Whitten, T. (1996). Effects of gender and situation on the perception of sexual harassment. *Sex Roles, 34*(1/2), 35–42.

Kraska, P. B., & Kappeler, V. (1995). To serve and pursue: Exploring police sexual violence against women. *Justice Quarterly, 12*(1), 85–111.

Las Vegas Sun. (2013, September 4) Nevada Capitol Police targeted in lawsuit. *Las Vegas Sun*. Retrieved from https://lasvegassun.com/news/2013/sep/04/capitol-police-officers-accused-sexual-harassment-/

Lee, R. D. Jr., & Greenlaw, P. S. (1995). The legal evolution of sexual harassment. *Public Administration Review, 55*(4), 357–364.

Lonsway, K. A., Cortina, L. M., & Magley, V. J. (2008). Sexual harassment mythology: Definition, conceptualization, and measurement. *Sex Roles, 58*, 599–615.

MacKinnon, C. A. (1979). *Sexual harassment of working women: A case of sex discrimination*. New Haven, CT: Yale University Press.

Martin, S. (1979). Policewomen and policewomen: Occupational role dilemmas and choices of female officers. *Journal of Police Science and Administration, 7*, 314–323.

Martin, S. E. (1994). "Outsider Within" the station house: The impact of race and gender on black women police. *Social Problems, 41*(3), 383–400.

Menard, K. S., Hall, G. C. N., Phung, A. H., Ghebrial, M. F. E., & Martin, L. (2003). Gender differences in sexual harassment and coercion in college students: Developments, individual and situational determinants. *Journal of Interpersonal Violence, 18*(10), 1222–1239.

Mitchell, K. (2016, August 22). Denver settles lawsuit by former top Michael Hancock aide for $200,000. *The Denver Post*. Retrieved from http://www.denverpost.com/2016/08/22/denver-settles-lawsuit-wayne-mcdonald-michael-hancock-aide/

Moore, D. L. (2015, April 23). While we focus on shootings, we ignore victims of police sexual assault. *Mic*. Retrieved from http://mic.com/articles/116216/the-type-of-police-brutality-no-one-is-talking-about#.VCUCcGTCc

Naff, K. C. (2001). *To look like America: Dismantling barriers for women and minorities in government*. Boulder, CO: Westview Press.

National Center for Women and Policing. (2003). Hiring and retaining women: The advantage to law enforcement agencies. Retrieved from http://womenandpolicing.com/pdf/newadvantagesreport.pdf

News-Gazette. (2008, September 25). Tolono officer alleges harassment. *News Gazette*. pp. A-7.

Noack, M. (2016). Police chief named in sexual harassment lawsuit. *Mountain View Voice*. Retrieved from http://www.mv-voice.com/news/2016/03/09/police-chief-named-in-sexual-harassment-lawsuit

Packman, D. (2010). *2010 Q3 national police misconduct statistical report*. CATO Institute. Retrieved from http://www.policemisconduct.net/2010-q3-national-police-misconduct-statistical-report/

Patrick, R. (2015, October 30). Officer sues St. Louis Police, supervisors, alleging he was sexually harassed, (October 30). *St. Louis Post-Dispatch*. Retrieved from http://www.stltoday.com/news/local/crime-and-courts/officer-sues-st-louis-police-supervisors-alleging-he-was-sexually/article_294a286d-509c-5381-91e4-f33d98bd1d39.html

Perry, T. (2014, February 26). San Diego's mayor-elect chooses a woman as police chief. *Los Angeles Times*. Retrieved from http://articles.latimes.com/2014/feb/26/local/la-me-ln-san-diego-police-chief-woman-20140226

Perry, T. (2014, March 23). DOJ agrees to review San Diego Police Department practices. *Los Angeles Times*. Retrieved from http://articles.latimes.com/2014/mar/23/local/la-me-ln-san-diego-police-audit-20140323

Pogrebin, M., Dodge, M., & Chatman, H. (2000). Reflections of African American women on their careers in urban policing: Their experiences of racial and sexual discrimination. *International Journal of the Sociology of Law, 28*, 311–326.

Pratt, G. (2014, February 5). Alsip settles sexual harassment suit against mayor for $120,000. *Chicago Tribune: Daily Southtown*. Retrieved from http://www.chicagotribune.com/suburbs/daily-southtown/news/ct-sta-alsip-sexual-harassment-settlement-st-0803-20160802-story.html

Quinn, B. A. (2002). Sexual harassment and masculinity: The power and meaning of "girl watching." *Gender and Society, 16*(3), 386–402.

Rabe-Hemp, C. (2008). Survival in an "all boys" club: Policewomen and their fight for acceptance. *Policing: An International Journal of Police Strategies & Management, 31*(2), 251–270.

Rudovsky, D. (2001). Law enforcement by stereotypes and serendipity: Racial profiling and stops and searches without cause. *Journal of Constitutional Law, 3*(1), 296–366. Retrieved from http://scholarship.law.upenn.edu/cgi/viewcontent.cgi?article=1419&context=jcl

Satzewich, V., & Shaffir, W. (2009). Racism versus professionalism: Claims and counter-claims about racial profiling. *Canadian Journal of Criminology and Criminal Justice, 51*(2), 199–226.

Scarborough, K. E., & Collins, P. A. (2002). *Women in public and private law enforcement*. Boston: Butterworth-Heinemann.

Schulz, D. (2004). *Breaking the brass ceiling: Women police chiefs and their paths to the top*. Westport, CT: Praeger Publishers.

Seklecki, R., & Paynich, R. (2007). A national survey of female police officers: An overview of findings. *Police Practice and Research, 8*(1), 17–30.

Spann, J. (2001). Dealing effectively with sexual harassment: Some practical lessons from one city's experience. *Public Personnel Management, 19*(1), 53–82.

Stinson, P. M. Sr., Liederbach, J., Brewer S. L. Jr., & Mathna, B. E. (2015). Police sexual misconduct: A national scale study of arrested officers. *Criminal Justice Policy Review, 26*(7), 665–690.

Stolberg, S. G. (2016. November 2). Why sexual harassment persists in politics. *New York Times*. Retrieved from https://www.nytimes.com/2016/11/03/us/politics/why-sexual-harassment-persists-in-politics.html

Sun Sentinel. (2016, January). Reports of sex assaults up at military academies. *Sun Sentinel: Palm Beach Edition*, Fort Lauderdale, FL, page 3A.

Swirko, C. (2015, December 9). GPD's Helmerson retires after sexual harassment investigation. *The Gainesville Sun*. Retrieved from http://www.gainesville.com/news/20151209/gpds-helmerson-retires-after-sexual-harassment-investigation

Taylor, T. (2003). Bath House John, Hinky Dink, and others: Chicago's history of graft and corruption. *History and Hauntings*. Retrieved from http://www.prairieghosts.com/graft.html

U.S. Equal Employment Opportunity Commission (EEOC). (1990, March 19). Policy guidance on current issues of sexual harassment, No: N-915-050 (Enforcement Guidance). Retrieved from http://www.eeoc.gov/eeoc/publications/upload/currentissues.pdf

Weinreich M. (2014, November 13). New Orleans police department under investigation for mishandling 90% of sex crime-related calls: Report. *New York Daily News*. Retrieved from http://www.nydailynews.com/news/national/new-orleans-police-botched-90-sex-crime-calls-report-article-1.2009714

Weiser, B. (2015, September 16). New York Times settles harassment suit by 3 female police officers. *New York Times*. Retrieved from http://www.nytimes.com/2015/09/17/nyregion/new-york-city-settles-harassment-suit-by-3-female-police-officers.html?_r=0

Whaley, S. (2013, December 20) State hearing officer upholds firing of former Capitol Police officer. *Las Vegas Review-Journal*. Retrieved from http://www.reviewjournal.com/news/state-hearing-officer-upholds-firing-former-capitol-police-officer

Wojciechowski, C. (2013). CPD officer sues sergeant for sexual harassment. *NBC Chicago*. Retrieved from http://www.nbcchicago.com/news/local/CPD-Officer-Sues-Sergeant-For-Sexual-Harassment-231091491.html

Xenos, S., & Smith D. (2001). Perceptions of rape and sexual assault among Australian adolescents and young adults. *Journal of Interpersonal Violence*, *16*(11), 1103–1119.

CHAPTER 9

WARS IN IRAQ AND AFGHANISTAN: CONTRACTOR CORRUPTION AND ELECTION CAMPAIGNS

Eric E. Otenyo and Parwez Besmel

ABSTRACT

The leadership of the Iraq and Afghanistan war has been criticized for reported cases of contractor corruption. This chapter examines the extent to which these wars have played out in the political agendas of candidates for President. The hypothesis is that while the two wars continue to be a key campaign issue in election cycles, the corruption narrative is a neglected part of the discourse. There are possible reasons for the disjuncture between United States (U.S.) positions against corruption by foreign governments and contractor behaviors within the defense industry, namely the impact of corruption on voters, candidates and other stakeholders. The chapter closes with lessons about the effects of corruption on agenda setting while also contributing to research on evaluation of private-public partnerships in public policy implementation and governance.

Keywords: Accountability; Afghanistan war; agenda setting; contractor corruption; Iraq war

Corruption, Accountability and Discretion
Public Policy and Governance, 163–181
Copyright © 2017 by Emerald Publishing Limited
All rights of reproduction in any form reserved
doi:10.1108/S2053-769720170000029010

INTRODUCTION

Reports about corruption in the military defense sector have been common since the American Revolutionary War (Cooper, 2003). Recent accounts of U.S. interventions overseas suggest profiteering and national pride happen regularly in American empire-building (Kinzer, 2017). In recent times, the media is replete with stories of contractor corruption involving many segments of the military. For example, from 2002–2013, the Departments of Defense and State awarded several contracts to private firms as part of Public-Private Partnerships (P3s) that have become a popular method for delivering public services and projects. Some of the most prominent P3 projects within the Department of Defense include military housing, provision of services on military bases, infrastructures which include highways, gas stations, offices and wastewater facilities in countries where the U.S. initiated efforts for reconstruction. However, several poorly managed contracts in the execution of war efforts in Afghanistan and Iraq have resulted in close to $60 billion in waste, suggesting a need for greater accountability in defense contracting (Arnoldy, 2011).

Regardless of the evidence of corruption, contracting out continues to be the norm in U.S. government-to-business transactions. It is estimated that close to 60% of the federal government budget goes toward payments on contracts with the private sector, and in many instances, agencies such as the Department of Energy, National Aeronautics and Space Administration (NASA) and Department of Defense traditionally rely on private providers. As Stillman (2010) observed, most of the major weapons are contracted out to private businesses, which now constitute a subsystem in policy implementation circles. Scholars acknowledge that corruption hinders innovation and reduces private investments because of perceptions that some companies are favored (Aidt, 2009; Mo, 2000). Corruption tends to also favor the upper class, thereby limiting opportunities for marginalized groups. That appears to also be true of defense contracts involving the U.S. and other countries.

What is unclear is why the corruption in defense spending is neglected as a prominent campaign issue. One explanation is that defining corruption is difficult and that many federal institutions have numerous approaches to managing accountability at programmatic levels. Scott (1972) posits that societal norms on what is corruption are normative, and for the highly-valued defense sector, there is a tendency to privilege public interest security goals over exposing flaws within operational contracts, particularly if one of the actors is within the famed military-industrial complex.

It may be that guardians of the public interest, especially party leaders, consider defense contracts as soft spots within governance discourses. This may explain the lack of operational definitions of corruption within party platforms. Transparency International (2017) limited its definition to "misuse of entrusted power for private gain," but the concept includes solicitation or acceptance by public officials of favors involving the use of public office. By relying on reports from investigative journalists and official public records, the chapter overcomes many of these challenges. Specifically, the content analysis in this chapter covers newspaper and magazine articles published from 2004–2016 and gives special attention to front-page coverage of items on corruption involving contractors and the Pentagon.

Knowing that the agenda-setting literature establishes a link between mass participation through voting and elite decision-making, we seek to understand the lack of appeal for scrutiny of corruption within the voting public which elects policymakers to govern the polity. More specifically, the question becomes, to what extent should defense contracting rise to a level of concern during campaigns for presidential elections? Essentially, the assumption is that if an issue is socially significant and relevant, then it will be more easily discussed on campaign trails and given a more formal and institutional presence. The assertion holds in conditions of western democratic traditions characterized by institutions for accountability. These institutions limit the discretion of federal bureaucrats to ensure public funds are not misused and wasted through fraud and corruption. In any event, when rampant corruption exists, it means legislative oversight must be strengthened through public participation. Thus, democracy requires corruption cases be included in election agendas and policy domains.

Research on agenda setting is expansive (Linz, 1990; Markowski, 2006). As Cobb & Elder (1972) noted, issues that rise to institutional levels are recognized within political systems as important. Such issues receive widespread attention and have a sizeable number of people recognizing the need for remedial action. In this light, we can decipher that public participation through mobilizing information on corruption and participating in elections injects accountability into the governance arena. The assumption is that contracting out to private firms should not transfer accountability out of the sphere of public deliberation. In other words, the actions of contractors should not be outside of the control of the power of the people who are engaged in public discussions over public policy agendas.

This explanation acknowledges the role of the media is critical in agenda setting. When the media exposes a story on corruption and abuse of office, the public can assign blame and consequences to specific offices, often that of the presidency. Dalton and Beck (1998) argue that the media plays a critical role in presidential agenda setting campaigns. According to Dearing and Rogers (1996), and McCombs (2004), the media provide information on public affairs, and when repeated in numerous outlets, influence public opinion. Stories highlighted on the front page have a greater chance to become campaign issues, especially if framing highlights the dangers of inaction. In many instances, news magazines, network televisions, the internet and other electronic media also cover corruption stories. Given the sophisticated nature of modern information and communication technologies (ICTs), many stories on electronic media paint enduring pictures in the minds of the attentive public. The images define issues that include perceptions of candidate trustworthiness and accountability. Given the correlation between media coverage and agenda setting, it is logical to infer that if stories on corruption become front-page news, the effects of corruption on agenda setting will be established.

This chapter examines the extent to which contractor corruption in the Iraq and Afghanistan wars have played out in the political agendas of presidential candidates. First, we briefly describe the nature of involvement of the government in Iraq and Afghanistan and the extent to which these wars have been described in presidential electoral politics. Second, we discuss some of the public-private partnerships and public discourses on corruption within the framework of elections. Third, we explain the impact of the corruption narrative on governance, especially in the context of policymaking and implementation effectiveness at the national level. In the latter case, we identify possible reasons for the disconnect between U.S. positions against corruption by foreign governments while turning a blind eye to corruption involving contractor corruption in the Departments of Defense and State.

WARS IN IRAQ AND AFGHANISTAN AND GENERAL CORRUPTION

U.S. diplomatic engagement in Afghanistan dates back to 1935. With the Soviet Union invasion of Afghanistan in 1979, American involvement intensified. In many ways, the roots of U.S. intervention in Iraq and Afghanistan are intertwined. The official line was that after 9/11, the U.S. invaded Afghanistan to arrest Saudi Arabian national Osama bin Laden, the mastermind of the attacks, and to eliminate the Taliban regime (Johnson & Manson,

2007; Williams, 2011). The mission to arrest bin Laden in Afghanistan failed for he moved with his Mujahedeen to Pakistan and other friendlier nations. America stayed in Afghanistan ostensibly to drive away the Taliban government, which hosted bin Laden, and to rebuild a friendlier administration in the occupied country.

In the case of Iraq, the 2003 war was based on allegations that Saddam Hussein was a threat to international peace and had stockpiles of weapons of mass destruction (WMD). The latter claim was never proven (Kessler, 2014). The reasons for the Bush-Cheney administration's invasion and occupation of Iraq have been the subject of many popular books. (Fallows 2006; Woodward, 2004). As a political campaign issue, the invasion of Iraq created conditions that favored the election of Barack Obama who as a senator opposed the war. He used the Iraqi war as a campaign tool against both Hillary Clinton's 2008 presidential campaign bid, and more poignantly, against the Republican Party, whose leader George W. Bush had made the decision to go to war with Iraq.

Outside of the political election process, general corruption, waste, and fraud have been linked to American efforts to reconstruct the Iraqi and Afghanistan economies. From 2002–2014, the U.S. Congress appropriated nearly $104 billion for the reconstruction of Afghanistan. Of this amount, the Department of Defense received $66 billion appropriated, which excludes the amounts spent on military operations and wasted monies (Chiaramonte, 2014; 2016; SIGAR, March 2015).The Congressional Commission on Wartime Contracting's Report issued in 2011 estimated that between $32–$60 billion was lost through waste and fraud (Engelhardt, 2015). By July 2016, Special Inspector John Sopko had inspected and investigated 355 companies and 401 individuals for debarment and suspension (SIGAR, July 2016). Over "141 criminal charges, 103 convictions and 91 sentences, and criminal fines, restitutions, forfeitures, civil-settlement recoveries" resulting in savings of $951 million were reported (SIGAR July 2016, pp. iv–v).

Among the reconstruction projects that were poorly implemented or found to have been funded without proper oversight were three industrial parks in the major cities of Kabul, Mazari-Sharif and Kandahar, the construction of a police academy in Iraq (contracted out to Parsons Corporation), the Khan Bani Saad Correctional Facility, and a gas station in Sheberghan (which cost $43 million while a similar one in Pakistan cost $500,000) (Corbin, 2015; SIGAR, 2015). Other reconstruction projects that were poorly implemented or found to have been funded without proper oversight included police stations in Afghanistan, a teacher training center in Sheberghan and numerous road and bridge projects that were incomplete or in disrepair even after millions of dollars were spent. Some of the infrastructure projects supervised and constructed by the U.S. Army Corps of Engineers became conduits for the transportation of drugs, including opium and heroin. In 2014, two companies, Supreme Foodservices GmbH and Supreme Foodservices FZE, were found guilty of devising and implementing a scheme to overcharge the United States so they could make profits over and above those provided by the $8.8 billion subsistence prime vendor (SPV) (U.S. Department of Justice, 2014). Instances of contracts being awarded to companies with bad reputations were reported in the case of DynCorp International, which received $2.8 billion in contracts for police infrastructure and equipment (Siegel, 2014; SIGAR, 2006).

In addition, the Agency for International Development's (USAID) efforts to fund roads in rural Afghanistan through subcontractors delivered questionable roads, which many observers also felt were overpriced, through corrupt deals involving Iraqi and Afghanistan field operators. Overall, investigative reporting noted there were many instances that "no Defense Department personnel can answer questions about" (Engelhardt, 2015). In addition, SIGAR (Sept. 2016, p. 6) confirmed that "poor oversight of contracting and procurement" were the driving force for corruption. There were also reports that Iraqi officials pocketed money meant for the recruitment of soldiers. Through 'ghost personnel' hires over 50,000 persons could not be accounted for, a factor that contributed to the strong performance of the Islamic State militants (Engelhardt, 2015).

CONTRACTING OUT AND CORRUPTION NARRATIVES IN THE CONTEXT OF ELECTIONS

Accounts of corruption following the invasions of Iraq and Afghanistan have been widely reported. In the next section, a few documented examples are highlighted to illustrate the specifics of the corruption, including the corporations involved and attendant political dimensions for governance. Chivers (2008) reported that in support of the war efforts in Afghanistan, the federal government contracted out the purchase of arms worth over $300 million in 2006 through a contract with a Miami, Florida-based company, AEY, Inc. The company became the main supplier of munitions to Afghanistan's army and police units. Although the deliveries were made, most were found to be more than 40 years old and determined by both the North Atlantic Treaty

Organization (NATO) and State Department to be unreliable. According to the *New York Times*, the contractor had been associated with entities on the federal list of groups suspected of dealing in arms trafficking (Chivers, 2008). Evidently, the Army contracting officials were pressured to contract with an "immature company to enter the arms deal on the Pentagon's behalf" (Schmitt, 2008, p. A12). This company had been investigated, suspended, and found by a congressional committee as having a poor performance record on previous contracts. Chivers (2008) captured the main problem with defense contracting on the international stage: "The international arms business operates partly in the light and partly in shadows, and is littered with short-lived shell companies, middlemen, and official corruption. Governments have tried to regulate it more closely for years, with limited success" (p. A1).

Perhaps the most discussed nexus between contractor corruption and political campaigns was that involving former Vice President Dick Cheney. Dick Cheney was Chief Executive at Halliburton from 1995 until 2000 before running on the Bush ticket. Although the Bush campaign maintained that Cheney cut his ties with Halliburton, an oil services and engineering firm, the administration gave the company preferential treatment with contracting deals in Iraq. In 2001, although competitive bidding for the supply of food, housing, fuel and other logistical products and services was done in a competitive setting, Pentagon auditors reported the company had overcharged for the products and services it supplied. In campaign remarks attributed to then-presidential candidate Senator John Kerry, the company is said to have overcharged the federal government even after benefitting from no-bid contracts (Rosenbaum, 2004). Cheney also received millions of dollars in bonuses. The Congressional Research Service found John Kerry's claims to be factually accurate (Rosenbaum, 2004).

In 2003, Halliburton's subsidiary, Kellogg Brown and Root, an engineering and construction company was awarded a sole-source contract from the Pentagon. The contract, giving the company rights to restore and operate Iraqi oil wells, was tagged at $7 billion. The administration and Government Accountability Office regarded the no bid contract as understandable since Halliburton was already on the ground. Besides, making the contract public could have been militarily challenging. Clearly, Cheney benefitted from the War in Iraq through his ties with Halliburton. Cheney's financial disclosure statements from 2001, 2002, and 2003 revealed he had received $1,997,525 from Halliburton; $1,451,398 in a bonus deferred from 1999 and additional monies in deferred salary. Cheney refused to provide an accounting of any communications he and his staff had with Halliburton.

Although several factors explain President Bush's win over John Kerry in the presidential election, the role played by the Iraq war is contentious. Brinkley (2004) and Skocpol (2004) suggest the war indirectly boosted Bush's re-election chances. On the other hand, Campbell (2005) and Pomper (2005) saw the war as having the effect of making the election a tight race. Regardless of the effect on voters, the war in Iraq became an important policy issue. The main concern for the public was the toll in terms of thousands of war casualties, especially on the American side. Since Bush won the election and outperformed his 2000 results, there is room to speculate that the drag was rather small and in terms of governance, any hints that defense contractors had benefitted from the war presented no major moral queries from the public.

In a widely-discussed case involving the Navy, a defense contractor nicknamed "Fat Leonard" (i.e. Leonard Glenn Francis) corrupted officials to receive favorable deals from government agencies. The press reported "Fat Leonard", a Singapore–based businessman, "showered Navy officers with gifts, epicurean dinners, prostitutes, and if necessary, cash bribes so they would look the other way while he swindled the navy to refuel and resupply its ships" (Whitlock, 2016). In the fall of September 2013, Francis was eventually arrested in San Diego. As *Washington Post* journalist Craig Whitlock (2016) states, his "arrest exposed something else that is still emerging three years later: a staggering degree of corruption within the navy itself."

Leonard Francis also seduced the Navy's 7th Fleet, an important unit that operated in the Pacific and Indian Oceans. Many members of the Navy gave him classified information on U.S. submarine movements. He was even privy to confidential contracting information and had access to files used by FBI agents probing him. In other words, Francis had infiltrated the law enforcement ranks. Francis pocketed more than $35 million from the Navy. Although a senior Naval Criminal Investigative Service (NCIS) official and a few enlisted officers pled guilty, the effect of the story could have been much larger if it was given as much publicity as the media gave to comparable criminal cases. But it did not, even though it involved sex, cigars, whiskey, more than 200 admirals under investigation, bribery, and other vices popular in the culture. Whitlock (2016) observed, "It was the worst national-security breach of its kind to hit the Navy since the end of the Cold War." Although the 7th fleet played a partial role in the Gulf Wars of the 1990s, we consider the corruption case in the context of the larger culture in defense contracting. Shockingly, these stories did not make it to the 2012 presidential campaign trail nor were they discussed in the open Senate confirmation hearings for nominees to positions such as Secretary of Defense. In another example, reported in the *Washington Post*, contractors were charged with trying to influence federal officials to win contracts (Babcock, 2006). Defense contractor Mitchell J. Wade admitted in federal court that he attempted to influence Department of Defense contracting officials. He gave campaign funds to some members of Congress, including Reps. Virgil H. Goode Jr. (R-Va) and Katherine Harris (R-Fla.). These congressional leaders represented districts where contractors had businesses.

These and other cases illustrate that there is evidence of corruption in contracts in nations where the American military is involved, but the forms of corruption vary in scope and type. The corruption is multidimensional and in some cases, involves quid pro quo transactions with elites in countries where the military operations occur. Therefore, the blame for corruption has to be examined more holistically. Speaking on *CBS's 60 Minutes,* former Afghanistan President Karzai acknowledged that corruption was rampant in his nation, but he was quick to blame American contractors when he stated: "The Soviets didn't give contracts to the relatives, brothers and the kin of the influential and high ups…the Americans did, and they continue to do, but we get blamed for it" (Pincus, 2012). Karzai stated that American corruption was even beyond what he had experienced during the 1980s when the Soviet Union occupied the country. The former president's claims were supported by other observers who criticized the U.S. government for poor management of contracts and misdirection of development aid funds to ill-conceived projects. Citing former Reagan administration official Anthony Cordesman, there was agreement in some scholarly communities that many of the projects focused more on spending amounts rather than results (Pincus, 2012). Karzai's successor President Ashraf Ghani also criticized corruption in defense contracts and centralized some of the local procurement decisions (Ghani, 2016).

EXPLAINING THE CORRUPTION NARRATIVE ON GOVERNANCE: AGENDA SETTING AND POLICY IMPLEMENTATION

Following the evidence above, we now offer possible explanations for why corruption in defense contracts has not moved through the political process to become a core campaign and governance issue in election cycles. We speculate the attention to corruption in the defense sector often takes a backseat in comparison to debates over going to war and the outcomes thereof. For starters, corruption as a governance issue lacks traction. Stated differently, it is popular for leaders to remind voters that politics should be localized first. This means that defense contracts have to have a direct impact on local affairs to gain traction as issues for electioneering. From data examined, the identified flaw in private-public partnerships, as narrated in popular media, lacked a frame that problematized corruption in contracts as a moral failure on the part of the U.S. government. Consistent with agenda setting literature, the issue of contractor corruption in the Afghanistan and Iraq wars was not concretely defined. The more the issue is broadly defined, the greater the likelihood of the issue remaining on the institutional agenda and becoming a matter of national interest. Corruption and deterioration of ethical values were not seen as relevant issues even though the manifestations of the wars were described as disastrous. There was no discourse about the nature of contractor corruption on the Iraqi and Afghan society or even on the morale of the U.S. Army which had to live with the consequences of collaborating with private contractors in missions abroad.

One of the reasons for the low salience relates to the common perception that corruption is a Third World issue. This is rather misleading and needs to be deconstructed. Transparency international (TI), which ranks countries on their degree of corruption, hardly focuses on sub-governments and, in most instances, gives more attention to corruption in developing countries. There is virtually no mention of TI rankings in American party platforms at any level of government. In 2015, the United States was ranked 16th out of 168 nations on the TI Corruption Perceptions Index (Transparency International, 2015). By comparison, Iraq was ranked 161st and Afghanistan 166th respectively. The United States' high placement suggests that the American political system is clean, but does not address the role of defense contractors in perpetuating corruption overseas.

While there are no credible and value-free ranking systems, one can hardly miss the rhetoric in presidential campaigns, especially in 2015-16 when candidate Donald Trump painted a different image of corruption in government. In numerous campaign speeches, he described opponents as corrupt. At one point, he acknowledged that he knew the *system* and had made contributions to many politicians. His attack on Democratic Party candidate Hillary Clinton was even more vicious on campaign trails, Twitter and other social media. Trump branded his opponent "crooked Hillary" (Spaeth, 2016). Trump told audiences across the country and during a nationally broadcast presidential debate that Hillary voted for the war in Iraq, and the war was a "mistake" (National Public Radio [NPR], 2016). Although Trump's positions on the war varied, he was nevertheless able to articulate to his followers his message that the war was a form of corruption and those who supported it were deficient in judgment.

Just before his 2016 election, presidential candidate Donald J. Trump boldly told Americans that he would "drain the swamp," impose congressional term limits, and eradicate corruption in the country (Trump, 2016). Many observers were not oblivious to his persistent narration of Washington D.C. as a place that required some form of cleansing from systemic corruption. Trump's opponents were quick to associate him with numerous unethical behaviors including swindling money from students at the defunct Trump University. Moreover, during his first week in office as president, a group of lawyers argued his actions were unethical and a violation of the Emoluments Clause. According to ethics experts, Trump's hotels and businesses received monies from foreign governments in violation of the spirit of the Emoluments Clause (Lipton & Liptak, 2017). In all instances, corruption seemed to be a less than a critical matter to change voting behaviors in the larger polity.

Perhaps another plausible explanation for the lackluster efforts in combatting corruption within the defense industry is to dig deeper and examine the military establishment itself. If corruption exists in defense contracts, why does the military condone these unethical behaviors? Stated differently, is there something in the military psyche that is averse to whistleblowing or outright public denunciation of reported instances of corruption? There are at least four arguments that may be considered as possible explanations. First, military leadership generally is anti-intellectual and its rank and file consider corruption discourses as a component of intellectualism. Matthews (2005) posits this anti-intellectualism tradition endures even in the age of ICTs. It is probable that individual officers may have been concerned about defense contracts but chose not to speak about it because it was an issue at odds with military strategy. Even those with contemplative minds are more driven by the military's view as an addendum to the American pioneer, "can-do mentality," which focuses more on defeating enemies in any frontier, including the mountains of Afghanistan and Iraq. Books on the Iraq and Afghanistan wars written by military men and women and also by keen observers of American militarism minimize contractor corruption. We include in this genre such works as Gutman (2010), Shimko (2010) and Bolger (2014). These volumes are excellent discussions on defense policy implementation but omit in-depth critical analyses of corruption in defense procurement. In the same tradition, Brooks (2016) demonstrates that there is a culture gap between government civilians and military contractors whose ethical standards are at odds with existing institutions during war times.

A second possible explanation is that the wars in Iraq and Afghanistan were fought at a time when the military's identity had reached a crisis. Since 2001, the U.S. military has been fighting stateless enemies, which has meant engagements went beyond the well-defined battlefields and often pushed military men and women into hunting terrorists hiding in neighborhoods. This shift in identity suggests a shift from military traditions that value adherence to duty and honor to be reconciled with behaviors that "win the hearts and minds" of civilians in combat zones. The mission to build nations, construct bridges, build schools, drill water wells, and so on inevitably required greasing the local elders and, perhaps, returning to patronage. Consistent with Watkins and Cohen's (2005) argument that the military has been steadily transitioning from a professional organization to a compliant bureaucracy, it is not hard to speculate that elements within the military may have no reason to question corruption within the establishment. After all, bureaucrats are known to act in their self-interest. Perhaps this explains why bureaupathology was condoned in the case of prisoner abuse at Abu Ghraib in Iraq.

The third explanation with a powerful appeal is the weak moral argumentation found in American constitutionalism. From an historic standpoint, the American Constitution originally turned a blind eye to those who faced discrimination. The mentality in the armed forces has continued to look at foreigners as "others," not protected by the constitution. As such, issues concerning corruption are, for the most part, construed to be outside of the military mission. In other words, if the Department of Defense is involved in corruption, it is not up to military men and women to bring these issues up for political debate. Rather, it is up to civilian leadership to respond to reported instances of corruption. For the rank and file military officer, their relationship to the constitution is different. Soldiers swear allegiance to the constitution and do their job to defend the constitution (Mattox, 2005). Therefore, regardless of the famed-pronouncements of an existing military-industrial complex, any reported forms of corruption are weighed against efficiency criteria. In other words, equipment procured, whether through a single source or other non-competitive bids, are not subject to political debate within the larger military body. Thus, if contracted civilian computer maintenance experts, fuel transporters, or others were procured through deals that would be judged as corrupt, the military still abides by its oath of allegiance to the constitution and accepts civilian oversight.

The fourth explanation relates to the relatively weak legal infrastructure governing defense contracts, which leads to weak oversight. Cordesman (2010) made this argument with regard to the Department of Defense's investigative arm. Moreover, the Foreign Corrupt Practices Act (1977), which requires American corporations to meet certain ethical standards has not deterred companies in the case of Iraq and Afghanistan from involving themselves in morally questionable transactions. New players in the defense contracting and reconstruction businesses have been shielded through defense contracts which the congressional Commission on Wartime Contracting investigated and found to be wasteful and, in some instances, fraudulent. For several years, giant corporations such as Lockheed-Martin, Boeing and Douglas grew out of their connections with the Department of Defense. These huge corporations have monopolies in the manufacture of certain categories of aircraft and weapon attendant systems. To enable these producers to function optimally, the first War Powers Act waived several restrictions on bureaucratic rules on contracting. The legal framework on defense contracts fails to determine the acceptable levels of profiteering within the industry. In other words, there is no clear indication as to what constitutes excessive profiteering within a section of the defense contracting enterprise. Following *United States v. Bethlehem Steel*, the Supreme Court deferred the control of profiteering to Congress which passed the Renegotiation Act (1942) in response (United States Supreme Court, 1942). In that statute, Congress made changes to contract negotiations to recognize and accept the legality of renegotiations over war-related contract payments considered as excessive (Marbury & Bowie, 1943). Kovacic and Schooner (2005), expressed similar concerns over the enduring legacy of excessive profit-making within civil-military relations and called for prudent management practices. Arguably, there is a weak managerial and legal infrastructure which allows defense contractors to exploit every inch of the loophole. These explanations suggest that the existence of weak mechanisms within civilian oversight and accountability institutions and the rank and file of the military add voice to civil society's concerns over corruption in the Department of Defense. Were military men and women, especially those in Iraq and Afghanistan, to reject corruption in procurement there is a possibility that the public could raise the issue of corruption in political campaigns and, perhaps, elevate the corruption discourse in American politics.

CONCLUSION

In conclusion, the unchartered ethical concerns manifested in the contracts awarded to various private businesses in the war-making and nation-building enterprises in Iraq and Afghanistan wars warrants ethical reflection in policy implementation. We know from various reports and accounts by TI that arms trade accounted for almost 40% of corruption in all global trade and that there were very few arms transactions that did not involve illegal actions (Feinstein, 2011a). As Andrew Feinstein (2011a) suggested, government action against corruption was less than satisfactory. He also contended global trade in arms was inherently lacking in transparency and was prone to corruption. "Governments protect corrupt and dangerous arms dealers as long as they need them and throw them behind bars when they are no longer useful." (Feinstein, 2011b, p. A21).

The question becomes, why does a corrupt form of business involving billions of dollars fail to retain a prominent place in election cycles? Comparisons with the war on drugs and other criminal activities, including politicians campaigning to be "law and order" presidents, are well documented. The realm of bribery in politics has resulted in the deaths of millions of people. The Iraq and Afghanistan wars are no exception. No doubt, campaign rhetoric on "arms deals" has existed in previous situations such as those involving the Reagan Contras and Iran exchanges. However, these activities were apparently not enough to receive sustained attention from the voting public. This finding suggests that elite framing of corruption needs to be meticulously targeted to generate enthusiasm among members of the voting public. Successful agenda-setting is a function of powerful messaging that is persuasive to a broad section of the public. Through party platforms and other messaging avenues, it is possible that even undecided voters seeking to change the culture of bureaucratic corruption in defense contracting can be swayed to join forces against waste and fraud.

With regards to Afghanistan, we concur with the remarks of investigative journalist Walter Pincus (2012): "When it comes to corruption in Afghanistan, the time may be now for the United States to look in the mirror and see what lessons can be learned from contracting out parts of that war." All indications have been that U.S. defense contractors abetted corruption and supported corrupt individuals within the local community. As Cooper (2003) hinted, contract management is riddled with suspicions of corruption and incompetence. In recent times, the U.S. ignored corruption and excused it by playing the counterterrorism card. In other words, support for some warlords and non-profits within Afghan society through subcontracts was a quid pro quo in exchange for fighting terrorism (Amiry, 2010; Felbab-Brown, 2012). Essentially, the U.S. cannot be a champion of good governance if a major part of its administrative apparatus is perceived to lack honesty. Good governance embodies both democratic governance and core values of administration such as transparency and honesty in public policy implementation. Pervasive corruption in defense contracting undermines the successful implementation of private-public partnerships and the survival of a healthy democracy. The correlation between government accountability and robust democratic governance applies to all nations, including the

United States. And since the accountability structures that are concerned with defense are fragmented, units within the department and Congress that authorize spending have to find common ground with the attentive public. Increasingly, the public has turned to social media, in addition to traditional media, to add a layer of forums through which oversight and public expectations are articulated.

Although the role of the media in investigating and reporting corruption in the defense sector is an offshoot from constitutional guarantees to freedom of speech and freedom of the press, the issue of corruption within the defense sphere is remarkably absent from the public discourse, especially within the context of political campaigns. In competitive democracies, the expectation is that elites frame an issue to encourage the public to weigh in on the impact of that issue, especially if the frame is repeated frequently enough (Chong & Druckman, 2007). The electorate's susceptibility to frames is expected and allows them to engage in the political process in a more meaningful way. Pertinent to this research, the presidential elections in 2004, 2008, 2012 and 2016 lacked strong anti-corruption platforms for competing political parties. Any content analysis of speeches related to the wars in Iraq and Afghanistan concerned strategy and failure on the part of incumbent leaders. The campaigns stayed away from giving voice to corruption involving the military and its civilian supervisors. For us, this amounts to a disconnect in bureaucratic behaviors. In some ways, the disjuncture is indicative of the differences between the Department of Defense's outlook and that of the Department of State and USAID, which for the most part run anti-corruption programs in developing countries, including Iraq and Afghanistan. Examining the corruption in defense contracts suggests the extent to which its influence on agenda-setting may be rather weak regardless of its consequences on wars or governance. We have offered a few reasons why we believe private-public partnerships in the conduct of foreign wars has not triggered sufficient outrage in either the civilian nor military establishment. The outrage is necessary because the opportunity costs of corruption are colossal and undermine our democratic institutions, which in the long run will lower the quality of administrative practices and policy implementation.

REFERENCES

Aidt, T. S. (2009). Corruption, institutions, and economic development. *Oxford Review of Economic Policy*, 25(2), 271–291.

Amiry, Q. (2010). Corruption and social trust in Afghanistan. *The Fletcher School-Al Nakhlah-Tufts University*. Retrieved from http://fletcher.tufts.edu/Al-Nakhlah/Archives/~/media/Fletcher/Microsites/al%20Nakhlah/archives/pdfs/Amiry%20Corruption%20and%20Social%20Trust%20in%20Afghanistan.pdf

Arnoldy, B. (2011). US commission finds widespread waste and corruption in wartime contracts. *The Christian Science Monitor*. Retrieved from http://www.csmonitor.com/World/Global-News/2011/0901/US-commission-finds-widespread-waste-and-corruption-in-wartime-contracts

Babcock, C. R. (2006, February 25), Contractor pleads guilty to corruption. *Washington Post*. Retrieved from http://www.washingtonpost.com

Bolger, D. P. (2014). *Why we lost: A General's inside account of the Iraq and Afghanistan wars*. New York, NY: Houghton Mifflin Harcourt.

Brinkley, A. (2004, November 21). What's Next? *The American Prospect*. Retrieved from http://prospect.org/article/whats-next-0

Brooks, R. (2016). *How everything became war and the military became everything: Tales from the Pentagon*. New York, NY: Simon and Schuster.

Campbell, J. E. (2005). Why Bush won the presidential election of 2004: Incumbency, ideology, terrorism, and turnout. *Political Science Quarterly*, *120*(2), 219–241.

Chiaramonte, P. (2014, July 28). War on waste: Pentagon auditor spotlights US billions blown in Afghanistan. Fox News.com. Retrieved from http://www.foxnews.com/world/2014/07/28/war-on-waste-pentagon-auditor-spotlights-us-billions-blown-in-afghanistan.html

Chiaramonte, P. (2016, Sep 13). US taxpayer billions lined pockets of corrupt Afghan warlords, says watchdog. Fox News.com Retrieved from http://www.foxnews.com/world/2016/09/13/us-taxpayer-billions-lined-pockets-corrupt-afghan-warlords-says-watchdog.html

Chivers, C. J. (2008, March 27). Supplier under scrutiny on aging arms for Afghans. *New York Times*, A1. Retrieved from http://www.nytimes.com

Chong, D., & Druckman, J. N. (2007). Framing public opinion in competitive democracies. *American Political Science Review*, *101*(04), 637–655.

Cobb, R., & Elder. C.D. (1972). *Participation in American politics: The dynamics of agenda-building*. Baltimore, MD: Johns Hopkins University Press.

Cooper, P. J. (2003). *Governing by contract: Challenges and opportunities for public managers*. Washington, DC: Congressional Quarterly Press.

Corbin, C. (2015, Dec.6). DOD spent $150 Mon private villas, security for 'handful' of employees in Afghanistan, watchdog claims. *Fox News*. Retrieved from http://www.foxnews.com/politics/2015/12/06/dod-spent-150m-on-private-villas-security-for-handful-employees-in-afghanistan-watchdog-claims.html

Cordesman, A. (2010). How America corrupted Afghanistan: Time to look in the mirror. *Centre for Strategic & International Studies*. Retrieved from https://www.csis.org/analysis/how-america-corrupted-afghanistan-time-look-mirror

Dalton, R. J., & Beck, P. A. (1998). A test of media-centered agenda setting: Newspaper content and public interests in a presidential election. *Political Communication*, *15*(4), 463–481.

Dearing, J. W., & Rogers, E. M. (1996). *Agenda – Setting*. Thousand Oaks, CA: Sage.

Engelhardt, T. (2015, Nov. 16). We got scammed by government contractors in Iraq and Afghanistan. *Moyers and Company*. Retrieved from http://billmoyers.com/2015/11/16/we-got-scammed-by-government-contractors-in-iraq-and-afghanistan/

Fallows, J. (2006). *Blind into Baghdad: America's war in Iraq*. New York, NY: Vintage.

Feinstein, A. (2011a). *The Shadow World: Inside the Global Arms Trade*, New York, NY: Farrar, Straus, and Giroux.

Feinstein, A. (2011b, Nov 21). Arms and the corrupt man. *The New York Times, Op-ed*, A 21. Retrieved from http://www.nytimes.com

Felbab-Brown, V. (2012). Slip-sliding on a yellow brick road: Stabilization efforts in Afghanistan. *Stability: International Journal of Security and Development, 1*(1),4–19.

Foreign Corruption Practices Act (FCPA) U.S. Department of Justice (2006). Retrieved from https://www.justice.gov/criminal-fraud/foreign-corrupt-practices-act

Ghani, A. M. (2016, May 5). *The way ahead for anti-corruption in Afghanistan. President's Speech at European Union conference*. The Islamic Republic of Afghanistan. Retrieved from http://www.afghanistan-vienna.org/2016/05/transcript-of-his-excellency-president-mohammad-ashraf-ghanis-remarks-at-european-union-conference/

Gutmann, M. C. (2010). *Breaking ranks: Iraq veterans speak out against the war.* Los Angeles, CA: University of California Press.

Johnson, T. H., & Mason, M. C. (2007). Understanding the Taliban and Insurgency in Afghanistan. *Orbis, 51*(1),71–89.

Kessler, G. (2014, Nov. 13). George W. Bush's claims on weapons found, and not found, In Iraq. Fact Checker. *Washington Post*. Retrieved from https://www.washingtonpost.com/news/fact-checker/wp/2014/11/13/george-w-bushs-claims-on-weapons-found-and-not-found-in-iraq/?utm_term=.60e155d0860d

Kinzer, S. (2017). *The Flag: Theodore Roosevelt, Mark Twain and the Birth of American Empire.* New York, NY: Macmillan.

Kovacic, W. E., & Schooner, S. L. (2005). A Modest Proposal to Enhance Civil/Military Integration: Rethinking the Renegotiation Regime as a Regulatory Mechanism to Decriminalize Cost, Pricing, and Profit Policy. *George Washington University (GWU) Law School Public Law Research Paper* No. 178.

Linz, J. J. (1990). The perils of presidentialism. *Journal of Democracy, 1*(1), 51–70.

Lipton, E., & Liptak, A. (2017, January 22). Foreign Payments to Trump Firms Violate Constitution, suit will claim. *The New York Times.* Retrieved from https://www.nytimes.com

Marbury, W. L., & Bowie, R. R. (1943). Renegotiation and procurement. *Law and Contemporary Problems. Duke University Law School Paper*, 218–234.

Markowski, R. (2006). Political accountability and Institutional Design in New Democracies. *International Journal of Sociology, 36*(2), 45–75.

Matthews, L. J. (2005). Anti-intellectualism and the army profession. In Snider, D. M., & Matthews, L. J.(Eds.). *The future of the army profession.* (pp. 61–93). New York: McGraw Hill.

Mattox, J. M. (2005). The Moral Foundations of Army Officership. In Snider, D. M., & Matthews, L. J. (Eds.). *The future of the army profession* (pp. 387–408). Boston, MA: McGraw-Hill.

McCombs, M. E. (2004). *Setting the Agenda: The Mass Media and Public Opinion.* Malden, MA: Blackwell.

Mo, P. H. (2001). Corruption and economic growth. *Journal of Comparative Economics, 29*(1), 66–79.

National Public Radio (NPR). (2016, Oct. 9). Fact Check: Clinton and Trump Debate for the 2nd time. Retrieved from http://www.npr.org/2016/10/09/497056227/fact-check-clinton-and-trump-debate-for-the-second-time

Pincus, W. (2012, Nov. 5). Afghan corruption and how the U.S. facilitates it. *The Washington Post.* Retrieved from https://www.washingtonpost.com

Pomper, G. M. (2005). The Presidential Election: The Ills of American Politics after 9/11. In Michael Nelson (Eds.) *The Elections of 2004*, (pp. 42–68). Washington, DC: Congressional Quarterly Press.

Rosenbaum, D. E. (2004, September 28). The 2004 Campaign: A closer look at Cheney and Halliburton. *The New York Times*. Retrieved from http://www.nytimes.com

Schmitt, E. (2008, June 25). Army Awarded Contract Unaware of Dealer's Past. *The New York Times*. Retrieved from http://www.nytimes.com

Scott, J. (1972). *Comparative Political Corruption*. Englewood Cliffs, NJ: Prentice-Hall.

Shimko, K. L. (2010). *The Iraq Wars and America's Military Revolution*. New York: Cambridge University Press.

Siegel, J. (2014). The real Winner of the Afghan War Is This Shady Military Contractor: *The Daily Beast*. Retrieved from http://www.thedailybeast.com/articles/2014/04/24/the-real-winner-of-the-afghan-war-is-this-shady-military-contractor.html

SIGAR Report (2006, April). Special Inspector General for Afghanistan Reconstruction. Quarterly Report to the United States Congress. Retrieved from https://www.sigar.mil/pdf/ quarterlyreports/2016-07-30qr.pdf

———— (March 2015). Special Inspector General for Afghanistan Reconstruction. Quarterly Report to the United States Congress. Retrieved from https://www.sigar.mil/pdf/Audits/ SIGAR-15

———— (2016, July 30). Special Inspector General for Afghanistan Reconstruction. Quarterly Report to the United States Congress. Retrieved from https://www.sigar.mil/pdf/ quarterlyreports/2016-07-30qr.pdf

———— (2016, Sept.). Special Inspector General for Afghanistan Reconstruction. Quarterly Report to the United States Congress. Retrieved from https://www.sigar.mil/pdf/

Skocpol, T. (2004, Dec. 20). *Looking Back, Looking Forward*. The Nation. Retrieved from https:// www.thenation.com/article/looking-back-looking-forward/

Spaeth, R. (2016, April 10). Donald Trump has come up with his Clinton nickname: "Crooked Hillary." *New Republic Magazine*. Retrieved from https://newrepublic.com/minutes/ 132765/donald-trump-come-clinton-nickname-crooked-hillary

Stillman, R. J. II., (2010). *Public Administration: Concepts and Cases*. Boston, MA: Cengage/ Wadsworth.

Transparency International (2015) Corruption Perception Index 2015. Retrieved from https:// www.transparency.org/cpi2015/

———— (2017). Anti-corruption center. What is corruption? Retrieved from https://transparency. am/en/resources/language-guide

Trump, D. (2016, Oct.18). Trump pledges to drain the swamp and impose congressional term limits. Presidential Candidate Donald Trump's website. Retrieved from https://www. donaldjtrump.com/press-releases/trump-pledges-to-drain-the-swamp

U.S. Department of Justice. (2014, Dec. 8). *Defense Contractor Pleads Guilty to Major Fraud in Provision of Supplies to U.S. Troops in Afghanistan. Justice News* [Press Release]. Retrieved from https://www.justice.gov/opa/pr/defense-contractor-pleads-guilty-major-fraud-provision-supplies-us-troops-afghanistan

United States v. Bethlehem Steel Corp. 315 U.S. 289 (1942). Retrieved from JUSTIA. https:// supreme.justia.com/cases/federal/us/315/289/case.html

Watkins, G. L., & Cohen, R. C. (2005). In their own Words: Army Officers Discuss Their Profession. In Snider, Don M and Lloyd J. Matthews. (Eds) *The future of the Army profession* (pp. 115–139.). Boston, MA: McGraw-Hill.

Whitlock. C. (2016, May 27). The Man who seduced the Navy's 7th fleet and the sting that revealed the trail of corruption. *Washington Post*. Retrieved from http://www.washingtonpost.com/sf/investigative/2016/05/27/the-man-who-seduced-the-7th-fleet/?utm_term=.78ec9029c1c9

Williams, B. G. (2011) *Afghanistan Declassified: A Guide to America's Longest War*. Philadelphia, PA: University of Pennsylvania Press.

Woodward, B. (2004). *Plan to Attack: The definitive account of the decision to invade Iraq*. New York, NY: Simon & Schuster.

PART IV

OVERSIGHT AND ACCOUNTABILITY

CHAPTER 10

CITIZENS UNITED AND POLITICAL ACCOUNTABILITY

Benjamin Bricker

ABSTRACT

This chapter examines the role that Citizens United v. FEC *(2010) has played in shaping the current system of election spending in the United States. In* Citizens United, *the Court determined that individual rights to speech and expression can flow into the corporate entities they join. This chapter argues that the Court's holding serves to redirect the focus of accountability away from those who seek to sway election outcomes through massive election spending and toward any efforts by government to regulate that type of spending. The practical result has been to allow for the creation of new organizations that can take in unlimited amounts of money while also effectively hiding the source of funds from disclosure. By muddying the waters of disclosure, these new entities – Super PACs and dark money organizations – lower the ability of citizens to maintain accountability over the electoral system. Finally, this chapter examines ways to encourage greater disclosure and accountability in government after* Citizens United.

Keywords: Accountability; *Citizens United*; democracy; election spending; Supreme Court

Corruption, Accountability and Discretion
Public Policy and Governance, 185–204
doi:10.1108/S2053-769720170000029011

INTRODUCTION

When David Bossie, head of the conservative activist group Citizens United, was contracted to produce *Hillary: The Movie*, a harsh documentary of Hillary Clinton's life and character, he wanted to run advertising for the film. The documentary itself may not receive favorable reviews, or much time in theatres, but if his organization could place advertisements on the major networks during the run-up to the 2008 presidential election, then the group's message would be seen by a wide audience. However, there was a problem with purchasing ads on television: Citizens United, a nonprofit corporation, sought to purchase the ads with its general treasury money, not its more regulated political action committee (PAC) money, and wanted to advertise during the 30-day period prior to the 2008 presidential primary elections. With the documentary considered an "electioneering communication" – that is, a communication intended to advocate for the election or defeat of a candidate – both the type of money used and the timeframe of the ads were not allowed under federal election and campaign finance laws.

Two years later, the Supreme Court heard Citizens United's legal challenge to those campaign finance laws. Ruling five to four in favor of Citizens United, the Court's decision fundamentally reshaped First Amendment constitutional law and upended the American political landscape. Almost overnight, *Citizens United v. FEC* (2010) became a lightning rod for public criticism of the role of money in politics and a new shorthand among some in society for judicial overreach. Ruling that corporations have First Amendment speech rights similar to private citizens, the Court majority determined that direct spending by corporations in an attempt to sway elections should not increase *quid pro quo* corruption or the appearance of corruption.

Though much of the discussion surrounding the case has focused directly on the role of money in politics and the appearance of corruption, there is an equally important aspect to the case – how *Citizens United* altered the system of accountability in American democracy. This chapter examines the case and its impact on several facets of political accountability. First, it examines the case holding itself, and how the Court's opinion functionally changes the focus of accountability in federal election law: by framing corporate activities as integral to the expression of individual liberties, the Court moved the legal burdens away from campaign spenders and toward governmental policies that regulate money in politics.

Second, the chapter examines the practical consequences of *Citizens United*. Perhaps most important, *Citizens United* has allowed for the creation of the Super PAC and "dark money" organizations, two new types of entities that can both take in and spend unlimited amounts of money while also effectively hiding the source of funds from disclosure. Both have critical effects for democratic governance. In a democracy, we expect our leaders to make decisions in the public interest; if not, they can be held accountable through the electoral process. In fact, the accountability function served by elections provides the defining feature of a democratic (as opposed to autocratic) regime (Schmitter & Karl, 1990). However, by muddying the waters of disclosure, Super PACs and dark money organizations effectively lower the ability of citizens to maintain accountability over the electoral system.

Third, this chapter outlines a path toward regaining accountability over election spending. These steps involve both private actions, including shareholder activism, and public actions, such as limiting the ability of corporations with foreign shareholders to engage in direct electoral spending. In addition, the Court has recently taken steps to limit political fundraising in judicial elections (*Williams-Yulee v. The Florida Bar*, 2015). The rationale provided by the Court could provide an opening to limit the extension of *Citizen United* going forward.

GETTING TO *CITIZENS UNITED*

The role of money in politics is nothing new: interest groups and corporations have long sought to gain advantages for their policies through donations to candidates for elected office. The last years of the nineteenth century were rife with tales of spending – licit and illicit – by the growing business interests in the United States. Wealthy Cleveland businessperson turned Republican Party chairperson Mark Hanna oversaw a fundamental transformation of campaign fundraising, developing an elaborate system in which big businesses were given "assessments" – required contributions – that had to be paid to the GOP (Sabato, 1984). In the 1896 presidential election, Hanna's system allowed business interests to coordinate decisively in favor of Republican William McKinley over the populist Democrat William Jennings Bryan, who sought the introduction of silver as an alternative monetary standard and the development of significant reforms to corporate business practices. Yet the GOP's behavior, specifically the unseemly connection between big business money and federal government policy, led to significant reform efforts aimed at reducing the potentially corrupting role of money in political campaigns.

In fact, the two great reform movements of the early twentieth century – the populists and the progressives – both sought to limit the role of money and campaign contributions in politics. President Theodore Roosevelt used his presidency to lead a reform effort to eliminate corporate funding for political campaigns. Though brought to the vice presidency by McKinley (over Hanna's objection), Roosevelt had for years argued against the corrupting influence of assessments and other efforts to fill political coffers with outside money (Roosevelt, 1892). Roosevelt's plan to publicly fund elections proved too much at the time, though Congress in 1907 did pass the first comprehensive national laws regulating spending and contributions in political campaigns, including a prohibition on corporate and banking contributions to federal election campaigns that was intended to clean up the perception of corruption in Congress.

Concerns over money in politics and accountability in government were raised again during the Watergate era, and led to the second major effort in campaign finance reform. The Watergate scandal and the publication of the Nixon Tapes brought to light not only a vast criminal effort to obtain information on political opponents, but also an extensive network of hidden money, funded by secret political contributions, to carry out the Nixon White House's campaign of break-ins, bugging, wiretapping, and other nefarious efforts to win re-election. The role of secret money as a source for the Nixon administration's criminal activities brought new urgency to campaign finance reform.

In response, a 1971 law, the Federal Election Campaign Act (FECA), was amended and strengthened in 1974. The 1974 amendments created the Federal Election Commission (FEC), an independent agency of government designed to monitor compliance with elections and facilitate the public disclosure of campaign financing and spending. The 1974 amendments also created important limits on two different avenues through which money travels in the political world. First, Congress placed strict limits on the *contributions* made to federal election campaigns. Second, Congress limited the amounts of money that campaigns can spend, as well as the amounts of money that private individuals could spend in an election (so-called *independent expenditures*). Both the contribution and expenditure limits were created by Congress to help eliminate new forms of corruption and the perception of corruption in the electoral system.

The 1970s also saw the Supreme Court take its first major steps to delineate the rules of campaign finance. The 1974 FECA amendments were immediately challenged, and in the landmark case *Buckley v. Valeo* (1976) the Court provided a partial victory for the campaign finance movement, upholding the law's limits on direct monetary contributions that individuals, unions, and corporations can make to candidates. However, the Court also struck down, on First Amendment free speech grounds, the limits that FECA placed on independent expenditures made by private citizens for political advocacy, as well as the limits placed on candidate campaign expenditures.

For years, this distinction between constitutionally protected expenditures and unprotected contributions served as the touchstone for campaign finance. Yet it did not stop the flow of campaign money. Instead, campaign contributions began to flow into other areas, including "soft money" – unlimited contributions to political parties that are intended to support party development and party messaging strategies. Additionally, *Buckley* stated that unions and corporations were only prohibited from using their general treasury funds to advance "express advocacy" for a candidate. However, these organizations could use their general treasury money to create "issue ads" – ads in which policy issues were promoted – as long as they did not also expressly advocate for or against a particular candidate (Coyle, 2013, p. 203).

The next round of major congressional campaign finance reform targeted both soft money and issue ads. The Bipartisan Campaign Reform Act of 2002 (also known as the McCain-Feingold Act) forbade national political parties, like the Democratic and Republican parties, from raising soft money donations. In addition, all non-political parties, specifically unions and corporations, were forbidden from using their general treasury funds for any "electioneering communications" focusing on a particular candidate within 60 days of a general election, or 30 days of a primary election. Finally, the funding sources for all such communications must be disclosed. These latter provisions were intended both to reduce the proliferation of issue ads and to allow for greater disclosure and accountability in the campaign funding process. Unions and corporations could still fund such ads, but only by using their more heavily regulated PAC money. It is this distinction between the heavily regulated PAC funds and the murkier corporate treasury funds that initially led Citizens United to challenge congressional and FEC regulatory policy on campaign spending.

CITIZENS UNITED AND CORPORATE SPENDING

Citizens United's legal campaign began during the 2008 presidential campaign season. Yet, the path Citizens United took to get their issue to the

Supreme Court was years in the making. The group had a long history with the FEC's election activity approval process before *Hillary: The Movie*. In 2004, Citizens United unsuccessfully requested the FEC to stop advertisements for Michael Moore's film *Fahrenheit 9/11*. Later in the year, Citizens United again sought out the FEC's judgment, this time about the group's plan to use the FEC commercial media exception to create its own documentary about 2004 Democratic presidential nominee John Kerry. Again, the agency rejected the group's request, concluding that Citizen United's film and its ads were effectively a ruse to get around federal election campaigning restrictions (Federal Election Commission, 2004).

After their unsuccessful efforts in 2004, Citizens United began fundraising for their next film project, *Hillary: The Movie*. However, David Bossie, the group's president, placed the funds raised for the Clinton documentary in the corporation's general treasury account, not its PAC account (Coyle, 2013). In addition, instead of seeking the FEC's approval for their film advertisements, Citizens United preemptively filed suit against the FEC in U.S. District Court, seeking an injunction to prevent the agency from enforcing the "electioneering communications" rules. In doing so, Citizens United was challenging years of federal law and Supreme Court precedent that placed limits on the ability of corporations to directly influence elections.

In *Austin v. Michigan State Chamber of Commerce* (1990), for example, the Court upheld legislation enacted by the state of Michigan that limited the ability of corporations to use their general treasury funds for direct political activity. The *Austin* majority focused on the unique problems of corporate election spending on the democratic political process. Unchecked, corporate entities can have a "corrosive" and "distorting" effect on the public debate due to the ease with which the corporate form can accumulate and spend "immense aggregations of wealth" (*Austin*, 1990, p. 660). These factors, the Court found, make corporations a wholly different type of speaker than individual citizens or other groups of speakers. That conclusion was reiterated in 2003 when the Court upheld the first major challenge to McCain-Feingold, ruling five to four in *McConnell v. FEC* (2003) that limits on soft money contributions and limits on advertising by corporations and unions were justified by the government's interest in preventing "the actual corruption threatened by large financial contributions" (*McConnell*, 2003, p. 137). These conclusions on the need to maintain accountability over outsized monetary interests in American elections stood as the bedrock of election spending law until *Citizens United*.

THE *CITIZENS UNITED* OPINION AND POLITICAL ACCOUNTABILITY

Citizens United's constitutional challenge was argued twice before the Supreme Court. The first oral argument, which took place in 2009, largely focused on whether McCain-Feingold's requirement that Citizens United disclose its list of donors for the film infringed the group's constitutional rights to free speech. However, on the last day of the Court's 2008–2009 term the justices issued an order asking the parties to prepare a new set of briefs on a broader question: whether the Court should explicitly overturn its earlier rulings in *Austin* and *McConnell* on the differential treatment given to corporate election spending. A second oral argument would be held in an extraordinary September session – one month before the Court's official term opened. With this new question, the ultimate outcome the Court would reach seemed preordained. The Supreme Court generally is limited to answering the questions it receives; by ordering re-argument on a new, broader question of its own devising, the Court seemed to be signaling that it wanted to use this case to overturn its past rulings on campaign finance and corporate election spending.

The Court's final opinion in *Citizens United v. FEC* was announced in January 2010, just over four months after the second round of oral arguments. Writing for a five justice majority, Justice Kennedy began by noting that corporations are at their essence simply "associations of citizens" – citizens who join together for a common purpose, much like the local choral society or the town Rotary Club (*Citizens United*, 2010, p. 313). Framing corporations as a simple aggregate of individual interests, Kennedy questioned why corporate spending on speech in the form of political advertisements should be treated differently than similar spending on speech done by individual citizens. Though corporations are fictitious persons, they nevertheless can speak on behalf of the individuals who choose to join the corporation. After concluding that individual rights can flow through a corporate entity, the Court then considered whether Congress and the FEC violated First Amendment free speech rights by regulating corporate political speech. Guided by their new framework of corporate rights, the Court ultimately determined the process that the law established, which authorized the FEC to determine whether *Hillary: The Movie* or any other corporate speech is expressly advocating the election or defeat of a candidate, had created an "ongoing chill on speech" that stifled political debate and violated the First Amendment (*Citizens United*, 2010, p. 336). *McConnell, Austin,* and significant parts of the McCain-Feingold Act regulating campaign spending were now overturned. Corporations and unions could now spend unlimited sums on independent election activities.

The logic of the Court can be criticized on several grounds. At first glance, it is unclear whether there is a real First Amendment problem to solve: individuals already hold free speech rights in their individual capacity and can express political speech fully, whether in the town square or by purchasing ads, without a corporation as intermediary (Kang, 2011, p. 245). Though Kennedy does not discuss this conundrum, the tenor of the opinion advances a distinct view of American governance, one in which the focus of legal responsibility should be directed away from corporations and unions and toward government regulations inhibiting speech – in any form, by any type of speaker. Breaking with Congress' long-held judgment that the vast wealth of many corporations can distort the political process, the *Citizens United* majority instead emphasized the constitutional responsibility of Congress to allow unfettered public debate.

The Court's discussion of First Amendment free speech concerns begins by detailing the hardships corporate speakers face – hardships that center on government-mandated record-keeping obligations and reporting disclosures. Under existing federal law, corporations that want to expressly advocate for or against a specific candidate in the immediate period before an election must set up a PAC. To the Court, however, a PAC is a "burdensome alternative" to direct speech that is both "expensive" to maintain and subject to "extensive regulations" (*Citizens United*, 2010, p. 337). Notably, PACs must maintain records of their donations and "file detailed reports with the FEC" specifying the amount of money they have received from donors, as well as any loans (*Citizens United*, 2010, p. 338). These required filings ultimately create a significant burden on the ability of corporations to speak. Kennedy proposes that the FEC's reporting requirements "might explain why fewer than 2,000 of the millions of corporations in this country have PACs" (*Citizens United*, 2010, p. 338). In other words, but for the burden of filing and maintaining records, more corporations would be entering the marketplace of electoral debate.

However, there is a reason why Congress chose to require detailed records for PAC donations, and regular public filings describing their political spending. Going back to the initial 1907 reforms, the purpose of congressional policy on campaign finance had been to ensure that corporations and unions remain accountable to the public for their spending in elections, and that they not use their outsized wealth to "unfairly influence" the electoral landscape

(*Austin*, 1990, p. 660). In *Citizens United*, though, Justice Kennedy's opinion downplays this concern by focusing narrowly on corruption as a *quid pro quo* relationship between politician and donor – that is, a direct exchange of money in return for a political favor, or outright vote buying. Intentionally or not, this narrowing helps advance the expansion of corporate speech. Though the need to prevent broad forms of corruption has guided constitutional law rulings since *Buckley*, the Court sidesteps that discussion by summarily concluding that the type of corporate election spending at issue in the case simply "will not cause the electorate to lose faith in our democracy" because such spending is *independent* of candidates. Thus, even if those corporate interests receive favored access or influence, "influence over or access to elected officials" does not equate to corruption and will not harm democracy (*Citizens United*, 2010, p. 359).

Though the majority opinion casts a skeptical eye toward congressional regulation of corporate spending on political speech, Kennedy's rationale nevertheless focuses on how the increased spending from these entities can increase political accountability. Kennedy explicitly states that more money, and thus more speech, in the political marketplace will provide the best way to "hold officials accountable to the people" (*Citizens United*, 2010, p. 339). Allowing corporate and union general treasury money to be used for political advertisements will enhance the flow of political ideas in the electoral marketplace, thus providing citizens a better opportunity to reach the best decision on policy issues and ultimately create a more enlightened citizenry.

Accountability also features prominently in the Court's answer to the charge that unlimited corporate and union election spending will be harmful to democracy. "With the advent of the Internet," Kennedy noted, "prompt disclosure of expenditures can provide shareholders and citizens with the information needed to hold corporations and elected officials accountable for their positions and supporters" (*Citizens United*, 2010, p. 370). Further, disclosure of campaign contributions mean that citizens will be able to see "whether elected officials are 'in the pocket' of so-called moneyed interests" (*Citizens United*, 2010, p. 370). In other words, if voters do not like the influx of campaign cash from corporations, they will be able to use disclosure requirements to punish those politicians who accept corporate contributions or who are benefited by outside, independent corporate spending in elections.

One major concern with Kennedy's conclusion is that the accountability link between elected officials and corporate contributions is severed with *independent* expenditures. If politicians do not want to be associated with the corporate speaker's independent message, they may have little recourse to prevent the broadcast of those independent messages. In the 1988 presidential campaign, for example, George H.W. Bush's campaign reportedly was not happy with the broadcast of the infamous "Willie Horton" ad, which was produced by an independent political group attempting to defeat the Democratic nominee Michael Dukakis (Meacham, 2015, pp. 341–42). The ad proved to be highly toxic, and was only shown a few times. Still, the Bush campaign was (and still is) tainted by the ad's implicit racism.

The majority opinion spurred a strong dissent, one that was equally focused on the connection between large corporate spending and political accountability. Writing for the four-justice minority, Justice John Paul Stevens emphasized the considerable dangers of unlimited speech by corporate and union interests in a participatory democracy – including corruption, bribery, and a lowering of trust in government. In fact, there are good reasons why Congress chose to differentiate corporations from individual citizens for electoral spending. Corporations are a legal fiction, an entity established to create economic efficiencies. Yet, because they are legal fictions, corporations also have natural limits in an electoral democracy. As both Sanford Schane (1987, p. 563) and Justice Stevens note, a corporation cannot vote, cannot run for office, and cannot go to prison for criminal misdoings. This leads to an inherent political accountability gap that necessitates regulation: a corporation could be used by its members to commit misdoings in the electoral or political process, yet the corporation itself cannot lose its liberty – the ultimate price individuals in society pay when they commit criminal acts. Shareholders in a corporation also gain legal limitations on their own liability for corporate acts, which could make corporate spending the preferred vehicle for stretching the bounds of political access. Similarly, the generic corporate form can be used to obscure, or hide, the spending done by the wealthiest members of society, while also providing them with outsized access to the marketplace of ideas.

Thus, the majority and dissent in *Citizens United* represent two different visions of political accountability. Justice Kennedy fuses the rights of individuals together with their corporations in a philosophical argument to provide increased public debate on policy choices, while Justice Stevens focuses more on the history of campaign abuse and distrust of government when corporate entities are given carte blanche to spend money to influence elections. And while Kennedy's majority opinion places faith in the ability of corporations to respond to the public's needs, Stevens emphasizes the need to defer to the informed choice made by the people's own representatives. Which vision has won out since 2010?

POST-*CITIZENS UNITED*: THE FALL OF CONTRIBUTION LIMITS

In fact, only weeks after the *Citizens United* decision, the DC Circuit Court of Appeals applied the principles of *Citizens United* in another campaign spending case, *SpeechNow.org v. FEC* (2010), which ultimately would pave the way for the establishment of the entity now known as the "Super PAC." SpeechNow.org was founded by David Keating, who at the time also was the Executive Director of the Club for Growth, a conservative free market organization that consistently has been one of the top outside spenders in national elections (Center for Responsive Politics, 2017). Because SpeechNow.org sought to campaign for and against certain political candidates, the FEC had determined the group to be a "political committee" under federal election law. This determination meant the group would be subject to limits on the amount of political contributions it could receive from any one individual – $5,000 per donor in any calendar year. SpeechNow's legal case challenged the principle that limited the amount of campaign donations to groups (like them) that try to *independently* influence elections.

Ruling just ten weeks after *Citizens United*, the DC Circuit Court determined that the free speech principles laid out in *Citizens United* meant the FEC could no longer impose limits on contributions to independent electoral groups like SpeechNow.org. Instead, campaign donors would now be able to give unlimited sums of money to these outside political organizations. In addition, the court also struck down the $69,900 aggregate limit on individual donations in any given year. SpeechNow also asked that because it was only planning to make independent expenditures, it be free of any obligation to provide a record of the names of its donors, though the DC Circuit rejected this second claim. The Supreme Court did not grant a writ of certiorari to the case on appeal, which left the elimination of limits on monetary contributions to independent political organizations as the default standard nationwide.

Within just a few weeks, the combination of *Citizens United* and *SpeechNow* dramatically altered the landscape of election spending. First, the Supreme Court determined corporations hold the same First Amendment rights that individuals have, allowing corporations the right to spend unlimited amounts of money directly from their general accounts (not their heavily regulated PAC accounts) to seek the election or defeat of specific candidates. Second, the DC Circuit Court applied the principles of *Citizens United* in a way that obliterated the long-standing distinction between contributions, which Congress can regulate, and political expenditures, which have had some amount of constitutional protection since *Buckley*. After *SpeechNow*, independent political advocacy organizations, including PACs, could begin to take in unlimited amounts of money from individuals and corporations to broadcast their message. The immediate result of this confluence was the introduction of the Super PAC, a new form of outside political spending organization that could accept unlimited amounts of money from private individuals, corporations, and other organizations.

Soon, Super PACs began to dominate the political world. Though these entities are, under the *SpeechNow* and *Citizens United* rules, prohibited from directly coordinating with individual candidates, it quickly became apparent that the views advanced by many Super PACs were virtual carbon copies of the specific candidates they (indirectly) support. The practical reality has been close (but not official) coordination between the messages of candidates and the Super PACs that back them, generally led by former intimates of the candidate running for office. In the 2012 presidential election season, the "Restore Our Future" Super PAC, a group founded in 2011 by several of Mitt Romney's former staffers, openly backed the Romney campaign, spending over $140 million on ads that both advanced the Romney agenda and criticized President Obama's policies (Eggen & Cillizza, 2011). Similarly, the "Priorities Action USA" Super PAC, cofounded in 2011 by former Obama staffer Bill Burton, spent over $65 million in the 2012 campaign against Romney. These sums of money raised and spent have not abated over time. During the first six months of 2015 alone, the "Right to Rise USA" Super PAC associated with Jeb Bush raised over $100 million, and spent nearly $84 million on pro-Bush advertising (Center for Responsive Politics, 2017). Overall, independent election expenditures have increased exponentially since *Citizens United*, from $143 million in spending during 2008 to $1.4 billion during the 2016 calendar year (Center for Responsive Politics, n.d.-a).

Super PACs also are required to provide disclosure of their donors to the FEC, though, much like Justice Stevens predicted, current rules make hiding donations quite easy. Super PACs can accept unlimited funds from limited liability corporations (LLCs), nonprofit corporations, and other associations, so individual donors who wish to remain anonymous can now simply establish a nonspecific, generic-sounding organization or LLC and contribute unlimited sums to Super PACs through that organization.

The close ties between candidates and the ostensibly independent Super PACs that back them belie the notion advanced in *Citizens United* that, because outside spending is independent of candidates, it cannot lead to the perception of corruption or lead to a lack of faith in our democracy. The deleterious effects of close coordination between large, often anonymous election ad spending and political position-taking can be seen in the general public: a 2012 survey conducted by the Brennan Center for Justice found 69% of respondents believed that allowing unlimited monetary donations will lead to increased corruption in government (Brennan Center, 2012). Further, the same study found 77% believed that big donors are favored over the interests of the general public in matters of public policy. In short, the American public does not share the belief animating *Citizens United* that independent electoral spending cannot corrupt officials.

Oddly, this faith in the incorruptibility of elected actors from outside spending was not even held by the Supreme Court in the year before *Citizens United*. In a case decided just before *Citizens United* was heard, the Court determined that one individual's outside – and outsized – expenditures in a judicial election could lead to a "serious risk" of actual bias in the courtroom. In that case, *Caperton v. Massey* (2009), Justice Kennedy wrote for the Court majority that the $3 million spent by Massey Coal CEO Don Blankenship to help elect a candidate running for a seat on the West Virginia State Supreme Court of Appeals did give rise to a serious risk of judicial bias. Blankenship's spending, which occurred almost exclusively through his independent political action committee, represented well over half of all spending in the judicial race, and came at a time when his company was appealing a $50 million contract dispute with Hugh Caperton to the state supreme court.

With Justice Kennedy writing the majority opinion, the Supreme Court determined that the vast sums of money Blankenship spent created "a serious risk of actual bias" in the legal process that violated Caperton's guarantees of fairness under the Constitution's Due Process Clause (*Caperton*, 2009, p. 1222). Further, Blankenship's effort to swing the election toward his favored candidate had a "significant and disproportionate influence" on the election outcome that could undercut the ability of citizens to believe that their legal system is fair and impartial (*Ibid.*).

Ultimately, the opportunity to extend *Caperton* was not taken just one year later. Kennedy noted differences in the remedy sought in each case: a recusal in *Caperton*, an injunction to permit speech in *Citizens United*. Still, at their core both cases involved attempts by outside actors to explicitly advocate for the election or removal of specific candidates. In the judicial elections context, the Court found the potential for harm, while in the executive and legislative electoral setting the principle that corporations can enhance democratic responsiveness prevailed.

THE RISE OF DARK MONEY

The path created by the *Citizens United* majority did not stop at the Super PAC. With *Citizens United* opening up corporate spending, and *SpeechNow.org* allowing unlimited contributions from corporations, unions, and individuals to independent groups, the next step for many political organizations was the search to keep the names of donors away from public disclosure – to keep the money that was flowing in hidden, or "dark." Because, despite their legal victories in the areas of campaign contributions and spending, both SpeechNow.org and Citizens United ultimately failed to gain court rulings allowing them to keep their donor lists away from the public eye.

In this search to avoid public disclosure of donations and spending, political groups began to discover the benefits provided by section 501(c)(4) of the IRS tax code, which provides tax-exempt status to "social welfare" organizations. Under the U.S. tax code, these social welfare organizations are provided with tax-exempt status if they are organized as not-for-profit and are "operated exclusively for the promotion of social welfare" (26 U.S.C. § 501). Thus, these groups cannot make political campaigning their primary activity (Internal Revenue Service, 2016). However, they are conferred an important benefit outside of tax exemption: unlike PACs and Super PACs, the list of donors to the organization *does not need to be made public*. Before *Citizens United*, 501(c)(4) status was generally reserved for civic organizations like the local Rotary Club or the Lions Club. Post-*Citizens United*, the number of organizations seeking 501(c)(4) status dramatically increased, with the IRS receiving nearly double the number of applications in 2012 as compared to 2010 (Dowling & Miller, 2014, p. 50).

Recognizing the ambiguity in what a "social welfare" organization is, major political fundraising organizations sought 501(c)(4) status, including Crossroads GPS, run by former Bush administration advisor Karl Rove, and Organizing for Action, the former fundraising arm of President Obama's 2012 reelection campaign (Sullivan, 2013). The rise of the 501(c)(4) and "dark money" had an immediate impact on the electoral landscape. The 100 highest spending nonprofit 501(c)(4)s spent nearly $95 million in 2010 alone, nearly

50% more than Super PACs spent during that same time (Beckel, 2012). In the 2016 election year, dark money groups spent nearly $184 million (Center for Responsive Politics, n.d.). Crossroads GPS provides an apt example of the new face of social welfare organizations post-*Citizens United*: when the organization was approved as a 501(c)(4) in February 2016, Crossroads had already reported donations of $330 million, while spending over $110 million on political activities (Gold, 2016).

The trend toward dark money continued into the 2016 presidential campaign. The 45Committee, a major 501(c)(4) operated by conservative activist and Chicago Cubs co-owner Todd Ricketts, provides a good illustration of the opacity of the dark money operations. Because it was designated a 501(c)(4), it was still not apparent by the end of the 2016 calendar year how much the organization has raised or spent, or who had contributed to the organization. It also was unclear who provided the funds for each organization's ad purchases and other political speech. In fact, a *Politico* story in late September 2016 stated that Ricketts was promoting the group to megadonors for its ability to "accept unlimited checks while keeping its donors' names secret" – a feature apparently attractive to many large donors because, according to the author's source in the fundraising world, "it's embarrassing to support Trump" (Vogel, 2016).

As the 2012 to 2016 election seasons show, the rise of dark money has led to a real erosion in the public's accountability over electoral spending. Recognizing the perception that money buys access, our campaign laws were created with an express purpose of requiring individuals to limit the amount of money individuals and entities can donate, and to require disclosure of contributions they make to candidates running for elected office. This disclosure allows the public to know, among other things, who is providing money to each candidate, and who is funding political advertisements and candidate statements. Thus, disclosure provides an assurance that corruption and access purchasing can potentially be monitored and detected. However, the system of campaign spending that originated with *Citizens United* has created a new political world in which 501(c)(4)s can keep donors and monetary contributions completely private, and Super PACs can take in unlimited contributions from shell companies that keep donors names undisclosed. Ultimately, citizens no longer know with certainty which individuals or associations are spending money to elect or defeat candidates, and how much they are spending. The waters of campaign spending, which were not entirely clear before *Citizens United*, are now a morass of unknown groups and unclear motives.

MAINTAINING PUBLIC ACCOUNTABILITY

Finally, it is worth considering how the Court's *Citizens United* opinion shifted the locus of decision making on election spending away from our elected actors in Congress and toward a series of nonelected actors – interest groups, the courts, and independent agencies of government.

One aftereffect of *Citizens United* was a flood of new constitutional litigation by groups seeking to expand the boundaries of the Court's new rule on corporate campaign spending. Soon, state laws that had limited corporate spending in elections were challenged and struck down (see *American Tradition Partnership v. Bullock*, 2012; *Free Enterprise Club's PAC v. Bennett*, 2011). Next came challenges to federal laws that set aggregate limits on individual campaign contributions. Following *SpeechNow.org*, the Court struck down these individual contribution limits in *McCutcheon v. FEC* (2014), allowing citizens to contribute money directly to an unlimited number of political campaigns, without being restricted by an overall spending cap. However, each new expansion of First Amendment political spending rights by the Supreme Court comes at a cost for democratic responsiveness, as those rulings foreclose any future action by Congress in that area. For example, a new law setting an aggregate limit on campaign contributions would almost surely fail, as the Court has constitutionalized the ability to contribute to an unlimited number of political campaigns. In addition, with each successive court ruling, the avenues through which the public can maintain accountability over electoral spending through their elected officials become narrower.

After *Citizens United*, the FEC assumed a more limited role in monitoring violations of election advocacy laws. Yet, with the rise of the Super PAC, the FEC took an even more prominent role in policing the boundary between independent and coordinated actions by outside groups. Similarly, the IRS was forced to determine whether thousands of new 501(c)(4) organizations were legitimate "social welfare" organizations or not. The resulting IRS plan, in which groups that described themselves with certain political phrases (like "tea party" or "We the People") were singled out for strict review, led to mass condemnation of the agency (Department of Treasury, 2013). Yet, whether it was foreseen or not by the DC Circuit, after *SpeechNow.org* the responsibility for making politically charged determinations in an evolving, still murky area of electoral campaigning was delegated to civil servants in our tax agency.

Thus, the over-judicialization of campaign finance has led to distinct accountability problems over public policy. After all, voters do not elect the

Supreme Court, not do they elect our independent oversight agencies; and while both gained power after *Citizens United*, they remain the least accountable of actors in government to the people for the choices they make. In fact, opinion polls since 2010 have consistently shown the public's desire to overturn *Citizens United*, yet the Court's response has only been to further open the tap for corporate and other outside political spending (Stohr, 2015). The result is particularly unfortunate in that congressional action to limit campaign contributions and electoral spending is arguably among the most selfless acts that members of Congress can make. They are, after all, the primary beneficiaries, directly or indirectly, of campaign spending, with incumbent elected officials the recipient of most campaign contributions. In 2008, the last election year before *Citizens United*, incumbents in both the House and Senate raised nearly three times as much money as challengers.

THE PROMISE FOR THE FUTURE: PROMOTING DISCLOSURE

Despite the onset of unlimited donations by often-anonymous donors, hope remains for increasing political accountability after *Citizens United*. Despite the practical outcome of *SpeechNow.org*, the Supreme Court has continued to promote the concept of disclosure as an antidote to corruption. Importantly, both SpeechNow.org and Citizens United lost their legal challenges to prevent the public from knowing any information about their donors. And in other recent cases, the Court has preserved the importance of public disclosures in campaigning and elections. In *Doe v. Reed* (2010), for example, an eight-Justice majority upheld the state of Washington's law requiring public disclosure of signed petitions. In that case, a group that sought to overturn the state's same-sex partner benefits law by ballot initiative also sought to keep their signatures out of public view. The Court determined the benefits of disclosure – protecting the integrity and reliability of the ballot initiative process – outweighed the speculative harm the petition signers might face from co-workers and neighbors knowing the signers were not supportive of rights for same-sex couples.

Similarly, in June 2016 the Court let stand a Delaware law requiring any organization producing election advertisements to disclose their donors. Though Justice Thomas's written dissent from the denial of certiorari called on the Court to reexamine the "harms" from monetary transparency laws that "justify eliminating disclosure requirements altogether" as a matter of constitutional law, only one other Justice (Samuel Alito) would have granted cert. (*Delaware Strong Families v. Denn*, 2016, p. 3).

Other efforts have focused on requiring disclosure of all shareholders in the corporation, or all shareholders who have donated money, as a way to ensure that foreign nationals are not among the donor pool. As FEC Commissioner Ellen Weintraub (2016) noted, foreign nationals have long been prohibited from donating to U.S. election campaigns. Justice Kennedy's opinion derived the corporate right to speech as a product of the associational rights of the corporation's individual members. Yet foreign nationals have no such right to speak given by our Constitution.

Shareholders of publicly traded corporations also can file shareholder resolutions to require disclosure of political donations and spending. The Center for Political Accountability has taken the lead in initiating political disclosure resolutions at annual shareholder meetings, which has led 305 companies (including more than half of the S&P 100) to publicly disclose their political spending in annual filings. These are excellent steps to improve disclosure and accountability, though this strategy cannot address the issue of the many nonpublic corporations, such as LLCs and nonprofit corporations like Citizens United, that are incorporated largely or solely to facilitate political spending.

Finally, the Supreme Court recently was forced to revisit its conclusions on political contributions and the perception of official corruption in a case involving state judicial elections. Florida judicial ethics rules bar candidates running for judicial office from personally soliciting funds – a rule that was challenged on the basis that it restricted core political speech. In *Williams-Yulee v. The Florida Bar* (2015), the Court determined that the First Amendment does not protect candidates for judicial office who seek to personally solicit campaign funds from donors. In this circumstance, the countervailing governmental interest in maintaining the integrity and neutrality of the judicial system was found to be compelling enough to prevent judicial candidates from engaging in this type of campaign fundraising. Noting that "the role of the judge differs from the role of politicians," Chief Justice Roberts concluded for the Court that such campaigning would harm "public confidence in the integrity of the judiciary" (*Williams-Yulee*, 2015, p. 12). Yet the rationale that "judges are not politicians" is questionable given the context of the case: if the executive, legislative, and judicial branches all are elected by the people, then candidates for judicial office should be no different from other elected office seekers. Thus, the public confidence argument developed in *Caperton* and extended in *Williams-Yulee* could be further extended to install greater regulation of campaign contributions and spending in all elections. With the Supreme Court taking the issue of campaign spending away from our elected actors in government, ultimately it will be up to the Court to reintroduce governmental regulation of political contributions and electoral spending.

REFERENCES

Beckel, M. (2012). Nonprofits outspent Super PACs in 2010. *Center for Responsive Politics.* Retrieved from http://www.opensecrets.org/news/2012/06/nonprofits-outspent-super-pacs-in-2

Brennan Center for Justice. (2012). *National survey: Super PACs, corruption, and democracy.* Retrieved from https://www.brennancenter.org/analysis/national-survey-super-pacs-corruption-and-democracy

Center for Political Accountability. (n.d.). Our impact. Retrieved from http://politicalaccountability.net/impact

Center for Responsive Politics. (n.d.-a). Outside spending. Retrieved from http://www.opensecrets.org/outsidespending/

Center for Responsive Politics. (n.d.-b). Dark money. Retrieved from http://www.opensecrets.org/darkmoney/

Center for Responsive Politics. (2017). 2016 outside spending, by Super PAC. Retrieved from http://www.opensecrets.org/outsidespending/summ.php?chrt=V&type=S

Coyle, M. (2013). *The Roberts Court.* New York, NY: Simon & Schuster.

Department of Treasury. (2013). Inappropriate criteria were used to identify tax-exempt applications for review. Retrieved from http://www.treasury/gov/tigta/auditreports/2013reports/201310053fr.html

Dowling, C., & Miller, M. (2014). *Super PAC! Money, elections, and voters after* Citizens United. Abingdon, UK: Routledge.

Eggen, D., & Cillizza, C. (2011, June 23). Romney backers start "Super PAC." *Washington Post.* Retrieved from https://www.washingtonpost.com/politics/romney-backers-launch-super-pac/2011/06/22

Federal Election Commission. (2004, October). Record, (30), 1–20.

Gold, M. (2016, February 9). IRS approves tax-exempt status of Crossroads GPS after more than five years. *Washington Post.* Retrieved from https://www.washingtonpost.com/news/post-politics/wp/2016/02/09/irs-approves-tax-exempt-status-of-crossroads-gps-after-more-than-five-years

Internal Revenue Code, 26 U.S.C. § 501 (2012).

Internal Revenue Service (2016). Political activity and social welfare. Retrieved from https://www.irs.gov/charities-non-profits/other-non-profits/political-activity-and-social-welfare

Kang, M. (2011). After *Citizens United. Indiana Law Review, 44,* 243–254.

Meacham, J. (2015). *Destiny and power: The American odyssey of George Herbert Walker Bush.* New York, NY: Random House.

Roosevelt, T. (1892, July). Political assessments in the coming campaign. *The Atlantic Monthly,* 103–105.

Sabato, L. (1984). *PAC power: Inside the world of political action committees.* New York, NY: W.W. Norton.

Schane, S. (1987). The corporation is a person: The language of a legal fiction. *Tulane Law Review, 61,* 563–609.

Schmitter, P., & Karl, T. (1990). What democracy is ... and is not. *Journal of Democracy, 2*(3), 75–88.

Stohr, G. (2015, September 28). Americans want Supreme Court to turn off political spending spigot. *Bloomberg.* Retrieved from https://www.bloomberg.com/politics/articles/2015-09-28/bloomberg-poll-americans-want-supreme-court-to-turn-off-political-spending-spigot

Sullivan, S. (2013, May 13). What is a 501(c)(4), anyway? *Washington Post.* Retrieved from https://www.washingtonpost.com/news/the-fix/wp/2013/05/13/what-is-a-501c4-anyway

Vogel, K. (2016, September 28). Secret money to boost Trump. *Politico.* Retrieved from http://www.politico.com/story/2016/09/secret-money-to-boost-trump-228817.

Weintraub, E. (2016, March 30). Taking on *Citizens United. New York Times,* p. A21.

COURT CASES

Austin v. Michigan State Chamber of Commerce, 494 U.S. 652 (1990).

American Tradition Partnership, Inc. v. Bullock, 132 S. Ct. 1307 (2012).

Buckley v. Valeo, 424 U.S. 1 (1976).

Caperton v. Massey, 556 U.S. 868 (2009).

Citizens United v. FEC, 558 U.S. 310 (2010).

Delaware Strong Families v. Denn, 579 U. S. ___ (2016).

Doe v. Reed, 561 U.S. 186 (2010).

Free Enterprise Club's PAC v. Bennett, 564 U.S. 721 (2011).

McConnell v. FEC, 540 U.S. 93 (2003).

McCutcheon v. FEC, 572 U.S. ___ (2014).

SpeechNow.org v. FEC, 599 F.3d. 686 (D.C. Cir. 2010).

Williams-Yulee v. The Florida Bar, 575 U.S. ___ (2015).

CHAPTER 11

JUDICIAL REVIEW

Elizabeth Erin Wheat

ABSTRACT

Under the doctrine of judicial review established by Marbury v. Madison
*(1803) and the Administrative Procedure Act (APA), courts retain the
power and authority to review legislative and executive actions and rule on
their constitutionality or legality. Courts may also review actions of judges
and lower court decisions. This is an important and necessary action to
maintain the checks and balances and separation of powers in the United
States (U.S.) political system. It is also critical for providing legal oversight and accountability. This chapter will first look at judicial review
historically including relevant statutes and cases, actions by the executive
branch, and efforts by Congress.*

*Additionally, the chapter will examine the relationship between judicial
review and public policy. Through laws passed by Congress or regulations
enacted by federal agencies, these branches of government draft policies
with the expectation the judicial branch will enforce them. The courts,
however, are to uphold the Constitution first and foremost, and rule on
the constitutionality of the laws and regulations. Judicial opinions can
have the effect of creating policy, which is a different purpose than the
Founding Fathers intended. After reviewing the court system, the chapter*

Corruption, Accountability and Discretion
Public Policy and Governance, 205–225
Copyright © 2017 by Emerald Publishing Limited
doi:10.1108/S2053-769720170000029012

will examine several issue areas where the court has been shaped by and in turn influenced public policy.

Keywords: Agency; courts; discretion; judicial review; oversight

INTRODUCTION

When the Founding Fathers drafted the Constitution, more attention was paid to Congress and to the executive than to the courts. The system of checks and balances in the Constitution was crafted in a way to give Americans a voice in policy through equal representation in the Senate and proportional representation in the House based on a state's population. Having fought for freedom from the British crown, the framers were wary of concentrating power in a single government leader. The expectation was that Congress, through the House and Senate, would be able to check any abuses of power by the president. The courts were to simply interpret the laws.

In Federalist No. 78, Alexander Hamilton wrote about the structure of the federal judiciary and its powers, or lack thereof. He characterized the judicial branch as the least dangerous branch because it had "no influence over either the sword or the purse…it may truly be said to have neither FORCE nor WILL, but merely judgment." Hamilton quotes Montesquieu who said, "Of the three powers […] the judiciary is next to nothing" (Bickel, 1986). This is the most cited of the Federalist Papers by U.S. Supreme Court justices (Coenen, 2007).

Federalist No. 78 also discusses judicial review. From Hamilton's perspective, the judiciary should evaluate whether laws passed by Congress are constitutional and in the event of a conflict between a state/federal law and the Constitution, the Constitution remains supreme. "The interpretation of the laws is the proper and peculiar province of the courts. A constitution is, in fact, and must be regarded by the judges, as a fundamental law. It therefore belongs to them to ascertain its meaning, as well as the meaning of any particular act proceeding from the legislative body" (Project Gutenberg, 2017). This was an essential safeguard to prevent abuses of power by Congress. "… It is far more rational to suppose, that the courts were designed to be an intermediate body between the people and the legislature, in order, among other things, to keep the latter within the limits assigned to their authority" (Project Gutenberg, 2017).

A debate between the Federalists, of which Hamilton was a part, and the Anti-Federalists was over the independence of federal judges and the ability of the legislature to review judicial decisions. The English system supported by the Anti-Federalists allowed Parliament to overturn decisions made by judges whereas Hamilton and the Federalists argued judges should be independent. He wrote:

> But it is not with a view to infractions of the Constitution only, that the independence of the judges may be an essential safeguard against the effects of occasional ill humors in the society. These sometimes extend no farther than to the injury of the private rights of particular classes of citizens, by unjust and partial laws. Here also the firmness of the judicial magistracy is of vast importance in mitigating the severity and confining the operation of such laws. It not only serves to moderate the immediate mischiefs of those which may have been passed, but it operates as a check upon the legislative body in passing them; who, perceiving that obstacles to the success of iniquitous intention are to be expected from the scruples of the courts, are in a manner compelled, by the very motives of the injustice they meditate, to qualify their attempts. This is a circumstance calculated to have more influence upon the character of our governments, than but few may be aware of (Project Gutenberg, 2017).

Marbury v. Madison (1803)

In 1803, the Supreme Court issued its opinion in *Marbury v. Madison*. This decision established judicial review—the power to declare an act of Congress unconstitutional (Foner & Garraty, 1991). The case originated in the remaining days of the Adams administration when he appointed William Marbury as justice of the peace for the District of Columbia. Adams' successor, Thomas Jefferson, ordered his new Secretary of State James Madison to not deliver the commission to Marbury and several other appointees. Three of the appointees joined Marbury when he petitioned for a writ of mandamus which "is an order from a court to an inferior government official ordering the government official to properly fulfill their official duties or correct an abuse of discretion" (Cornell University Law School, 2017e). If Marbury received the writ, John Marshall, appointed by Adams to the Supreme Court, would be required to deliver the Senate-approved commissions.

Based on the Judiciary Act of 1789, Congress gave the Supreme Court original jurisdiction beyond what Article III of the Constitution provided. Section 13 of the Judiciary Act allowed Marbury to file his writ and it was this statute that Chief Justice John Marshall had to rule on in the case (Haas, 2017). In the majority opinion, Marshall writes Marbury did have a legal right and was entitled to the commission. However, he states that Congress exceeded its authority when it granted the Supreme Court original jurisdiction for writs of mandamus in these kinds of situations. Marshall rules the Judiciary Act unconstitutional and wrote:

> The authority, therefore, given to the supreme court, by the act establishing the judicial courts of the United States, to issue writs of mandamus to public officers, appears not to be warranted by the constitution...

> It is emphatically the province and duty of the judicial department to say what the law is. Those who apply the rule to particular cases, must of necessity expound and interpret the rule. If two laws conflict with each other the courts must decide on the operation of each (*Marbury v. Madison*, 1803).

Marbury does not receive his commission and by declaring the Judiciary Act unconstitutional, the Supreme Court stated its right to judicial review. When the Supreme Court released the opinion, President Jefferson expressed his strong disapproval on several occasions. In a letter to Spencer Roane in 1819, Jefferson wrote, "If this opinion be sound, then indeed is our Constitution a complete *felo de se* [act of suicide] ... The Constitution on this hypothesis is a mere thing of wax in the hands of the judiciary, which they may twist and shape into any form they please" (Jefferson, 1819). To Congressman Nathaniel Macon he wrote:

> [How] to check these unconstitutional invasions of ... rights by the Federal judiciary? Not by impeachment in the first instance, but by a strong protestation of both houses of Congress that such and such doctrines advanced by the Supreme Court are contrary to the Constitution; and if afterwards they relapse into the same heresies, impeach and set the whole adrift. For what was the government divided into three branches, but that each should watch over the others and oppose their usurpations? (Jefferson, 1821).

One year before his death, Jefferson wrote to Edward Livingston, "This member of the Government [the federal judiciary] was at first considered as the most harmless and helpless of all its organs. [See, for example, Federalist 78.] But it has proved that the power of declaring what the law is, *ad libitum*, by sapping and mining slyly and without alarm the foundations of the Constitution, can do what open force would not dare to attempt" (Jefferson, 1825).

Since *Marbury*, judicial review remains controversial with the court taking an active role in interpreting a policy's constitutionality and also declaring what laws and policies it can review. If the court is able to say what laws passed by Congress are constitutional, then it can heavily influence which laws become policy and which ones do not. Congress and the executive branch retain the authority to enact new laws and overturn decisions by the judicial branch. As the next section illustrates with segregation cases, the court shaped policy by upholding "separate but equal" while later assisting with desegregation by ordering integration of public schools and transportation. The next section will review cases such as these expanding judicial review followed by examples of the courts exercising this power over Congress and the executive.

JUDICIAL REVIEW PRECEDENTS

Following *Marbury*, courts have built on judicial review, expanding it to state or civil cases if the case arises under a federal or constitutional law (*Martin v. Hunter's Lessee*, 1816), expanding it to state criminal cases (*Cohens v. Virginia*, 1821), and extending review to actions by the state, executive, judicial, or legislature if they are unconstitutional (*Cooper v. Aaron*, 1958) (Haas, 2017). The impact of *Marbury* and the other cases expanding judicial review can be observed in education law, civil liberties and rights, free speech, criminal law, and others. A few cases will be highlighted here.

There are a series of cases involving judicial review of race-related state and federal laws. After the Emancipation Proclamation of 1863 and Northern victory in the Civil War, Congress became deeply divided over Reconstruction policies. When Reconstruction officially ended in 1877, white-dominated Southern state legislatures enacted laws to disenfranchise blacks through Jim Crow policies, making the de facto segregation into de jure segregation. This occurred in situations such as school, movie theaters, transportation, housing, and even drinking fountains. *Plessy v. Ferguson* (1896) upheld a state law in Louisiana mandating "equal but separate" railway cars for blacks and whites. The 7-1 opinion issued by the Supreme Court argued state law violated neither the privileges and immunities clause nor the equal protection clause of the Fourteenth Amendment, thus establishing the "separate but equal" legal policy and practice of segregation (*Plessy v. Ferguson*, 1896). The policy implication of this decision was the legalization of segregation in the United States. In *Brown v. Board of Education of Topeka* (1954), the Supreme Court struck down the "separate but equal" law for public education because it violated the equal protection clause of the Fourteenth Amendment. In the unanimous opinion, the justices held that "separate but equal" facilities were inherently unequal and that the segregation of public education created a sense of inferiority among African-American children that could have long-lasting impacts (*Brown v. Board of Education of Topeka*,

1954). In 1967, the court heard *Loving v. Virginia* and ruled on the constitutionality of a Virginia state law prohibiting interracial marriage. In a unanimous opinion, the justices held the state law unconstitutional under the due process clause of the Fourteenth Amendment and said it had no legitimate purpose "independent of invidious racial discrimination" (*Loving v. Virginia*, 1967). The Supreme Court heard another significant race in education case in 1978 with the *Regents of the University of California v. Bakke* decision. Allan Bakke, a 32-year-old white man, was repeatedly rejected from medical school at UC-Davis and challenged the university's affirmative action that required sixteen spots be held for qualified minority students. Though there was no majority opinion, the court ordered Bakke's admission to law school. Four justices held the university use of strict racial quotas violated the Fourteenth Amendment while four different justices held it was constitutional to use race as one of several factors in the admissions process (*Regents of the University of California v. Bakke*, 1978).

In response to these rulings from the judicial branch, Congress and the executive branch responded with the Civil Rights Acts of 1957, 1960, 1964, 1968, 1991, and 2004 prohibiting different forms of discrimination; Executive Order 11246 in 1965 establishing affirmative action for government contractors; Executive Order 12898 in 1994 calling for addressing environmental justice issues in minority and low-income communities; the Voting Rights Act of 1965 prohibiting racial discrimination in voting; and the Fair Housing Act of 1968 prohibiting housing discrimination (Congress on Racial Equality, 2014). Additional cases challenging these laws were brought back before the courts by states, individuals, and organizations such as the NAACP, illustrating the continuously evolving relationship of judicial review and policymaking.

Judicial review has also been used in criminal law. In the first application of the "exclusionary rule" which prohibits the use of evidence obtained in violation of the Constitution, the Supreme Court reviewed whether police actions violated this rule in a search and seizure case (Cornell University Law School, 2017a). The unanimous opinion in *Weeks v. United States* (1914) held that the police search of Weeks' home, seizure of his private property without a search warrant, then the use of this evidence against Weeks, violated Fourth Amendment protections (*Weeks v. United States*, 1914). Following the *Gideon v. Wainwright* (1963) decision, individuals charged with a felony who cannot afford an attorney in criminal cases must be provided one by the state. Florida state law at the time only had to provide counsel for defendants charged with capital crimes and this case extended Sixth Amendment protections to felony defendants in state courts (*Gideon v. Wainwright*, 1963). Another landmark ruling of judicial review in a criminal case is *Miranda v. Arizona* (1966).

Ernesto Miranda was arrested and questioned about his involvement in a rape and kidnapping. After hours of questioning and multiple interrogation techniques, Miranda confessed. His attorney argued, and the police admitted, that Miranda had not been advised of his Fifth Amendment right from self-incrimination. The constitutional question for the court to answer was whether Fifth Amendment protections extended to police interrogation of suspects. In a 5-4 opinion, the Supreme Court held Miranda's constitutional rights had been violated and statements obtained in this manner could not be used against an individual at trial. From this case, the "Miranda rights" to remain silent, any statements made can be used against an individual, and the right to an attorney must be explained to a suspect and the suspect has the option to waive those rights or exercise them and stop all police questioning until counsel arrives (*Miranda v. Arizona*, 1966).

With these criminal cases, similar to the race-related ones above, the courts enacted policies to hold police accountable and preserve constitutional due process of the law. They also attempted to standardize treatment of suspected criminals throughout the country, so a citizen in one state would have the same rights as a citizen in another. Supreme Court precedents apply to every state meaning that once they issue a majority decision, it becomes the law of the land unless overturned by Congress or the President. This is a powerful tool in shaping public policy and improving accountability among law enforcement and administration.

JUDICIAL REVIEW IN STATUTES: THE ADMINISTRATIVE PROCEDURE ACT AND THE NATIONAL ENVIRONMENTAL POLICY ACT

The Administrative Procedure Act (APA)

The APA explains the rules and procedures federal agencies must follow including how they develop, publish, and implement policy. Passed in 1946, the APA governs agency decision-making, divides actions into rules and orders published in the *Federal Register*, specifies procedures agencies must follow, and gives a standard for judicial review of agency action (U.S. Government, 2017).

Judicial review under the APA (5 U.S.C. 7, §701–706) has three standards: substantial evidence, arbitrary and capricious, and statutory interpretation (Cornell University Law School, 2017b). Under §706, courts can review a challenge to final agency action, review a non-discretionary action, a case where other administrative remedies have been exhausted, and if a case is ripe for review (Cornell University Law School, 2017c). When applying the arbitrary and capricious standard, courts will look at whether the agency relied on factors Congress did not intend for it to consider (statutory interpretation), if the agency failed to consider a key aspect of the problem, if the agency action was unreasonably delayed or unlawfully withheld, if the agency offered an explanation that runs counter to the evidence in the record, and if the rule is so implausible it could not be explained by a difference in view or by agency expertise (Cornell University Law School, 2017d). If the court decides an agency failed part of the review or made an error, the court can set aside or vacate the rule until the agency corrects the action.

One landmark case where judicial review of agency action was conducted is *Chevron v. the Natural Resources Defense Council (NRDC)* (*Chevron v. NRDC*, 1984). This case established the precedent of agency deference and the "Chevron two-step." In *Chevron*, the EPA developed a rule under the Clean Air Act (CAA) to implement permit requirements allowing states to adopt a plant-wide definition of the term "stationary source," known as the bubble concept of net emissions. This would allow a plant to modify or replace a piece of equipment without getting a new permit if overall plant emissions did not increase. The NRDC and other environmental groups challenged this rule arguing it ran counter to the intent and purpose of the CAA. The D.C. Circuit Court of Appeals set aside the regulation as inappropriate for an agency, but the Supreme Court overturned the verdict in a unanimous ruling. Justice John Paul Stevens wrote the opinion and created a two-step process for evaluating agency interpretations that occurred in rulemaking and formal adjudications. In the first step, a court must ask if the statute in question is clear. If it is, then the court must apply the statute. If it is not, then the court proceeds to the second step of asking if the agency interpretation of the statute is "permissible" or reasonable. If their interpretation is reasonable, then the court must defer to the agency's decision because they are the experts in the situation. In *Chevron*, Justice Stevens and the majority felt the agency's interpretation was reasonable and thus upheld the rule. This case became an important precedent for the courts when reviewing agency action.

Chevron became an important precedent for the courts when hearing cases involving agency decision-making. By calling for deference to the agencies, the *Chevron* court emphasized its preference for policies written by these agencies as experts in the policy area. The case made it more difficult for parties challenging an agency rule or regulation on substantive grounds. It also made statutes passed by Congress or Executive Orders issued by a president more important because these set the foundation for regulations enacted by the agencies, thus shaping what policies could be challenged legally.

National Environmental Policy Act (NEPA)

Within environmental law, many of the statutes were purposely designed to include review by the courts. One example of this is the National Environmental Policy Act of 1969 (NEPA). NEPA's purpose is to make every federal agency consider the effects of their actions on the environment. It puts forth a process by which any federal agency planning a major project with a significant impact on the quality of the human environment, must prepare an environmental impact statement (EIS) (Environmental Protection Agency, 2017). The two main questions regarding review under NEPA are as follows: If an agency has complied with NEPA requirements of preparing an EIS: did Congress intend for the courts to also consider an agency's decision on the merits be reviewed under substantive provisions of NEPA; and if the decision is subject to scrutiny by the courts, what is the standard of review? ("Judicial Review," 1973).

§101b of NEPA states, "In order to carry out the policy set forth in this Act, it is the continuing responsibility of the Federal Government to use all practicable means, consistent with other essential considerations of national policy, to improve and coordinate Federal plans, functions, programs, and resources..." (Ferrey, 2013, p. 85). §102 tells federal agencies to incorporate the §101 policies into their planning and decisions with §102(2)(C) requiring consultation with other federal agencies that have jurisdiction or expertise in environmental impacts. If a federal agency's actions may have a significant effect on the environment, an EIS must be prepared (Environmental Protection Agency, 2017b). The EIS is the foundation of decision-making by federal agencies when it comes to environmental issues and leads to more lawsuits than any other environmental law (Rasband, Salzman, & Squillace, 2009, p. 260).

Since its passage, the courts have upheld NEPA, reviewing actions (or inaction) by federal agencies. The first major case testing NEPA was decided in 1971 with the D.C. Circuit case of *Calvert Cliffs' Coordinating Committee v. United States Atomic Energy Commission* (1971). Calvert Cliffs Coordinating Committee challenged the Atomic Energy Commission's (AEC) policy applying §102's procedural requirements of the EIS. The AEC required applicants seeking to build a nuclear power plant to submit a "detailed statement" evaluating the potential environmental impact along with their licensing application. However, the AEC argued the EIS did not need to be considered by the licensing board, disregarding the statute's purpose of informing agency decision-making. The circuit court held that NEPA requires an agency to consider environmental factors at every important stage of its decision-making. Subsequent cases including *Strycker's Bay Neighborhood Council v. Karlen* (1980) and *Robertson v. Methow Valley Citizen Council* (1989) affirmed that NEPA is a procedural statute and does not require a specific substantive result (*Strycker's Bay Neighborhood Council v. Karlen*, 1980; *Robertson v. Methow Valley Citizen Council*, 1989).

If an agency has complied with the procedural requirements of the statute, it is not required to choose a specific pro-environment option and the court's power of judicial review in these cases is limited under NEPA. When reviewing NEPA cases, courts use a "reasonableness" standard that weighs evidence from the plaintiff and the agency, and the court determines if the agency's decision over whether not to prepare an EIS was reasonable. Since the *Citizens to Preserve Overton Park, Inc. v. Volpe* (1971) ruling, the courts apply this standard to informal agency decisions. The Supreme Court has also held that "once an agency has made a decision subject to NEPA's procedural requirements, the only role for a court is to insure that the agency has considered the environmental consequences" (Ferrey, 2013, p. 86; *Robertson v. Methow Valley Citizen Council*, 1989). The court can review an agency's final decision under other environmental statutes, though, and under the "arbitrary and capricious" provision of the APA (Rasband, Salzman, & Squillace, 2009, p. 262). If an agency's decision fails to comply with the NEPA provisions or is deemed "arbitrary and capricious," the agency risks having its decision challenged court and possibly overturned. The statute gives standing to interested parties who want to hold the agency accountable for their actions.

A final important area of judicial review under NEPA is standing and possible injunctive relief. NEPA lacks a citizen suit provision, so plaintiffs must make a claim under §10 of the APA to gain standing. In *Marsh v. Oregon Natural Resource Council* (1989) and *Winter v. Natural Resources Defense Council, Inc.* (2009), the court held that existence of a NEPA violation does not mean there will be available injunctive relief (Ferrey, 2013, p. 132). "[A] Preliminary injunction is an extraordinary remedy never awarded as of 'right' and 'plaintiffs must demonstrate that irreparable harm is likely if the injunction does not issue and that the balance of the harms favors plaintiffs'" (Ferrey, 2013, p. 132). Courts must use a four-part standard for injunctive relief, which includes the following: "irreparable injury, remedies available at law are inadequate, balance of hardships, and the public interest would not be disserved by a permanent injunction" (Ferrey, 2013, p. 132; *Monsanto Co. et al, v. Geertson Seed Farm, et al.*, 2010).

As NEPA and the APA illustrate, judicial review enables accountability of federal agencies and can help both the public and agencies ensure compliance with existing laws. These statutes emphasize following correct procedures, but over time the courts have clarified how and when substantive issues can be ruled on as well. As supported by the sample of cases listed here and differences in litigant resources, it is difficult to successfully win a court case against an agency on substantive or procedural grounds. NEPA and the APA give organizations, individuals, states, or other interested parties the legal authority to challenge agencies, though, and to hold them accountable for following procedures and upholding the substance of the statutes within their jurisdiction. These laws are important tools for each branch of government and outside actors working to shape public policy.

JUDICIAL REVIEW OF THE EXECUTIVE BRANCH

Throughout history, presidents and their administrations have also been subject to judicial review. For some, the scandal and court involvement ended their time in office. This section will look at the Teapot Dome scandal, Watergate, and President Bill Clinton's affair with Monica Lewinsky and address its implications for public policy and accountability.

Teapot Dome

Warren Harding briefly served as president from March 4, 1921–August 2, 1923 before suddenly dying of a heart attack in San Francisco. His administration is characterized as scandal-ridden because of the criminal actions of some appointees and Cabinet members, though Harding himself was not involved in any of the corruption (History Channel, n.d.). One of the most infamous is the Teapot Dome scandal involving Secretary of the Interior Albert Bacon Fall.

Teapot Dome is located north of Casper, Wyoming and was named for a rock formation resembling a teapot. Another feature of the area is an oil field of 9,481 acres, designated Naval Petroleum Reserve Number Three in 1915 by presidential executive order in the event the Navy needed emergency fuel reserves (Department of the Interior National Park Service, 1974).

Though the least productive of the three naval reserves, Teapot Dome became the most famous.

The Secretary of the Interior manages oil leasing on public lands and is responsible for overseeing the competitive bidding process. Fall leased the naval lands to private oil companies both at a low rate and without going through the required bidding process. While this is allowed under the Mineral Leasing Act of 1920, accepting bribes to bypass the competitive leasing is not (Bureau of Land Management, 2007). On April 7, 1922, Secretary Fall announced lease of the Teapot Dome reserve to Mammoth Oil Company, which was run by Henry Sinclair and the lease of oil rights in Elk Hills to the Pan-American Oil Company owned by E.L. Doheny (Cherny, 2017). Parties objecting to the leases claimed they were granted without the required competitive bidding (Department of the Interior National Park Service, 1974). Shortly after the lease was granted, Senator Thomas J. Walsh launched an investigation and uncovered the scandal. The investigation took 18 months and hearings started in October 1923. Fall resigned in March 1923.

In early 1924, E.L. Doheny, an oil tycoon in Southern California, confessed to offering Fall a $100,000 bribe. Though Doheny was acquitted of making the bribe, Fall was convicted of accepting it and sentenced to a year in jail, making him the first Cabinet member to go to prison. The court found Fall accepted a total of $409,000 in bribes. Secretary of the Navy Edwin Denby resigned, and the Attorney General Harry Daughterty resigned as part of the Republican efforts to reorganize leading up to the 1924 and 1928 presidential elections (Department of the Interior National Park Service, 1974). In 1927, the Department of the Interior transferred jurisdiction of the Teapot Dome reserve to the Navy and both Doheny's leases and the Wyoming leases were cancelled.

The Teapot Dome scandal illustrated corruption throughout the Interior and between companies it was required to monitor. It involved civil and criminal trials, and ultimately led to conviction of a Cabinet official. Federal agencies were put on notice by the court that they were not above or excluded from judicial review and that corruption would not be excused.

President Richard Nixon & Watergate

Due to actions taken by seven individuals on June 17, 1972, public perceptions of the presidency were never the same. The individuals were members of Nixon's Committee to Re-Elect the President who broke into the Democrat National Committee (DNC) headquarters in the Washington, D.C. Watergate building.

They were arrested for trying to wiretap phones and steal classified documents (History Channel, n.d.). Though not conclusively involved with the break-in, President Nixon's involvement in the cover-up led to his ultimate resignation.

Historical accounts differ on the extent to which Nixon was personally involved or knowledgeable about the break-in, but afterwards, Nixon led the attempts to cover-up the illegal actions. The White House released 1,254 pages of transcripts, which included 46 presidential conversations about Watergate on April 31, 1974, detailing talks Nixon had with staff including counsel John Dean. Nixon and Dean discussed various payment methods totaling $1 million to meet the blackmail demands of the reelection committee-affiliated burglars (Woodward & Bernstein, 1974). A portion of a conversation from March 21, 1973 reads as follows:

"How much money do you need?" the President asked Dean…

"I would say these people are going to cost a million dollars over the next two years," Dean replied.

"We could get that," the President continued. "On the money, if you need the money you could get that. You could get a million dollars. You could get it in cash. I know where it could be gotten. It is not easy, but it could be done. But the question is who the hell would handle it? Any ideas on that?" (Nixon Presidential Library and Museum, n.d.)

In addition to the bribery payments, Nixon worked to prevent the FBI from investigating the burglary by asking the Central Intelligence Agency (CIA) for help, firing staff members who refused to cooperate with him, and destroying evidence (History Channel, n.d.). Asking the CIA to hinder the FBI's investigation was an abuse of presidential power and his handling of tapes from the Oval Office conversations constituted obstruction of justice.

Nixon argued he did not have to turn over the Oval Office tapes to investigators under executive privilege while Judge John J. Sirica, members of the Senate investigating committee, and Independent Special Prosecutor Archibald Cox disagreed (History Channel, n.d.). The Supreme Court ordered Nixon to turn over the tapes in July 1974 in a unanimous opinion and he finally complied in August 1974 (Watergate.info, 1974). Nixon resigned on August 9, 1974 when his specific role in the scandal became public and the Senate was likely to impeach him. He was never prosecuted for Watergate. Five of the burglars pled guilty to avoid a trial while the other two were convicted and sentenced. President Gerald Ford pardoned Nixon for any crimes he "committed or may have committed" during his presidency in Proclamation 4311 (History Channel, n.d.; American Presidency Project, 1974).

Nixon's connection to the cover-up of Watergate fed into growing political mistrust at the time over Vietnam. Mistrust in the president has continued since his administration and Nixon's abuse of presidential power forever changed the way Americans viewed the office (Zelizer, 2014). It was a powerful action of judicial review by trial judge Sirica and later by the Supreme Court.

President Bill Clinton: Whitewater and Monica Lewinsky

In 1995, a twenty-one-year old woman named Monica Lewinsky became an unpaid White House intern for Chief of Staff Leon Panetta. Less than six months later, Lewinsky and President Bill Clinton began an affair (AllPolitics, 1998). Around the same time, Kenneth Starr had been appointed as an independent counsel to investigate Clinton's involvement in the Whitewater real estate case. Upon finding insufficient evidence to support the investigation, Starr shut it down in December 1997 (NPR, 2010).

Lewinsky's affair came out through a separate lawsuit against President Clinton where Paula Jones sued him on sexual harassment charges. Lewinsky claimed that in meeting with the president about the Jones suit, he encouraged her to be "evasive" in her answers. As part of this case, Lewinsky's filed statement denied any affair with Clinton. Clinton also denied the affair in his deposition. Upon learning of Lewinsky's denial, her friend and Pentagon co-worker Linda Tripp contacted Starr claiming she had evidence of an affair between Clinton and Lewinsky. Tripp had begun taping her conversations with Lewinsky in the fall of 1997 and they included Lewinsky discussing her affair with the president. She gave the tapes to Starr who requested an expansion of his Whitewater investigation from the DOJ. This led to judicial review of a president and his staff's actions. As the investigation progressed, Starr requested subpoenas for many of Clinton's staff and aides and Lewinsky requested immunity for her testimony against the president (AllPolitics, 1998).

The White House legal team argued Clinton and his staff should be shielded from testifying in the Lewinsky case because of executive privilege. On March 20, 1998, President Clinton invoked executive privilege, but Judge Norma Holloway ruled against his claim on May 5, 1998 (Baker & Schmidt, 1998). By June, the President's defense team drops their appeal of Judge Holloway's ruling, but continues arguing for attorney-client privilege to keep advisor Bruce Lindsey from answering questions posed by Kenneth Starr and to keep notes from late White House Deputy Counsel Vince Foster from being released. The Clinton legal team also argued for the "protective function" privilege for members of the Secret Service. In a 6-3 ruling, the Supreme Court held that attorney-client privilege extended beyond death, and thus Foster's notes of conversations he had with his lawyer were exempt from being used in Starr's investigation. Conversations with Bruce Lindsey, presidential friend and confidant, were not protected and he was called before the grand jury. Regarding the protective function argument, the U.S. Court of Appeals held that the agents must testify before the grand jury, upholding Judge Holloway's ruling (AllPolitics, 1998).

Judge Susan Webber Wright dismissed the Paula Jones civil lawsuit on April 1, 1998, shifting the legal and media focus to the Lewinsky case (AllPolitics, 1998). On August 17, 1998, Clinton made history by becoming the first president to testify before a grand jury while in office. House Judiciary Committee Chairman Henry Hyde (IL-Republican) announced the committee would consider a resolution on September 24, 1998 to start impeachment proceedings (AllPolitics, 1998; King, Franken, & Curley, 1998). In response to calls for resignation or a plea bargain, President Clinton said, "The right thing to do is for us all to focus on what's best for the American people...And the right thing for me to do is what I'm doing. I'm working on leading our country, and I'm working on healing my family" (King, Franken, & Curley, 1998).

The House of Representatives voted on December 20, 1998 to impeach President Clinton on charges of perjury (misleading a federal grand jury during the Lewinsky case) and obstruction of justice. The vote in favor of impeachment for perjury (228-206) occurred primarily on party lines. The obstruction of justice vote was closer (221-212) with 12 Republicans voting no and five Democrats voting yes. Five Democrats broke ranks to vote with the Republicans while five Republicans crossed party lines to support the Democrat opposition to impeachment. Two additional charges, one for perjury in the Jones case and one for abuse of power with testimony to questions from the House Judiciary Committee, failed. Clinton was only the second president in American history to be impeached along with Andrew Johnson in 1868 (Mitchell, 1998). The Senate failed to secure the necessary 67 votes to force Clinton's removal from office and he was thus acquitted of all charges.

The Clinton-Lewinsky affair and impeachment process was a unique case of judicial review by the courts. When speaking before the Senate after the impeachment deliberations, Supreme Court Chief Justice William Rehnquist gave a glimpse of the situation in saying, "I underwent the sort of culture shock that naturally occurs when one moves from the very structured [atmosphere] of the Supreme Court to what I shall call, for want of a better phrase, the more free-form environment of the Senate" (Baker & Dewar, 1999). Long-term effects of this case include limits to executive privilege/presidential immunity and a realization that courts will not shy away from reviewing any official's actions while in office, including a president.

JUDICIAL REVIEW OF CONGRESS

The political system in the United States provides for checks and balances, which include congressional oversight over actions by the executive branch. As the presidential cases illustrate, Congress plays an important role in accountability and promoting good governance in the American political system. In this section, "Lawyergate" under President Bush will be covered.

On December 7, 2006, the DOJ took a dramatic and unprecedented step by firing nine U.S. attorneys in the mid-term. The prosecutors included Daniel Bogden (Nevada), Paul Charlton (Arizona), Margaret Chiara (Michigan), Bud Cummins (Arkansas), Todd Graves (Missouri), Carol Lam (California), John McKay (Washington), Kevin Ryan (California), and David Iglesias (New Mexico) (Department of Justice, 2008). It is common practice for an incoming administration to request resignations of U.S. attorneys from the prior administration, but firings in the middle of a presidency were highly unusual. The Bush administration argued they were due to performance issues, but reviews of most of the prosecutors showed they had received outstanding performance evaluations for competence. These firings were allowed by a provision in the PATRIOT Act of 2001, granting a President the authority to appoint "interim" attorneys for an indefinite period without Senate confirmation. Prior to this provision, interim appointments were limited to 120 days (Zagorin, 2007).

One of the fired attorneys, David Iglesias, a Navy commander, defense lawyer, and the inspiration for Tom Cruise's character in *A Few Good Men*, argued the firing was due to political pressure. Iglesias remarked, "I didn't give them what they wanted. That was probably a political problem that caused them to go to the White House or whomever and complain that I wasn't a team player" ("Fired U.S.," 2007). Iglesias claimed Senator Pete Domenici (R-New Mexico) pressured him when Iglesias said he would not be filing indictments on Democrats after the 2006 election. Domenici acknowledged the call, but denied any coercion. Fired attorney H.E. "Bud" Cummings said he received a threatening email from the DOJ warning any fired attorney about speaking to the media or agreeing to testify before Congress. The DOJ denied this memo. Fired attorney John McKay said an aide to Doc Hastings (R-Washington), Chairman of the House Ethics Committee, contacted him.

The aide allegedly asked questions about McKay's investigation into the 2004 election of Democrat Governor Christine Gregoire. Hastings' office and his aide denied McKay's claims (Zagorin, 2007).

Despite denying any involvement, the DOJ released documents showing the White House had started the process of the dismissals and that they were, in fact, heavily influenced by perceptions of the attorneys' political loyalties. Documents from President Bush and White House advisor Karl Rove also included complaints over the prosecutors not pursuing voter fraud cases. In March 2007, Attorney General Alberto Gonzales accepted responsibility for the firings of the U.S. attorneys, saying, "I acknowledge that mistakes were made here. I accept that responsibility...I stand by the decision, and I think it was a right decision" (Eggen & Kane, 2007). Gonzales and the White House blamed his Chief of Staff D. Kyle Sampson for communicating poorly with Congress. In the documents released by the DOJ, a plan by Sampson explained how the lawyers would be fired, a rating system weighting political loyalty, and how to best prepare for the political backlash (Serrano, 2007). Sampson resigned on March 12, 2007.

Following Gonzales admission, Senator Charles Schumer (D-New York) was the first Democrat to call for Gonzales' resignation. Representative Darrell Issa (R-California) defended the administration, but concurred with Schumer, "...if someone led us astray, they should resign, and I don't care how high it is, anyone involved with this cover-up of giving us the truth needs to step down.... I am including anybody who would mislead, deliberately mislead the Congress... If it's the attorney general who had a hand in it, then he has to step down" (Eggen & Kane, 2007). Additional members of Congress from both parties called for the resignation and began working on removing Gonzales of his right to avoid Senate oversight when appointing interim prosecutors. Republican Senator John Ensign of Nevada said, "Everybody who's appointed by the White House understands that they serve at the pleasure of the president...a good leader does not just dismiss somebody for no good reason, especially if you haven't done your job in the first place. And I don't feel that the U.S. attorney general's office did their job in the first place"(Eggen & Kane, 2007). Gonzales resigned August 2007, two weeks after Rove stepped down and several months before Harriet Miers resigned. President Bush argued Gonzales' resignation was a political exercise while Democrat senators including Schumer and Reid cheered his departure from the DOJ (Myers, 2007).

Shortly before the 2008 presidential election, the DOJ Inspector General (IG) issued a report titled "An Investigation into the Removal of Nine U.S. Attorneys in 2006." The IG concluded the process used to dismiss the attorneys was "arbitrary" and "fundamentally flawed" (Department of Justice, 2008). In 2010, the DOJ closed the investigation without filing any charges. "Evidence did not demonstrate that any prosecutable criminal offense was committed with regard to the removal of David Iglesias...the investigative team also determined that the evidence did not warrant expanding the scope of the investigation beyond the removal of Iglesias" (Associated Press, 2010b). In the letter from the DOJ to Congress, Special Prosecutor Nora Dannehy stated the DOJ's failure to investigate claims against Iglesias showed, "an undue sensitivity to politics on the part of DOJ officials who should answer not to partisan politics but to principles of fairness and justice" (Associated Press, 2010a).

"Lawyergate" illustrates the importance of judicial review by Congress through the Senate Judiciary Committee and by the DOJ as it reviews its own handling of government prosecutors. Scholars argued the long-term impact of this controversy could be threats to the independence of federal law enforcement officials and greater scrutiny of political motivations in prosecutions of indictments (Coyle, 2007).

CONCLUSION

Dating back to *Marbury v. Madison*, judicial review has been an important tool for the courts to hold branches of government accountable while also providing them with discretion in applying laws and case precedents to contemporary issues. The Founding Fathers created a separation of powers among the three branches of government, but also wanted to make sure the branches of government could check and balance each other. Through statutes such as the APA and NEPA and an extensive body of case law, the authority of judicial review helps courts promote legal and effective public policy. Moving forward, we can hope the legal system will continue exercising its authority to review Congress, the President, federal agencies, and itself.

REFERENCES

AllPolitics. (1998). *A chronology: Key moments in the Clinton-Lewinsky saga*. Retrieved April 1, 2017, from http://www.cnn.com/ALLPOLITICS/1998/resources/lewinsky/timeline/
American Presidency Project. (1974, September 8). *Proclamation 4311-granting pardon to Richard Nixon*. Retrieved from http://www.presidency.ucsb.edu/ws/?pid=4696

Associated Press. (2010, July 21a). *Justice Dept. opts not to file charges for Bush-Era U.S. attorney firings.* Retrieved from http://www.foxnews.com/politics/2010/07/21/justice-dept-opts-file-charges-bush-era-attorney-firings.html

Associated Press. (2010, July 22b). Justice Dept. won't file charges in Bush-era firings of U.S. attorneys. *Washington Post.* Retrieved from http://www.washingtonpost.com/wp-dyn/content/article/2010/07/21/AR2010072105670.html

Baker, P., & Dewar, H. (1999, February 13). The Senate acquits President Clinton. *Washington Post,* Politics. Retrieved from http://www.washingtonpost.com/wp-srv/politics/special/clinton/stories/impeach021399.htm

Baker, P., & Schmidt, S. (1998, May 6). President is denied executive privilege. *Washington Post,* Politics. Retrieved from http://www.washingtonpost.com/wp-srv/politics/special/clinton/stories/starr050698.htm

Bickel, A. M. (1986). *The Least Dangerous Branch: The Supreme Court at the Bar of Politics* (2nd ed.). Yale University Press.

Brown v. Board of Education of Topeka, 347 U.S. 483 (May 17, 1954). Retrieved from https://www.oyez.org/cases/1940-1955/347us483

Bureau of Land Management. (2007, August 7). *Mineral Leasing Act of 1920.* Retrieved from https://www.blm.gov/style/medialib/blm/ut/vernal_fo/lands___minerals.Par.6287.File.dat/MineralLeasingAct1920.pdf

Cherny, R. W. (2017). *Graft and oil: How Teapot Dome became the greatest political scandal of its time.* Retrieved from https://www.gilderlehrman.org/history-by-era/roaring-twenties/essays/graft-and-oil-how-teapot-dome-became-greatest-political-scand

Chevron U.S.A., Inc. v. Natural Resources Defense Council, Inc., 467 U.S. 837 (May 31, 1983). Retrieved from https://www.oyez.org/cases/1983/82-1005

Citizens to Preserve Overton Park v. Volpe, 401 U.S. 402 (Mar. 2, 1971). Retrieved from http://caselaw.findlaw.com/us-supreme-court/401/402.html

Coenen, D. T. (2007). Fifteen Curious Facts about the Federalist Papers. *Popular Media.* Retrieved from http://digitalcommons.law.uga.edu/cgi/viewcontent.cgi?article=1001&context=fac_pm

Congress on Racial Equality. (2014). *Key civil rights related acts, laws and amendments to U.S. Constitution.* Retrieved from http://www.coreonline.org/History/history_links.htm

Cornell University Law School. (2017a). *Exclusionary rule.* Retrieved from https://www.law.cornell.edu/wex/exclusionary_rule

Cornell University Law School. (2017b). *5 U.S. Code Chapter 7 — Judicial Review.* Retrieved from https://www.law.cornell.edu/uscode/text/5/part-I/chapter-7

Cornell University Law School. (2017c). *5 U.S. Code § 704 — Actions reviewable.* Retrieved from https://www.law.cornell.edu/uscode/text/5/704

Cornell University Law School. (2017d). *5 U.S. Code § 706 — Scope of review.* Retrieved from https://www.law.cornell.edu/uscode/text/5/706

Cornell University Law School. (2017e). *Mandamus.* Retrieved from https://www.law.cornell.edu/wex/mandamus

Coyle, M. (2007, April 27). Scandal over U.S. Attorneys' firing could cloud other cases. *The Legal Intelligencer.* Retrieved from http://www.thelegalintelligencer.com/id=900005554868/Scandal-Over-US-Attorneys-Firing-Could-Cloud-Other-Cases?slreturn=20170302140738

Department of Justice (2008). *An investigation into the removal of nine U.S. attorneys in 2006.* Retrieved from https://oig.justice.gov/special/s0809a/final.pdf

Department of the Interior National Park Service. (1974, December). *National Register of Historic Places inventory-nomination form*. Retrieved from https://npgallery.nps.gov/pdfhost/docs/NRHP/Text/74002028.pdf

Eggen, D., & Kane, P. (2007, March 14). Gonzales: 'Mistakes were made' but Attorney General defends firings of eight U.S. Attorneys. *Washington Post*. Retrieved from http://www.washingtonpost.com/wpdyn/content/article/2007/03/13/AR2007031300776_pf.html

Environmental Protection Agency. (2017). *National Environmental Policy Act review process*. Retrieved from https://www.epa.gov/nepa/national-environmental-policy-act-review-process

Ferrey, S. (2013). *Environmental law: Examples and explanations* (6th ed.). New York: Wolters Kluwer Law & Business.

Fired U.S. attorney alleges political pressure. (2007, February 28). *Dallas Morning News*, Nation. Retrieved from https://web.archive.org/web/20070530041944/http://www.dallasnews.com/sharedcontent/dws/news/nation/stories/030107dnnatattorney.398bb40.html

Foner, E., & Garraty, J. A. (Eds.). (1991). Marbury v. Madison. Retrieved from http://www.history.com/topics/marbury-v-madison

Gideon v. Wainwright, 372 U.S. 335 (Mar. 18, 1963). Retrieved from https://www.oyez.org/cases/1962/155

Haas, S. (2017). Judicial review. Retrieved from https://nationalparalegal.edu/JudicialReview.aspx

History Channel. (n.d.). *Warren G. Harding*. Retrieved from http://www.history.com/topics/us-presidents/warren-g-harding

History Channel. (n.d.). Watergate scandal. Retrieved from http://www.history.com/topics/watergate

Jefferson, T. (1819, September 6). *Thomas Jefferson to Spencer Roane*. Retrieved from http://press-pubs.uchicago.edu/founders/documents/a1_8_18s16.html

Jefferson, T. (1821, November 23). *From Thomas Jefferson to Nathaniel Macon*. Retrieved from https://founders.archives.gov/documents/Jefferson/98-01-02-2444

Jefferson, T. (1825, March 25). *From Thomas Jefferson to Edward Livingston*. Retrieved from https://founders.archives.gov/documents/Jefferson/98-01-02-5077

Judicial review: NEPA and the courts. (1973). *Duke Law Journal*, *193*, 301–317. Retrieved from http://scholarship.law.duke.edu/cgi/viewcontent.cgi?article=2437&context=dlj

King, J., Franken, B., & Curley, A. (1998, September 24). *Judiciary Committee schedules vote on impeachment inquiry*. Retrieved from http://www.cnn.com/ALLPOLITICS/stories/1998/09/24/starr.report/

Loving v. Virginia, 388 U.S. 1 (June 12, 1967). Retrieved from https://www.oyez.org/cases/1966/395

Marbury v. Madison, 5 U.S. 137 (1803). Retrieved from https://www.law.cornell.edu/supremecourt/text/5/137

Miranda v. Arizona, 384 U.S. 436 (June 13, 1966). Retrieved from https://www.oyez.org/cases/1965/759

Mitchell, A. (1998, December 20). Impeachment: The Overview – Clinton impeached; He faces a Senate trial, 2D in history; Vows to do job till term's "last hour". *New York Times*, U.S. Retrieved from http://www.nytimes.com/1998/12/20/us/ impeachment-overview-clinton-impeached-he-faces-senate-trial-2d-history-vows-job.html

Monsanto Co. v. Geertson Seed Farms, No. 09-475 (9th Cir. June 21, 2010). Retrieved from https://www.supremecourt.gov/opinions/09pdf/09-475.pdf

Myers, S. L. (2007, August 27). Embattled Attorney General resigns. *Washington Post*. Retrieved from http://www.nytimes.com/2007/08/27/washington/27cnd-gonzales.html

National Public Radio. (2010, February 16). *"Clinton vs. Starr": A "definitive" account*. Retrieved from http://www.npr.org/templates/story/story.php?storyId=123653000

Nixon Presidential Library and Museum. (n.d.). *Watergate trial conversations.* Retrieved from https://www.nixonlibrary.gov/forresearchers/find/tapes/watergate/trial/transcripts.php

Plessy v. Ferguson, 163 U.S. 537 (May 18, 1896). Retrieved from https://www.oyez.org/cases/1850-1900/163us537

Project Gutenberg. (2017). *The Federalist Papers.* Retrieved from https://www.congress.gov/resources/display/content/The+Federalist+Papers#TheFederalistPapers-78

Rasband, J., Salzman, J., & Squillace, M. (2009). *Natural resources law and policy* (2nd ed.). New York: Foundation Press.

Regents of the University of California v. Bakke, 438 U.S. 265 (June 26, 1978). Retrieved from https://www.oyez.org/cases/1979/76-811

Robertson v. Methow Valley Citizens, 490 U.S. 332 (May 1, 1989). Retrieved from https://supreme.justia.com/cases/federal/us/490/332/case.html

Serrano, R. A. (2007, March 14). E-mails detail goals in firing U.S. attorneys. *Los Angeles Times.* Retrieved from http://articles.latimes.com/2007/mar/14/nation/na-emails14

Strycker's Bay Neighborhood Council v. Karlen, 444 U.S. 223 (Jan. 7, 1980). Retrieved from http://caselaw.findlaw.com/us-supreme-court/444/223.html

United States Government. (2017). *Federal Register.* Retrieved from https://www.federalregister.gov

Watergate info. (1974, July 24). *Supreme Court orders Nixon to hand over tapes.* Retrieved from http://watergate.info/1974/07/24/supreme-court-orders-nixon-release-white-house-tapes.html

Weeks v. United States, 232 U.S. 383 (Feb. 24, 1914). Retrieved from https://www.oyez.org/cases/1900-1940/232us383

Woodward, B., & Bernstein, C. (1974, May 1). Nixon debated paying blackmail, clemency, 'keep cap on bottle'. *Washington Post*, Watergate 25, p. A01. Retrieved from http://www.washingtonpost.com/wp-srv/national/longterm/watergate/articles/050174-2.htm

Zagorin, A. (2007, March 7). Why were these U.S. Attorneys fired? *Time.* Retrieved from http://content.time.com/time/nation/article/0,8599,1597085,00.html

Zelizer, J. (2014, July 7). *Distrustful Americans still live in age of Watergate.* Retrieved from http://www.cnn.com/2014/07/07/opinion/zelizer-watergate-politics/

CHAPTER 12

NATIONAL SECURITY WHISTLEBLOWERS AND THE JOURNALISTS WHO TELL THEIR STORIES: A DANGEROUS POLICY DANCE OF TRUTH-FINDING, TRUTH-TELLING, AND CONSEQUENCE

Maria A. Moore, John Huxford and
Jennifer B. Bethmann

ABSTRACT

At a time when governmental corruption seems rife and administrations grow ever more secretive, the whistleblower is a crucial resource in journalism's attempts to make accountable those who wield power. Yet despite legislation that is meant to protect employees and officials who expose wrongdoing, a governmental "war on whistleblowers" has made the hazards faced by many whistleblowers increasingly grim. This chapter explores the

Corruption, Accountability and Discretion
Public Policy and Governance, 227–246
Copyright © 2017 by Emerald Publishing Limited
All rights of reproduction in any form reserved
doi:10.1108/S2053-769720170000029013

role of the journalist/whistleblower collaboration in disclosing important, but sensitive, information involving national security. In discussing case studies of those who have braved the government's anger, we examine not only the circumstances of these breaches, but also their political and legal repercussions.

Keywords: whistleblower; journalism; investigative reporting; leaker; Espionage Act

BACKGROUND

With Barack Obama's election in 2008, advocates for whistleblowers were optimistic that protection for those who spoke out against governmental and corporate corruption would be expanded. Candidate Obama had promised to "strengthen whistleblower laws to protect federal workers who expose waste, fraud, and abuse of authority in government" (Change.gov, 2008, para. 20). This pledge bore fruit; three key legislative initiatives were passed under Obama's administration — the economic stimulus package, the financial reform bill, and health care reform — and all included enhanced provisions to protect whistleblowers. Moreover, in 2016, safeguarding the act of whistleblowing continued to be one of the rare issues to have the support of both Democrats and Republicans. Such support indicated that both parties seemed "eager to tell the public that whistleblowers are vital weapons in the battle against waste, fraud, and abuse in both the public and private sectors" (Hertsgaard, 2016, p. 52).

Yet despite these successes, the hazards faced by many whistleblowers have become increasingly grim. For all its expressions of support, the Obama administration was aggressive in its prosecution of national security whistleblowers (those who work for an agency in the intelligence community), with more prosecutions being made under Obama than in all previous presidential administrations combined (Shane, 2011). Equally troubling, this period saw an unprecedented use of the Espionage Act of 1917 to prosecute six individuals who allegedly disclosed sensitive information to *journalists* (Horton, 2010), an act that historically was reserved for the prosecution of those who disclosed national secrets to foreign governments. Additionally, the Obama administration followed the Bush administration's lead in trying to pressure reporters into identifying the anonymous sources behind headline-making stories about national security (Downie, 2013). It has been argued that this "war on whistleblowers" has succeeded in intimidating not only journalists' sources, but also investigative journalists themselves (Papandrea, 2014). Serious consequences await those who participate in certain types of whistleblowing.

Essentially, the government has made a sharp policy distinction between two types of whistleblowers — *bad* whistleblowing, which pertains to anything relating to national security, and *good* whistleblowing that deals in non-security matters, particularly relating to financial issues. In this stark binary, good whistleblowers often find their path through regulation and the courts. The public may hear only the broad results of good whistleblowing reported in the media due to the issue being handled internally (Norris, 2013). Alternately, those the government regard as bad whistleblowers routinely rely on journalists and media outlets to achieve an ending of consequence.

This chapter focuses on the supposed bad whistleblowers prosecuted during the Obama administration, their journalist collaborators, and their prosecution under the Espionage Act or the Intelligence Identities Protection Act (IIPA). John Kiriakou, Jeffrey Sterling, and Thomas Drake may not be household names to the average U.S. citizen, but each was a member of the U.S. intelligence community, each leaked classified information to journalists to expose governmental wrongdoing, and each was prosecuted under the Espionage Act while Obama was in office.

DEFINING WHISTLEBLOWING

Historically, the term whistleblowing has conflicting meanings. Dasgupta and Kesharwani (2010) defined it as "the disclosure by organization members (former or current) of illegal, immoral, and illegitimate practices under the control of their employers to persons and organizations that may be able to effect action" (p. 12). Equally, it has been considered as an act of principled dissent that can influence both policy agenda and public opinion (Moore, Huxford, & Hopper, 2014), with such dissent arising from an ethical concern an employee perceives as contradictory to his or her understanding of the organization's legal or ethical responsibilities. The organizational dissenter becomes the whistleblower when the individual seeks external disclosure of a perceived act of negligence or deliberate wrongdoing (Graham, 1986). This growing body of literature has framed whistleblowers as ethical heroes or "guardians of public accountability" (Grant, 2002; Ravishankar,

2003), a kind of "moral David who stands up against the dominant power of a corrupt Goliath, that image being particularly relevant to certain acts of whistleblowing within corrupt political institutions" (O'Sullivan & Ngau, 2014, p. 405). From this perspective, whistleblowers, as knowledgeable insiders, constitute an invaluable mechanism for improving government transparency (Rosenbloom, 2003).

Another view of the whistleblower, sometimes promulgated by targeted organizations, is that of a malcontented individual ruthlessly pursuing their own agenda at the expense of their colleagues and employer (Firtko & Jackson, 2005). In government, these individuals are labeled as "enemies of the state" due to their disregard of the law, and direct violation of state's authority by leaking classified data without going through proper channels of authority (Delmas, 2015). Yet the whistleblower may feel that he or she has no other option but to look outside the organization, having attempted and failed to address the problem using internal channels (Jubb, 1999). For many, the most viable route is to disclose their information to a journalist.

JOURNALISM'S ROLE

Ellison, Keenan, Lockhart, and Schaick (1985) suggest several reasons why whistleblowers favor the media in making their disclosures; it makes supporting documents public, and releases information at an appropriate time while also avoiding the need for the whistleblower to reveal their identity. Going to the news media may be especially effective in those cases where the whistleblower attempts to remain anonymous. Studies have shown that when the whistleblower remains anonymous internally or externally but does not seek out the media, it may lessen the credibility of the information given and undermine any impact for change (Miceli & Near, 1992). The media provides a legitimizing platform for those who wish to reveal information to the public.

Whistleblowers are more likely to turn to the news media when their accounts of wrongdoing are ignored internally, when top management is involved in the wrongdoing, or when they fear retaliation from management above their own supervisors. Media whistleblowers particularly fear reprisals from senior management (Callahan & Dworkin, 1994). Whistleblowers are also more motivated to speak to journalists when the observed wrongdoing threatens health or safety, and when the fraud or illegal behavior involves large sums of money (Perry, 1990). The news media is perceived to have the power to influence the public agenda by being able to publicize the whistleblower's complaint and apply pressure to the organization, while also protecting the whistleblower's anonymity (Callahan & Dworkin, 1994).

Equally compelling are the reasons for the news media to embrace the whistleblower. Stories emerging from such leaks are likely to fulfill many of the characteristics that make an incident newsworthy (Jamieson & Campbell, 1992). These characteristics include *personalization* — in whistleblowing, either of an individual charged with wrongdoing or, on occasion, on the consequences to the whistleblower themselves; normative *deviance* — events that involve the violation of social and legal norms; and the key attributes of *conflict* and *drama* (Huxford & Moore, 2011). Beyond these qualities, the typical whistleblower exposé may be seen as crucial to journalism's remit as public watchdog (Overholser & Jamieson, 2005; Schudson, 1995). In the words of *The New York Times* journalist Glenn Greenwald (2013):

> Given how subservient the federal judiciary is to government secrecy claims, it is not hyperbole to describe unauthorized leaks as the only real avenue remaining for learning about what the U.S. government does — particularly for discovering the bad acts it commits. (para. 3)

From this perspective, investigative reporting may be regarded as a basic means by which the news media fulfills its constitutional duties under the First Amendment (Aucoin, 1997), with the prime purpose of the press to "make power accountable" (Entman, 2005, p. 48).

However, the journalist/whistleblower collaboration is a dance fraught with dangers for both partners, with the bulk of whistleblower statutes not protecting disclosures made outside of official channels. As Papandrea (2014) explains:

> The lack of protection for public disclosures is most likely based on the belief that whistleblowers who truly care about correcting wrongdoing — as opposed to self-aggrandizing or publicity — are more likely to report misconduct internally within the government agency than to a reporter. (p. 487)

Consequently, those who leak information through the news media may be particularly vulnerable to the backlash whistleblowers typically endure (Callahan & Dworkin, 1994). Retaliation by authorities can come in many forms, from threats and isolation to physical assault (Devine, 1999). Rothschild and Miethe (1999) found that 69% of whistleblowers lost their jobs or were forced to retire, 68% received negative job performance evaluations, and 64% were blacklisted from getting another position in the same field.

Journalists should be aware they may be entering dangerous terrain when they take on a whistleblower exposé. Shield laws that protect the journalist are uneven across the country and maintaining the source's anonymity may not be protected legally, with instances on record of journalists being jailed for refusing to divulge this information (Reporters Committee, n.d.). Yet at the same time, failing to honor a pledge to protect a whistleblower's identity can lead to the reporter and their organization being sued (Ragusa, 1993). Worse, there is little formal training of journalists on how to navigate the difficult journalist/whistleblower relationship (Huxford & Moore, 2011).

INTELLIGENCE COMMUNITY WHISTLEBLOWING: OBAMA'S EXCEPTION

Divulging secrets to the news media is a hazardous undertaking, especially when the case involves what the government regards as bad whistleblowing. The dichotomy between good and bad acts of whistleblowing has been carefully framed in public statements, with strong negative sentiment directed toward the latter. As broadcast on ABC News, CIA director Leon Panetta stated, "Disclosure of classified information to anyone not cleared for it — reporters, friends, colleagues in the private sector or other agencies...does tremendous damage to our work. At worst, leaks endanger lives," (Leon Panetta Warns, 2011, n.p.). Those in the news media have not missed the message. As Jonathan Alter, a reporter for *Newsweek*, observed: "Obama had one pet peeve that could make him lose his cool...leaks" (Alter, 2010, p. 154). On October 7, 2011, the administration created an Insider Threat Task Force, tasked with developing "a government-wide program for insider threat detection and prevention to improve protection and reduce potential vulnerabilities of classified information from exploitation, compromise or other unauthorized disclosure" (The White House, 2011, para. 13), justifying the action as a national security imperative.

It is apparent those who leak information involving national security do so at their peril, yet whistleblowing continued to make headlines. In the second half of this chapter, we focus on case studies of whistleblowers and journalists who have braved the government's anger, and examine not only the circumstances of these breaches, but also their policy, political and legal repercussions.

THE CASES

Over the past decade, many high profile and important whistleblowing cases have grabbed headlines and raised the political temperature. Pentagon analyst

Lawrence Franklin, convicted in 2005 of leaking information about U.S. policy toward Iran to the American Israel Public Affairs Committee, former F.B.I. employee Shamai Leibowitz, convicted of disclosing classified information to a blogger in 2009, and Stephen Jin-Woo Kim, charged with leaking information about North Korea to Fox News in 2010, and others are worthy of note. However, for the purposes of this chapter, we have chosen to explore three stand out cases whose impact has been substantial: Jeffrey Sterling, Thomas Drake, and John Kiriakou.

Jeffrey Sterling 2015

Jeffrey Sterling, a former-CIA officer, was convicted in January 2015 of leaking classified information to *The New York Times* journalist James Risen. The government argued that the leaked information — attributed to Sterling, although he consistently denied the allegation — had effectively shut down an important program designed to sabotage the Iranian nuclear program and had placed the lives of those working with the CIA at risk (Apuzzo, 2015). Risen, a Pulitzer Prize winner, included the information in his book *State of War*, which detailed how the CIA paid a Russian scientist to try to get faulty nuclear plans to Iranian officials (Zapotosky, 2016).

Sterling's relationship with the CIA had long been turbulent. In August 2000, he became the first-ever black case officer to sue the agency for racial discrimination, a case eventually dismissed amid fears that a trial would reveal state secrets (Solomon, 2015). In March 2002 — two months after Sterling was fired by the CIA — Risen wrote about the discrimination suit in *The New York Times* (Risen, 2002). In the espionage trial, the Justice Department argued that Sterling had been motivated by vindictiveness, revealing details to Risen to get back at an agency with which he had been feuding (Apuzzo, 2015; Zapotosky, 2015b).

Sterling was convicted under the Espionage Act, and sentenced to three and a half years in prison. However, with Risen refusing to reveal his source, Sterling's conviction was largely circumstantial. Telephone records and emails showed that Sterling and Risen had talked frequently, and prosecutors argued that only Sterling had the information, the motive, and the opportunity to leak it to Risen (Apuzzo, 2015; Zapotosky, 2015b).

Legal and Political Outcomes
This case is notable for the aggressive efforts made against Risen to reveal his sources, with the journalist's lengthy struggle to avoid testifying about those

sources turning the case into a rallying point for news organizations and free speech advocates. Risen insisted he would go to prison rather than break his sources' anonymity. Ultimately, following a court decision that Risen would not be pressed on his source's identity if he agreed to testify in court, prosecutors opted not to call Mr. Risen to the stand.

However, the case set what many news organizations saw as an unsettling precedent when a Federal Appeals court ruled that — the first amendment notwithstanding—reporters had no protection against subpoenas compelling them to give testimony in criminal cases. An appeal to the Supreme Court to overturn this judgment was rejected (Greenslade, 2014; Liptak, 2014). In a statement, the Reporters Committee for Freedom of the Press said the ruling: "sends an undeniable chill through current and future news sources who would want to come forward with information essential to the well-being of the community and the country" (as cited in Greenslade, 2014, para. 6).

Thomas Drake 2011

Thomas Drake, a former senior executive at the National Security Agency (NSA), was indicted under the Espionage Act on ten felony charges of retaining classified information, obstruction of justice, and making false statements. The charges could have sent him to prison for the rest of his life. However, they were dropped after prosecutors were ordered to show allegedly classified material to the jury, and the case fell apart. The result was a misdemeanor plea bargain of "exceeding the authorized use of a computer" (Zetter, 2011, para. 1) for which Drake received one year of probation and community service. Drake's problems with the agency began when he attempted to alert his superiors and Congress to what he saw as illegal activities, waste and mismanagement at the NSA. His concerns centered on an intelligence gathering system codenamed Trailblazer, a project that would cost billions, and would later be abandoned. His concerns, voiced through official whistleblower-reporting channels, had little result, so he took his allegations to the press via reporter Siobhan Gorman at *The Baltimore Sun* (Gorman, 2006; Mayer, 2011). He was cautious, using an encrypted e-mail to communicate with Gorman, but his leak of unclassified information was discovered (Wise, 2011). Although eventually receiving only a mild penalty for the misdemeanor charge, Drake paid a heavy price for his act of whistleblowing. He was arrested at gunpoint, stripped of his security clearance, and all but ruined financially and professionally (Goodman, 2012).

Legal and Political Outcomes

The Drake case is now regarded as an embarrassment for the Department of Justice, and a cautionary tale for those who pursue government whistleblowers. The judge who passed a token sentence on Drake was caustic about the handling of the case, both in terms of the major charges being dropped on the eve of the trial, and of the long delay Drake suffered in awaiting conviction. Suggesting the accused had gone through "years of hell," Judge Richard Bennett said it was "unconscionable" that an American citizen should be left "waiting two and a half years after their home is searched to find out if they're going to be indicted or not" (Nakashima, 2011, p. A02).

At the same time, the criticisms of Drake and others about issues surrounding the Trailblazer project were eventually validated. Prompted by these protests, a "highly classified study" (Smith, 2011, p. A07) by the Defense Department's internal watchdog upheld the complaints. Danielle Brian, executive director of the Project on Government Oversight claimed, "This is just more evidence that the government never should have prosecuted Thomas Drake," (as cited in Smith, 2011, p. A07). She continued, "We should be thankful that Mr. Drake had the courage to stand by his convictions and do what was best for the country" (p. A07).

In contrast to several other whistleblowing cases, journalist Siobhan Gorman of *The Baltimore Sun* was not heavily implicated in the Drake legal battle. The original indictment did not name either the reporter or the newspaper (Shane, 2010). Although these details later emerged in court records, Gorman was neither charged nor called to testify. Gorman went on to win a national journalism award for her investigative series of articles on the NSA, later moving to *The Wall Street Journal* (Bishop, 2011). Meanwhile, Drake received the 2011 Ridenhour Truth-Telling Prize and has since become a powerful spokesman on whistleblowing issues; being used, for example, as an expert source in news coverage of the Snowden affair (Nakashima, 2013). He has also written, and contributed to, opinion articles on whistleblowing in national newspapers, including *The Washington Post* (Drake, 2011) and *USA Today* (Loomis, Wiebe, Drake, Binney, & Roark, 2014).

John Kiriakou 2012

John Kiriakou, a former CIA covert agent, pleaded guilty in October 2012 to disclosing classified information, and was sentenced to 30 months in prison (Shane, 2013). A decade earlier, Kiriakou had been part of the team that captured Abu Zubaydah, the first big target in the Al-Qaeda hierarchy after the terrorist attacks of 9/11.

His crime, prosecuted under the Intelligence Identities Protection Act (IIPA), was giving journalists the names of two former colleagues who interrogated detainees using harsh practices including waterboarding. In 2007, Kiriakou became central to the debate surrounding interrogation tactics after giving an interview to Brian Ross on ABC News (Esposito & Ross, 2007a; Esposito & Ross, 2007b). He said in his interview:

> Like a lot of Americans, I'm involved in this internal, intellectual battle with myself weighing the idea that waterboarding may be torture versus the quality of information that we often get after using the waterboarding technique, and I struggle with it. (2007b, p. 6)

He continued by suggesting that although waterboarding had proven effective and "probably saved lives" (Warrick & Eggen, 2007, p. A01), the United States should abandon the technique because "we're Americans and we're better than this" (Esposito & Ross, 2007a, p. 29).

After the interview, Kiriakou became a source for other journalists investigating the use of torture by the U.S. government. Over the next year, he gave the name of one former colleague to an unnamed freelance reporter — who never published the name, but allegedly passed it on to a legal team defending Guantanamo Bay detainees — and revealed the identity of another former colleague to Justin Jouvenal, a reporter for *The New York Times*. He pleaded guilty to the leak made to the freelancer; the charge related to *The New York Times* was dropped (Jouvenal, 2013). In an interview with Steve Coll (2013) of *The New Yorker*, Kiriakou discussed possible motivations behind his prosecution.

> At the C.I.A., "you don't ever talk to the press and you don't talk about dirty laundry, and I did. And there were players involved in the Counterterrorist Center, where I was working, who have very long memories. They were going to make sure I got punished." (as cited para. 16)

Legal and Political Outcomes

The national debate on waterboarding that Kiriakou helped to fuel eventually led to the practice being outlawed. President Obama signed an executive order in 2009 banning the use of torture by any government agency, this being codified into law in the National Defense Authorization Act of 2015 (Crook, 2009). Only those interrogation techniques outlined in the Army

Field Manual are considered legal — and these do not include waterboarding (U. S. Department of the Army, 2006). However, the current president, Donald Trump, is on record as wanting to reinstate waterboarding and similar techniques. He asserted during a presidential primary debate, "I would bring back waterboarding, and I would bring back a hell of a lot worse than waterboarding" (Trump, 2016, p. 39).

For those who pursue whistleblowers, the renewed use of the IIPA constituted a significant success. In a statement to CIA employees, then-Director David H. Petraeus (2012) said, "This case yielded the first IIPA successful prosecution in 27 years, and it marks an important victory for our Agency, for our Intelligence Community, and for our country" (para. 2).

DISCUSSION

Famously, Benjamin Franklin (1755/1963) warned the public, "those who would give up essential Liberty, to purchase a little temporary Safety, deserve neither Liberty nor Safety" (p. 242). But the trade-off between these fundamental values has only grown more complex in the 21st century. As we have seen, the Obama administration was careful to draw a stark distinction between those who disclosed information associated with national security—in its eyes acts of bad whistleblowing — and leaks in other, often less contentious, areas where whistleblowing is broadly regarded as socially worthy.

Even in the news media there is some ambivalence over those who leak government secrets — especially secrets dealing with national security. In 2015, *CounterPunch* published an insightful article about the increasing hostility toward whistleblowers from members of the elite Washington press corps (Hanrahan, 2015). Similarly, it is notable that a leaked story regarding a plan to sabotage the Iranian nuclear program — the basis of journalist James Risen's book — was rejected by *The New York Times* after consultation with government officials (Pincus, 2011). As Randall Eliason (2014) wrote in a column in *The Washington Post*, "Although the government no doubt classifies too much material, there is a core of true national security information that does need to be confidential" (p. A15). So, while the initial reaction of many is to leap to the defense of those who pierce the veil surrounding government secrets, there may be valid reasons to treat national security disclosures differently. Not all leakers reveal information about government misconduct (illegal, unethical, violating public interest), and might not deserve protection. It may be argued that Bradley Manning's data-dump of 700,000 classified documents via WikiLeaks in 2009, for example, might not merit protection (Poulsen, 2013).

A whistleblower may not have all the facts or understand the larger context of an issue, leading their perception of wrongdoing to be incorrect. For example, using information allegedly supplied by Sterling, Risen described an operation to sabotage the Iranian nuclear program as botched and "reckless," in part because the flaws in the nuclear plans were easily detectable. However, evidence described by *The Washington Post* reporter Walter Pincus (2015) that emerged during the trial suggested otherwise. These documents appeared to show the intent had always been to offer plans that were clearly incomplete, acting as a hook "to get the Iranians to stay in touch" (p. A15). The reporter concluded, "The Sterling case should be a lesson that not all secret information passed to journalists is totally true, and that government claims that such information may be inaccurate are not totally false" (p. A15).

Similarly, John Kiriakou, while helping to focus attention on waterboarding with his ABC news interview, also added to the confusion over its effectiveness. Although Kiriakou had not been present during the interrogation he described, the former CIA officer stated the prisoner had started cooperating with investigators within 35 seconds of being waterboarded, and "from that day on he answered every question" (Stelter, 2009, p. A1). Kiriakou had also suggested that, although ethically reprehensible, waterboarding had "probably saved lives" (Warrick & Eggen, 2007, p. A01) by preventing "maybe dozens of attacks" (as cited in Pincus, 2015, p. A15). These claims, repeated across dozens of broadcasts and newspaper articles, were contradicted in 2009 when a newly declassified Justice Department memo said Zubaydah had been waterboarded at least 83 times (Savage, 2012; Shane, 2009). Moreover, little or no useful extra information may have been gained by such harsh methods (Pilkington, 2013).

Nonetheless, the arguments in favor of national security whistleblowing remain strong. Exposing illegality, waste, abuse of authority and gross mismanagement might be even more critically important in national security than in other areas of government and the private sector where whistleblowing is more acceptable. The belief, among some critics, that whistleblowers who truly care about correcting wrongdoing rather than simply looking for self-aggrandizement are more likely to report misconduct internally than leak to a reporter (Duffy & Freeman, 2011) quickly runs aground when case studies are examined. In the three cases described in this chapter, two turned to journalists only after internal whistleblowing failed. Moreover, in the case of Sterling, previous attempts to "do the right thing" through internal dissension were used as ammunition by prosecutors to suggest the whistleblower had a long record of troublemaking and a motive of vengeance (Apuzzo, 2015; Zapotosky, 2016).

The list of governmental misdeeds that have been brought into public scrutiny through the whistleblower/journalist collaboration is impressive; from torture by waterboarding to domestic wiretapping. And given this, it is unsurprising that such an enterprise will raise the ire of those in charge. A good deal of truth may be found in Glenn Greenwald's (2013) contention:

> the most basic precepts of human nature, political science, and the American founding teach that power exercised in the dark will be inevitably abused. Secrecy is the linchpin of abuse of power. That's why those who wield political power are always driven to destroy methods of transparency. (para. 9)

Given this, the act of whistleblowing, regardless of its sometime flaws and compromises, remains essential if democracy is to flourish. Reporter Declan Walsh of *The New York Times*, calling leaks "the unfiltered lifeblood" of investigative journalism, put it in a nutshell: "They may come from difficult, even compromised sources, be ridden with impurities and require careful handling to produce an accurate story. None of that reduces their importance to journalism" (as quoted in Sullivan, 2013, p. 12).

IMPLICATIONS OF A NEW ADMINISTRATION

Whatever obstacles the whistleblower/journalist collaboration may have faced under the policies of previous administrations, it now seems certain these will serve as merely a prelude to a still more aggressive reaction from the Trump administration. Only weeks after taking office in 2017, President Donald Trump decried embarrassing leaks about private conversations with foreign leaders in Australia and Mexico — in particular, leaks about communications with Russia's ambassador, which led to his National Security Advisor, Michael Flynn's resignation (Nelson, 2017). The information about Trump and Flynn's private communications with foreign leaders could be considered classified and therefore illegal to disclose without authorization. Steven Aftergood, a government secrecy expert surmised "the situation is different for a leaker, who unilaterally violates presidential instructions. Such a person places himself at risk of administrative or criminal penalties" (as quoted in Nelson, 2017, para. 7).

The policy approach enacted in the Obama administration, to prosecute national security leakers under the Espionage Act, might also be deployed by this new administration. In his first month in office, Trump asked the Justice Department to investigate, as he vowed to go after, those "low-life leakers" whom he considers "criminal" (Trump, 2017, para. 1). Prosecuting the leakers is possible as the Justice Department could use the Espionage Act to charge the administration official who leaks national defense information (Goodwin, 2017). In a press conference in January 2017, Trump demanded an apology from *The New York Times*; not for getting facts wrong, but rather for reporting accurately on confidential information that the government did not want the public to know. Gregg Leslie, legal defense director of the Reporters Committee for Freedom of the Press, was troubled by the demand. "There's no way they should apologize for accepting and printing leaked information" (as cited Goodwin, 2017, para. 19). He continued, "The American people deserve that. We need to know what's really going on, not just what the White House press office says is happening" (para. 19).

Early signs are evident that the new Trump Administration may also be exploring ways to gut protections enacted during the Obama era for so-called good whistleblowers via the Dodd-Frank Whistleblower Act — compensating and protecting those who revealed wrongdoing in the financial sector as overseen by the Securities Exchange Commission (SEC). This is despite the fact that billions of taxpayer dollars have been recovered by the SEC's investigations into fraud exposed by whistleblowers. A memo leaked to *The New York Times* authored by the House Financial Service Committee recommends greatly limiting the scope of oversight of big publicly traded companies (Rappeport, 2017).

Journalists were quickly treated with scorn and skepticism by the new administration. As Julian Zelizer (2017) of CNN editorialized, the first war declared by the new president was a war on journalists. In his first full day as president, Trump took direct aim at the reporters covering the White House. Standing in the headquarters of the CIA, newly sworn-in President Trump prioritized attacking journalists, declaring, "they are among the most dishonest human beings on earth, right?" (Trump, 2017). The administration has, on occasions, blocked participation of some journalists from press briefings, including those from *The New York Times*, CNN, and *The Guardian*. *The New York Times* editor Dean Baquet said, "Nothing like this has ever happened at the White House in our long history of covering multiple administrations" (as cited in Helmore, 2017). Dan Rather, retired CBS anchor and journalist, posted on Facebook:

> The barring of respected journalistic outlets from the White House briefing is so far beyond the norms and traditions that have governed this republic for generations, that they must be seen as a real and present threat to our democracy. (personal communication, February 24, 2017)

The most telling early indicator that the journalist/whistleblower relationship may be becoming more critical for holding government to account is an unprecedented secure website for whistleblowers launched by *USA Today* in partnership with the Freedom of the Press Foundation. The website "uses an encrypted and anonymous computer network known as Tor, and routes internet connections through a series of different computers around the globe, making it largely untraceable" (*USA Today*, 2017, para. 3). The site is available to anyone who wants to share information with reporters assigned to cover local, state or national government beats. Trevor Timm, director of the Freedom of the Press Foundation, claimed, "Trump's election has created a sense of urgency among news organizations to find better ways to protect their sources" (as cited in *USA Today*, 2017, para. 5). Similarly, in discussing the intent of the site, Joanne Lipman, *USA Today*'s Chief Content Officer, argued, "Investigative reporting is core to our mission. This tool will improve our ability to connect sources and journalists to better hold public officials and civic institutions accountable" (para. 10).

Whistleblowers and their journalist counterparts work to navigate a complex and dangerous dance of truth-finding and truth-telling, an enterprise fraught with multiple levels of consequence. As recent political and organizational climates indicate, extra vigilance is necessary to protect those wishing to disclose vital information to the public.

A CONCLUDING CAUTION

This chapter was written as the Obama era concluded and the Trump era began. While the Obama administration acted aggressively against those who leaked national security information, it also set in place stronger policy protections for financial whistleblowers, resulting in positive conclusions for both the public and those who disclosed the information. The Trump administration's early declaration of war on whistleblowers and the journalists who report on the information gleaned may evolve into unchartered policy territory. The authors encourage the reader to consider this chapter's content as a moment in time in early 2017.

REFERENCES

Alter, J. (2010). *The promise: President Obama, year one.* New York, NY: Simon and Schuster.

Apuzzo, M. (2015, January 26). C.I.A. officer is found guilty in leak tied to *Times* reporter. Retrieved from http://www.nytimes.com/2015/01/27/us/politics/cia-officer-in-leak-case-jeffrey-sterling-is-convicted-of-espionage.html?_r=0

Aucoin, J. (1997). Historiographic essay: The investigative tradition in American journalism. *American Journalism, 14*(3-4), 317–329. doi:10.1080/08821127.1997.10731926

Bishop, T. (2011, June 15). NSA employee accused of leaking information sentenced to probation. Retrieved from http://www.baltimoresun.com/news/maryland/bs-md-thomas-drake-sentencing-20110715-story.html

Callahan, E. S., & Dworkin, T. M. (1994). Who blows the whistle to the media, and why: Organizational characteristics of media whistleblowers, *American Business Law Journal, 32*(2), 151–84. Retrieved from http://onlinelibrary.wiley.com/journal/10.1111/(ISSN)1744-1714

Change.gov, the office of the president elect. (2008). *The Obama/Biden Plan.* Retrieved from http://web.archive.org/web/20130425082834/http://change.gov/agenda/ethics_agenda/

Coll, S. (2013, April 1). The Spy who said too much: Why the administration targeted a C.I.A. officer. Retrieved from http://www.newyorker.com/magazine/2013/04/01/the-spy-who-said-too-much

Crook, J. R. (2009). President issues executive order banning torture and CIA prisons. *The American Journal of International Law, 103*(2), 331–334. doi:10.2307/20535157

Dasgupta, S., & Kesharwani, A. (2010). Whistleblowing: A survey of literature. *Journal of Corporate Governance, 9*(4), 57–70. Retrieved from http://www.iupindia.in/Corporate_Governance.asp

Delmas, C. (2015). The ethics of government whistleblowing. *Social Theory & Practice, 41*(1), 77–105. doi:10.5840/soctheorpract20154114

Devine, T. M. (1999). The whistleblower protection act of 1989: Foundation for the modern law of employment dissent. *Administrative Law Review, 51*(2), 531–579. Retrieved from http://www.jstor.org/stable/40709996?seq=1#page_scan_tab_contents

Downie, L., Jr. (2013, October 10). The Obama administration and the press. Retrieved from https://cpj.org/reports/2013/10/obama-and-the-press-us-leaks-surveillance-post-911.php

Drake, T. (2011, August 26). At what price national security? *The Washington Post*, pp. A13.

Duffy, M. J., & Freeman, C. P. (2011). Unnamed sources: A utilitarian exploration of their justification and guidelines for limited use. *Journal of Mass Media Ethics, 26*(4), 297–315. doi:10.1080/08900523.2011.606006

Eliason, R. (2014, September 2). No free pass for a free press. *The Washington Post*, pp. A15.

Ellison, F., Keenan, J., Lockhart, P., & Schaick, J. V. (1985). *Whistleblowing research: Methodological and moral issues.* New York, NY: Praeger Publishers.

Entman, R. M. (2005). The nature and sources of news. In G. Overholser & K. Hall Jamieson (Eds.), *Institutions of American democracy: The press* (pp. 48–65). New York, NY: Oxford University Press.

Esposito, R., & Ross, B. (2007, December 10-a). *"CIA – Abu Zubaydah" Interview with John Kiriakou: Tape 1*. Retrieved from http://abcnews.go.com/images/Blotter/brianross_kiriakou_transcript1_blotter071210.pdf

Esposito, R., & Ross, B. (2007, December 10-b). *"CIA – Abu Zubaydah" Interview with John Kiriakou: Tape 2*. Retrieved from http://abcnews.go.com/images/Blotter/brianross_kiriakou_transcript2_blotter071210.pd

Firtko, A., & Jackson, D. (2005). Do the ends justify the means? Nursing and the dilemma of whistleblowing. *The Australian Journal of Advanced Nursing, 23*(1), 51–56. Retrieved from http://www.ajan.com.au/

Franklin, B. (1963). Pennsylvania assembly: Reply to the governor, November 11, 1755. In L. W. Labaree (Ed.), *The papers of Benjamin Franklin, Volume 6: April 1, 1755 through September 24, 1756* (p. 242). New Haven, CT: Yale University Press. (Original work published 1755.)

Goodman, A. (2012, March 21). *NSA whistleblower Thomas Drake prevails against charges in unprecedented Obama admin crackdown*. Retrieved from http://www.democracynow.org/2012/3/21/in_unprecedented_obama_admin_crackdown_nsa

Goodwin, L. (2017, February 16). *Can Trump make good on his pledge to prosecute leaks?* Retrieved from https://www.yahoo.com/news/can-trump-make-good-on-his-pledge-to-prosecute-leaks-231846572.html

Gorman, S. (2006, May 18). *NSA rejected system that sifted phone data legally: Dropping of privacy safeguards after 9/11*. Retrieved from http://articles.baltimoresun.com/2006-05-18/news/0605180094_1_surveillance-national-security-agency-well-informed

Graham, J. W. (1986). Principled organizational dissent: A theoretical essay. *Research in Organizational Behavior, 8*, 1–52. Retrieved from https://www.journals.elsevier.com/research-in-organizational-behavior

Grant, C. (2002). Whistleblowers: Saints of secular culture. *Journal of Business Ethics, 39*(4), 391–399. Retrieved from http://www.jstor.org/stable/25074853

Greenwald. G. (2013, January 27). *Kiriakou and Stuxnet: The danger of the still-escalating Obama whistleblower war*. Retrieved from https://www.theguardian.com/commentisfree/2013/jan/27/obama-war-on-whistleblowers-purpose

Greenslade, R. (2014, June 3). US Supreme Court refuses to help *New York Times* reporter facing jail. Retrieved from https://www.theguardian.com/media/greenslade/2014/jun/03/press-freedom-new-york-times

Hanrahan, J. (2015, March 25). *Whistleblowers and the press heavyweights*. Retrieved from http://www.counterpunch.org/2015/03/25/whistleblowers-and-the-press-heavyweights/

Helmore, E. (2017, February 25). *Trump's media war threatens journalists globally, protection group warns*. Retrieved from https://www.theguardian.com/us-news/2017/feb/25/trump-media-war-committee-protect-journalists-warning

Hertsgaard, M. (2016). *Bravehearts: Whistle blowing in the age of Snowden*. New York, NY: Hot Books.

Horton, S. (2010, August). *Obama's war on whistleblowers*. Retrieved from http://harpers.org/blog/2010/08/obamas-war-on-whistleblowers/

Huxford, J., & Moore, M. A. (2011). Teaching journalism students about confidential whistleblower sources: An analysis of introductory news writing textbooks, *Journal of College Teaching & Learning, 8*(10), 2–16. Retrieved from https://www.cluteinstitute.com/journals/journal-of-college-teaching-learning-tlc/

Jamieson, K. H., & Campbell, K. K. (1992). *The Interplay of influence: News, advertising, politics and the mass media*. Belmont, CA: Wadsworth.

Jouvenal, J. (2013, January 25). *Former CIA officer John Kiriakou is sentenced to 30 months in prison for leaks*. Retrieved from https://www.washingtonpost.com/local/former-cia-officer-john-kiriakou-sentenced-to-30-months-in-prison-for-leaks/2013/01/25/49ea0cc0-6704-11e2-9e1b-07db1d2ccd5b_story.html

Jubb, P. B. (1999). Whistleblowing: A restrictive definition and interpretation. *Journal of Business Ethics, 21*(1), pp. 77–94. Retrieved from https://link.springer.com/journal/10551

Leon Panetta warns CIA employees: No more OBL raid leaks [Video file]. (2011, May 19). Retrieved from http://abcnews.go.com/blogs/politics/2011/05/leon-panetta-warns-cia-employees -no-more-obl-raid-leaks

Liptak, A. (2014, June 3). *Supreme Court rejects appeal from Times reporter over refusal to identify source*. Retrieved from https://www.nytimes.com/2014/06/03/us/james-risen-faces-jail-time-for-refusing-to-identify-a-confidential-source.html?_r=0

Loomis, E., Wiebe, K., Drake, T., Binney, W., & Roark, D. (2014, January 16). We need real protection from the NSA. *USA Today*, pp. 8A.

Mayer, J. (2011, May 23). *The secret sharer: Is Thomas Drake an enemy of the state?* Retrieved from http://www.newyorker.com/magazine/2011/05/23/the-secret-sharer

Miceli, M. P., & Near, J. P. (1992). *Blowing the whistle: The organizational and legal implications for companies and employees*. New York, NY: Lexington Books.

Moore, M. A., Huxford, J., & Hopper, K. M. (2014). Whistleblower as news source: A complex relationship examined through a survey of journalists' attitudes. *Journal of Applied Journalism & Media Studies, 3*(3), 355–374. doi:10.1386/ajms.3.3.355_1

Nakashima, E. (2011, July 30). Judge slams prosecutors' handling of leak suspect. *The Washington Post*, pp. A02.

Nakashima, E. (2013, June 10). NSA contractor's self-outing puts him in spotlight. *The Washington Post*, pp. A04.

Nelson, S. (2017, February 15). *Trump fumes over 'criminal' leaks as culprits risk harsh penalties*. Retrieved from http://www.usnews.com/news/articles/2017-02-15/trump-fumes-over-criminal-leaks-as-culprits-risk-harsh-penalties

Norris, M. (2013). Bad leaker or good whistleblower – A test. *Case Western Reserve Law Review, 64*(2), 693–710. Retrieved from http://scholarlycommons.law.case.edu/caselrev/vol64/iss2/15

O'Sullivan, P., & Ngau, O. (2014). Whistleblowing: A critical philosophical analysis of the component moral decisions of the act and some new perspectives on its moral significance. *Business Ethics: A European Review, 23*(4), 401–415. doi:10.1111/beer.12058

Overholser, G., & Jamieson, K. H. (Eds). (2005). *Institutions of American Democracy: The Press*. New York, NY: Oxford University Press.

Papandrea, M. R. (2014). Leaker traitor whistleblower spy: National security leaks and the first amendment. *Boston University Law Review, 94*(2), 449–544. Retrieved from http://lawdigitalcommons.bc.edu/

Perry, J. L. (1990). *The organizational consequences of whistleblowing*. Unpublished manuscript, Department of Public and Environmental Affairs, Indiana University, Bloomington, Indiana.

Petraeus, D. H. (2012, October 23). *Message from the director: Former officer convicted in leak case, a statement to employees of the Central Intelligence Agency*. Retrieved from https://www.cia.gov/news-information/press-releases-statements/2012-press-releasese-statements/statement–former-officer-convicted.html

Pilkington, E. (2013, May 30). *CIA whistleblower John Kiriakou shares prison experience in open* letter. Retrieved from https://www.theguardian.com/world/2013/may/30/cia-whistle-blower-john-kiriakou-open-letter-prison

Pincus, W. (2011, June 5). A CIA operation, a reporter and an ongoing ordeal. *The Washington Post*, pp. A09.

Pincus, W. (2015, January 27). Trial alters 'reckless' view of CIA mission. *The Washington Post*, pp. A15.

Poulsen, K. (2013, April 16). *Wikileaks and the massive data dump that rocked the Pentagon.* Retrieved from https://www.wired.com/2013/04/wikileaks/

Ragusa, J. W. (1993). Biting the hand that feeds you: The reporter-confidential source relationship in the wake of Cohen v. Cowles Media Company. *John's Law Review, 67*, 125–144. Retrieved from http://heinonline.org/

Rappeport, A. (2017, February 9). *Consumer watchdog faces attack by House Republication.* Retrieved from https://nyti.ms/2k9DJ0L

Ravishankar, L. (2003, February 4). *Encouraging internal whistleblowing in organizations.* Retrieved from https://www.scu.edu/ethics/focus-areas/business-ethics/resources/encouraging-internal-whistleblowing/

Reporters committee for the freedom of the press. (n.d.). Retrieved from http://www.rcfp.org/jailed-journalists

Risen, J. (2002, March 2). *Fired by C.I.A., he says agency practiced bias. The New York Times,* pp. A13.

Rosenbloom, D. (2003). *Administrative law for public managers.* Boulder, CO: Westview Press.

Rothschild, J., & Miethe, T. (1999). Whistle-blower disclosures and management retaliation: The battle to control information about organization corruption. *Work and Occupations, 26*(1), 107–128. doi:10.1177/0730888499026001006

Savage, C. (2012, January 25). Ex-C.I.A. officer's path from terrorist hunter to defendant. *The New York Times*, pp. A20.

Schudson, M. (1995). *The power of news.* Cambridge, MA: Harvard University.

Shane, S. (2009, April 19). *Waterboarding used 266 times on 2 suspects.* Retrieved from http://www.nytimes.com/2009/04/20/world/20detain.html

Shane, S. (2010, April 15). *Former N.S.A. official is charged in leaks case.* Retrieved from http://www.nytimes.com/2010/04/16/us/16indict.html

Shane, S. (2011, September 5). *Leak offers look at efforts by U.S. to spy on Israel.* Retrieved from http://www.nytimes.com/2011/09/06/us/06leak.html?pagewanted=all

Shane, S. (2013, January 5). *Ex-officer is first from C.I.A. to face prison for a leak.* Retrieved from http://www.nytimes.com/2013/01/06/us/former-cia-officer-is-the-first-to-face-prison-for-a-classified-leak.html?pagewanted=all

Smith, R. J. (2011, June 23). Classified report upheld Drake complaint. *The Washington Post*, pp. A07.

Solomon, N. (2015, May 27). *Jeffrey Sterling vs. the CIA: An untold story of race and retribution.* Retrieved from http://www.huffingtonpost.com/norman-solomon/jeffrey-sterling-vs-the-c_b_7449246.html

Stelter, B. (2009, April 28). How '07 ABC interview tilted a torture debate. *The New York Times*, pp. A1.

Sullivan, M. (2013, March 10). The danger of suppressing the leaks. *The New York Times, Sunday Review*, pp.12.

The White House, Office of the Press Secretary. (2011). Fact Sheet: Safeguarding the U.S. Government's Classified Information and Networks [Press release]. Retrieved from https://obamawhitehouse.archives.gov/the-press-office/2011/10/07/fact-sheet-safeguarding-us-governments-classified-information-and-networ

Trump, D. (2016, February 6). *Republican debate*, Goffstown, NH: St. Anselm College. Transcript retrieved from https://www.nytimes.com/2016/02/07/us/politics/transcript-of-the-republican-presidential-debate-in-new-hampshire.html?_r=0

Trump, D. (2017, February 16). *Press conference* [Streaming video]. Washington, DC. Retrieved from http://www.cnn.com/videos/politics/2017/02/16/trump-press-conference-full.cnn

United States Department of the Army. (2006, September). *Human intelligence collector operations*. (Field Manual 2-22.3). Washington, DC: Author.

United States v. Sterling, 1:10-cr-00485-LMB Document 115-2 (June 21, 2011). Retrieved from http://www.fas.org/sgp/jud/sterling/062111-risen115.pdf

USA Today. (2017, February 22). *USA Today* launches secure whistle-blower site. Retrieved from http://usat.ly/2lvJVm3

Warrick, J., & Eggen, D. (2007, December 11). Waterboarding recounted; Ex-CIA officer says it 'probably saved lives' but is torture. *The Washington Post*, pp. A01.

Wise, D. (2011, August). *Leaks and the law: The story of Thomas Drake*. Retrieved from http://www.smithsonianmag.com/history/leaks-and-the-law-the-story-of-thomas-drake-14796786/?no-ist

Zapotosky, M. (2015, April 21-b). *Federal prosecutors urge 'severe' sentence for ex-CIA officer in leak case*. Retrieved from https://www.washingtonpost.com/local/crime/federal-prosecutors-urge-severe-sentence-for-ex-cia-agent-in-leak-case/2015/04/21/4c8d1f5e-c001-4757-9b2a-50adf23b8d3c_story.html?utm_term=.c7857c05bdf7

Zapotosky, M. (2016, February 21). *He was fired from the CIA and jailed for a leak. Now he's trying to hang on*. Retrieved from https://www.washingtonpost.com/news/post-nation/wp/2016/02/21/he-was-fired-from-the-cia-and-jailed-for-a-leak-now-hes-trying-to-hang-on/?utm_term=.7f7ae5c091ec

Zelizer, J. (2017, January 25). President Trump's dangerous war on the media, CNN.com, Retrieved from http://www.cnn.com/2017/01/25/opinions/trumps-war-on-media-zelizer-opinion/

Zetter, K. (2011). NSA whistleblower to plead guilty to misdemeanor. Retrieved from https://www.wired.com/2011/06/drake-pleads-guilty/

INDEX